Orkney's Lifeboat Heritage

Orkney's Lifeboat Heritage

NICHOLAS LEACH

TEMPUS

To Sarah

Acknowledgements

Du ring the writing of this book I have received assistance from many people and express my gratitude to them all. The lifeboat crews and personnel at the Orkney lifeboat stations were very supportive and helpful with the following providing answers to my many requests: at Longhope, Coxswain Kevin Kirkpatrick, Mechanic John Budge, Second Coxswain Angus Budge, Lifeboat Operations Manager Dr Tony Trickett MBE and Alex Norquoy; at Stromness, Lifeboat Operations Manager Captain William J. Duncan, and former Coxswain John Banks; at Kirkwall, Lifeboat Operations Manager Captain Graeme Smith, Coxswain Geoff Gardens and Mechanic Dupre Strutt; and at Stronsay, William Miller. Shetland Coastguard manager Neville Davis facilitated photographic opportunities and was of much help. For assistance with photographs, information and suggestions for improvements to the contents I am grateful to Jeff Morris, John Harrop, Phil Weeks, Tony Denton, Donald Budge, Andy Anderson, William Miller, Kieran Murray, Martin Fish, John Pagni and Paava Antila. David Mackie, of Orkney Photographic Archives, was extremely helpful in supplying photographs and information, and I am grateful to him for his considerable assistance. The staff at Orkney Library also provided information and facilities for research. Finally, on a personal note, I am grateful as always to Sarah for her continued support throughout the writing of this book, and companionship during our memorable visits north to enjoy all that Orkney has to offer.

Nicholas Leach, Birmingham, January 2007

First published 2007

Tempus Publishing Limited
The Mill, Brimscombe Port,
Stroud, Gloucestershire, GL5 2QG
www.tempus-publishing.com

© Nicholas Leach, 2007

The right of Nicholas Leach to be identified as the Author
of this work has been asserted in accordance with the
Copyrights, Designs and Patents Act 1988.

British Library Cataloguing in Publication Data.
A catalogue record for this book is available from the British Library.

ISBN 978 0 7524 3896 2

Typesetting and origination by Tempus Publishing Limited
Printed in Great Britain

Front cover: *Longhope lifeboat 16m Tamar* Helen Comrie *passing Cantick Head lighthouse on Hoy. (Nicholas Leach)*

Frontispiece: *52ft Arun* The Queen Mother *off Hoy; she served at Longhope from 2004 to 2006. (Nicholas Leach)*

Overleaf (p.6): *Kirkwall lifeboat* Margaret Foster *on exercise. (Nicholas Leach)*

Contents

CHAPTER ONE

Orkney's Maritime Traditions

Orkney is a group of over seventy islands of which about twenty are inhabited. These islands lie approximately 15km off the northern-most tip of Scotland, separated from Caithness by the sometimes treacherous Pentland Firth, a narrow channel through which the waters of the Atlantic and the North Sea ebb and flow. The islands are low lying with households scattered over the arable land, with two main centres of population on the mainland, Stromness and Kirkwall. Of the other islands, Westray, Sanday, Rousay and Stronsay are the largest to the north, while Hoy and South Ronaldsay make up the southern group.

The islands lie on an important sea route for Atlantic shipping, within easy reach of Scandinavian and northern European ports. Orkney's history is inextricably linked with the sea and maritime activities. Ever since the first settlers arrived on this fertile archipelago over 6,000 years ago, the sea has played an important part in shaping the lives of the islands' inhabitants. The islands belonged to Norway and then Denmark up until the fifteenth century, when they came under the sovereign power of Scotland. Many place names, such as Hoy, derive from Old Norse, spoken in the islands until the seventeenth century but which gradually disappeared after Norse law was abolished in 1611.

During the seventeenth and much of the eighteenth centuries, the Orkney earldom estates were leased by the king to a series of Earls of Morton until a wealthy army contractor, Sir Lawrence Dundas, bought the estate in 1766. The lands were eventually sold off to sitting tenants during the twentieth century as a result of punitive estate taxation after the First World War. The other major Orkney land owner, the Bishopric Estate, was broken up in private leases to incoming Scots after the Reformation of the Church in 1560. As baronial and Church control of the land and power was eroded, the merchant lairds became the dominant group in the islands. These resident lairds received most of their rents in kind from impoverished tenants, acquiring goods such as malt and meal, feathers and hides, the surplus which was exported in frail trading vessels to Shetland, Norway, Holland and the east coast ports of Britain. The frequent wars in which Britain was engaged with other European powers curbed foreign imports and, as a result, Orkney became Britain's main supplier of kelp, the burnt residue of seaweed which provided essential chemicals for the nation's expanding glass and soap industries. As seaborne trade between Orkney and its neighbouring nations expanded, trading and ship-operating played an increasingly important role in the economic life of the islands as more and more islanders became involved in seafaring.

Orcadians could escape the poverty of the islands' farm dominated economy by working for the Hudson's Bay Company, whose fur trading ships called at Stromness en route for Canada each summer from the late seventeenth century. Many did so and by the end of the eighteenth century three-quarters of the workforce at the fur trading posts were Orcadians. Many young Orkneymen also signed on for hazardous trips with the East Coast-based Arctic whalers which called at the islands from about the 1750s to engage crewmen, chiefly skilled oarsmen, for their whale-catchers. During the nineteenth century, commercial fishing was developed and reached its height with the herring fishing boom of the 1890s. The start of regular steamship services to Aberdeen and Leith opened up a ready market for cattle which helped farming to prosper.

Orkney's strategic location was of importance in the nineteenth century as convoys of British trading vessels took advantage of the natural anchorage provided by Scapa Flow which, during the twentieth century's two world wars, became the Navy's northern anchorage. Here, in 1919, the interned German High Seas Fleet was scuttled to prevent it falling into enemy hands. During the Second World War, the island's population was supplemented by thousands of service men and women who came to defend the anchorage. After the end of the war, the uneconomical small farms merged into larger farms which, with increased mechanisation, greatly reduced rural employment. To counter this, fish farming was developed and a fleet of deep sea trawlers built up. The depopulation of the outer isles has been a gradual but continual process, despite improvements in inter-island transport with the ro-ro ferry system. The latest development has seen, during the latter decades of the twentieth century, an expansion of the tourist industry, helped by improved connections to the mainland, with new museums and interpretation centres being built. The islands' economy in the post-war years, particularly since the 1970s, was further boosted with the coming of the oil industry to Orkney.

The Perils to Shipping

The islands that make up Orkney have always proved to be an extreme hazard to shipping. Many ships have been wrecked on the islands, caught out by a variety of problems, usually in severe weather. However, in the eighteenth century when the islanders' lives were particularly hard, shipwrecks could provide unexpected bounty and the chance of acquiring goods from a wrecked ship was often too good an opportunity to pass up. On 18 November 1740, when the Dutch East Indiaman *Suecia* was driven ashore onto a reef to the south of North Ronaldsay by a gale, the locals were in luck as the vessel carried an extremely valuable cargo including silk, cotton goods and saltpetre. Forty-five men, including the captain, had died on the *Suecia's* voyage from India and, of the remaining eighty-five on board when the ship was wrecked, only forty-four survived. A few days after being wrecked, the ship broke up completely and large quantities of cargo washed ashore. Admiralty Court officials could not reach North Ronaldsay in time to prevent pilfering, so many islanders seized on the chance of personal gain including one James Graham 'who ran away with a boatful of goods in the night time.'

Tales such as this are common, although less so in Orkney than in other parts of the British Isles. Locals would often go to a wreck with the intention of plundering the cargo and anything else they could gain, including timber from the vessel's hull, but only if they had the chance. This practice, known as wrecking, was quite widespread during the eighteenth century, although tales that false lights were exhibited to lure vessels onto the shore to plunder the cargo and even murder the survivors may be exaggerated. The practice gradually ceased during the nineteenth century as customs and Coastguard officers became more efficient at enforcing the laws against it. However, the lighthouse engineer Robert Stevenson wrote that, in Orkney, 'Shipwrecks were regarded with indifference if not with complacency. Property fell into the hands of wreckers,' adding that he had seen 'a park paled round chiefly with cedar-wood and mahogany from the wreck of a Honduras-bound ship and in one island, after the wreck of a ship laden with wine, the inhabitants have been known to take claret to their barley-meal porridge.'

Help to vessels navigating the archipelago came first in the form of lighthouses, which marked the most dangerous of Orkney's cliffs, shoals and skerries. The first lighthouse in the islands was built on North Ronaldsay, to mark the way around the north-east corner of the archipelago, and was originally suggested by the Kirkwall schoolmaster Murdo O. Mackenzie in 1757. However, it was not until more than three decades later, as the routes around the

Orkney Lifeboats and Lighthouses

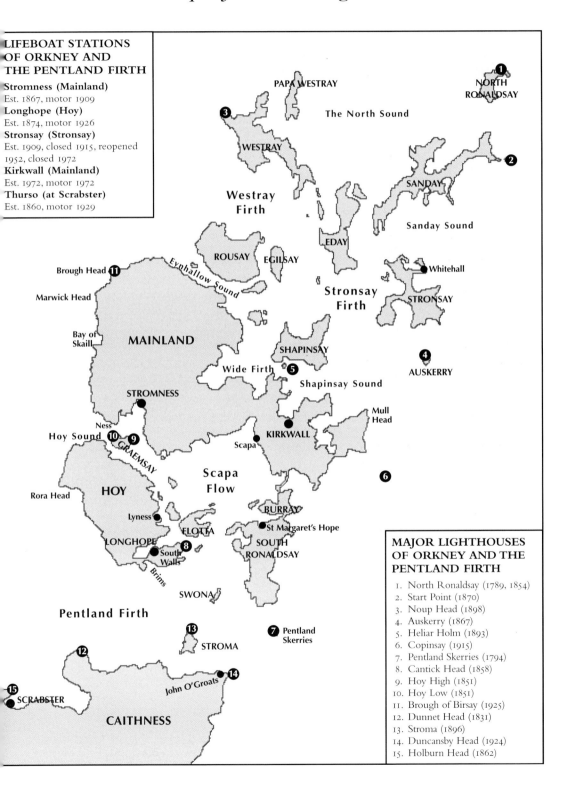

LIFEBOAT STATIONS OF ORKNEY AND THE PENTLAND FIRTH

Stromness (Mainland)
Est. 1867, motor 1909
Longhope (Hoy)
Est. 1874, motor 1926
Stronsay (Stronsay)
Est. 1909, closed 1915, reopened 1952, closed 1972
Kirkwall (Mainland)
Est. 1972, motor 1972
Thurso (at Scrabster)
Est. 1860, motor 1929

PAPA WESTRAY

The North Sound

NORTH RONALDSAY

WESTRAY

SANDAY

Westray Firth

Sanday Sound

ROUSAY   EGILSAY

EDAY

Whitehall

Brough Head

Marwick Head

Eynhallow Sound

Stronsay Firth

STRONSAY

Bay of Skaill

MAINLAND

SHAPINSAY

Wide Firth

AUSKERRY

Shapinsay Sound

STROMNESS

Mull Head

Ness

Hoy Sound   GRAEMSAY

KIRKWALL

Scapa

Rora Head   HOY

Scapa Flow

Lyness

BURRAY

St Margaret's Hope

FLOTTA

South Walls

LONGHOPE

SOUTH RONALDSAY

Brims

SWONA

Pentland Firth

STROMA

Pentland Skerries

John O'Groats

SCRABSTER

CAITHNESS

MAJOR LIGHTHOUSES OF ORKNEY AND THE PENTLAND FIRTH

1. North Ronaldsay (1789, 1854)
2. Start Point (1870)
3. Noup Head (1898)
4. Auskerry (1867)
5. Heliar Holm (1893)
6. Copinsay (1915)
7. Pentland Skerries (1794)
8. Cantick Head (1858)
9. Hoy High (1851)
10. Hoy Low (1851)
11. Brough of Birsay (1925)
12. Dunnet Head (1831)
13. Stroma (1896)
14. Duncansby Head (1924)
15. Holburn Head (1862)

The first lighthouse in Orkney was built at North Ronaldsay in 1789 and was replaced by this tower in 1854 which had a greater range than the earlier one. It was built to provide seafarers with the maximum warning of the local danger spots. (Orkney Photographic Archives)

north of Scotland and Orkney became more widely used, that the construction of lighthouses was considered seriously. The wars with France at the end of the eighteenth century forced shipping to find an alternative route to the English Channel and the northern route thus developed. An Act of Parliament passed in 1786 called for the construction of four lighthouses around Scotland's coastline, which would 'conduce greatly to the Security of Navigation and the Fisheries' to be built at Kinnaird's Head, North Ronaldsay, Scalpa in the Hebrides and on the Mull of Kintyre. By this Act, the Northern Lighthouse Board (NLB) was established and since then its commissioners have been responsible for building and maintaining the lighthouses of Scotland.

The North Ronaldsay light, built at Kirk Taing, was first shown, along with that at Eilean Glas, on 10 October 1789. It had taken more than a year to build, and proved something of a challenge to the engineers and masons of the time despite their use of the latest in lighting systems. The success of the new light was soon apparent and led to calls for further lights around Orkney. In particular, a light was needed for the Pentland Firth, and the cluster of rocks lying at the eastern end of the Firth known as the Pentland Skerries was chosen as the site for the next light. Two towers were built here, 60ft apart, one 80ft in height and the other 60ft, and they were first lit on 1 October 1794. The towers were heightened in the 1820s, but in 1895 the lower light was discontinued.

With the improvements in navigation around Orkney resulting from the construction of the two lighthouses, more and more vessels ventured north, but this highlighted the dangers presented by Sanday. In a letter to the commissioners, the Revd William Grant, of Cross Parish,

Sanday, listed twenty-two shipwrecks that had occurred in the area between 1788 and the early years of the nineteenth century, making clear the need for a light. Although a tower had been built at Start Point, on the eastern extremity of the island, it remained an unlit beacon and Grant pointed out that it was useless unless lit as most wrecks occurred at night. So, in 1806, the tower was fitted with the first revolving apparatus in Scotland.

With the new light at Start Point, that at North Ronaldsay was considered redundant and so was extinguished in 1809 although the tower remained as a beacon. Removing this light proved to be an error as the island, with its dangerous shoals, still required its own lighthouse. Almost fifty years passed before the mistake was rectified by when the sea around North Ronaldsay had been surveyed and a site for a new tower at Dennis Head chosen to give maximum warning of the Reef Duke and Seal Skerry. Work began in 1852 and by 1853 North Ronaldsay had what is still the highest, at 139ft, land-based lighthouse in the British Isles. In 1889, the red brick tower was painted with two white bands for use as a day mark.

The lighthouses at North Ronaldsay, Start Point and the Pentland Skerries had all been built with the purpose of making the passage to the north, south and east around Orkney safe, but ships coming from the west had a more difficult approach. Negotiating the strong tides in Hoy Sound before reaching a safe anchorage in Stromness harbour required skilful seamanship. To ease the situation, aids to navigation in Hoy Sound were therefore provided with the construction of the Hoy High and Low Lights in the 1840s on the island of Graemsay,

Start Point lighthouse was built to mark the eastern tip of Sanday and was first lit in 1806. Although the round stone tower was originally painted white, vertical black stripes were later added to give it a more distinct appearance. (Orkney Photographic Archives)

midway between Stromness and Hoy. Designed by Alan Stevenson, who succeeded his father as engineer to the NLB, the two towers were first exhibited in 1851.

The building of lighthouses in and around Orkney continued during the latter half of the nineteenth century. On Hoy, a lighthouse was built at Cantick Head, on the south-east coast of the island in 1858, to make a safe passage into Longhope and Scapa Flow. Lengthy correspondence between Trinity House and the Board of Trade regarding the specification, character of light and building tenders delayed the start of construction work until February 1856, with the light being first exhibited on 15 July 1858. A 22m white-painted tower was built. A light with a nominal range of eighteen miles was exhibited and it was was automated in 1991. In 1864, work began on a lighthouse on the uninhabited island of Auskerry, three miles south of Stronsay. Completed in 1866, this marked the entrance to Stronsay Firth. In 1893, after the grounding of the steamer *St Rognvald* on the Head of Work in Shapinsay, a lighthouse was built at Heliar Holm, marking Shapinsay Sound on the east side of the islands. Five years later, another lighthouse was completed on Noup Head, at the most westerly point of Westray, to indicate the dangerous submerged North Shoal. To complete the lighting of the area with major lighthouses, a light was established on Copinsay in 1915, guarding the south side of the Stronsay Firth and operating in conjunction with Auskerry lighthouse. Since 1895, the NLB has established eleven minor lighthouses in Orkney to mark the less busy island passages and inshore hazards. The NLB also maintained a depot at Stromness, from which successive lighthouse tenders were operated, until October 2004 when it was closed.

Lifeboats and Rescues

Despite improvements in navigation and measures such as the building of lighthouses, ships were still wrecked and lives and property lost. The small coasting vessels of the eighteenth and nineteenth centuries were ill-equipped to cope with long journeys. They were often poorly built and maintained as well as being reliant upon and at the mercy of weather, wind

The lighthouse at Heliar Holm was completed in 1893 to the design of David A. and Charles Stevenson, the renowned Scottish lighthouse designers. (Nicholas Leach)

and tide. Many operated with inexperienced crews who found navigation difficult, a problem compounded by the inaccuracy of charts. Consequently, shipowners and masters were frequently faced with their ships wrecked and both crews and cargoes lost. Few sailing vessels ventured as far north as Orkney because the seas around the islands were so dangerous, a fact highlighted by three wrecks that occurred in the space of forty-eight hours in April 1830. During the night on 8 April, the Wick schooner *Edina* was totally wrecked on the west side of the island of Stroma, while the following day in dense fog two other vessels, *Aesceili* and *Anna*, were stranded off the north end of the island. The crews were saved, but only with great difficulty.

With the number of schooners, brigs and sloops increasing, particularly on the busy trade routes of the east coast, attempts to remedy the situation were made and the idea of a shore-based boat, ready to put to sea to help those in distress, was proposed in the 1790s. This idea was turned into reality by a group of gentlemen in Newcastle who employed local boatbuilder Henry Greathead of South Shields, at the mouth of the Tyne, to construct the first purpose-built lifeboat. Greathead went on to build over thirty lifeboats, all about 30ft in length with ten oars, a curved keel and double-ended hull. The first lifeboats in Scotland were built to his design and stationed at Ayr, Aberdeen, Montrose, Arbroath and St Andrews in the early 1800s, the major ports where the largest concentrations of shipping could be found and therefore where most shipwrecks occurred. However, lifeboats were stationed no further north than Aberdeen for at least another half century because shipping casualties were too infrequent and the necessary local finance was not available.

In 1824 a national body responsible for coordinating the building and operating of lifeboats, the Royal National Institution for the Preservation of Life from Shipwreck (RNIPLS), was established. After initially being quite successful at increasing the number of lifeboats around the country, by the 1840s the organisation's efforts started to falter through lack of funds. The Institution found raising money for lifeboats difficult and enjoyed limited success in providing a nationwide lifeboat service until the 1850s. Reforms and improvements, including the adopting of a new title, Royal National Lifeboat Institution (RNLI), were implemented providing a new impetus during the latter half of the nineteenth century. A new design of lifeboat, the self-righter, was developed and, with greater funds available to it, the newly reformed and renamed Institution was able to increase lifeboat provision throughout the British Isles, including turning its attention to life-saving in the northern isles. During the 1860s and 1870s, many new lifeboat stations opened in Scotland. A lifeboat was sent to Scrabster, near Thurso on the southern shore of the Pentland Firth, in 1860 and seven years later the first lifeboat for Orkney arrived at Stromness.

Considering the dangers of the seas around Orkney and the north of Scotland, why did it take until the 1860s, more than four decades after the founding of the RNIPLS, for lifeboats to be stationed in the area? Firstly, although the frequency of wrecks justified the building of lighthouses, only a relatively modest amount of shipping actually passed through the area compared to other parts of the British Isles and, until the latter part of the nineteenth century, ships were seen relatively infrequently. Secondly, rowing and sailing lifeboats were insufficiently powerful to deal with the conditions in which they were likely to be needed. So, even if they had been ready and available, the help they could offer to ships in distress would have been restricted by their limited range. Thirdly, insufficient finance was forthcoming at a local level due to the relative poverty of Orkney's largely rural communities and so the construction of lifeboats and lifeboat houses was not a priority. Lastly, in some circumstances, locally operated boats were already available to help vessels in distress, thus obviating the need for purpose-built lifeboats.

CHAPTER TWO

Orkney's First Lifeboat Stations

The first lifeboat on Orkney was stationed at Stromness, one of the principal harbours
and towns of Orkney. Stromness was described in the 1860s as 'a picturesque little town,
built of grey stone, on the side of a hill overlooking a secure and landlocked harbour,
and commanding a magnificent panoramic view of some of the interior sounds and islands of the
archipelago.' The bay of Stromness, known as Hamnavoe, offered a sheltered, deep-water anchorage
that opens into Hoy Sound and well protected by the granite ridge of Brinkie's Brae. The town
developed along the water's edge and, by the 1790s, had grown into a settlement of more than
220 houses. Its main function has always been as a port and outlet for local industries, such as kelp
and herring. Ships attempting to reach the Atlantic en route to North America, attracted by the
passage north of the British Isles during the Napoleonic Wars, called at Stromness whose situation
made it an ideal port for provisioning vessels. All kinds of vessels were hosted including Royal
Navy ships and whalers destined for Arctic waters. The Hudson's Bay Company, established by
royal warrant to trade with native people of America, had its ships calling annually at Stromness
between 1702 and 1892 to recruit men. Today, Stromness retains its links with the sea by playing
host to the ferries linking Orkney with Scrabster on Scotland's North Coast.

By the middle of the nineteenth century the town had expanded sufficiently to support
a lifeboat station, although it was established only after tragedy had been witnessed in the
vicinity of the port. On 1 January 1866, the emigrant ship *Albion*, with 100 passengers and
crew on board, became a total wreck at the Point of Oxan on the island of Graemsay, south
of Stromness. The ship struck near the lighthouse and many local boats were immediately
launched from Graemsay to try to save the ship's passengers and crew. Most of the schooner's
passengers were brought to safety, but one small boat, with ten from *Albion* as well as local
man Joseph Mowatt, capsized in the heavy seas with the loss of all on board. The tragedy
highlighted the need for a lifeboat in the area and, as a direct result of the wreck which
had been witnessed by many local people, a number of meetings were held to discuss the
possibility of forming a lifeboat station.

The request came at a time when the RNLI was expanding its operations. During the
1850s the Institution had been reorganised and by the 1860s, with increasing resources, was in
a better financial position than at any time hitherto. The establishment of a station at Stromness
in 1867 was part of this expansion. The process to get the station established began with a
request to the RNLI's Committee of Management in London. Local man J.M. Garrick wrote
to the Institution and, in response, the Inspector of Lifeboats, Capt. John Ward, visited the
area in August 1866. He recommended the formation of a station and that a 33ft ten-oared
self-righting type lifeboat be sent. The station was to cover most of the north and west side of
Orkney and become the most northerly of the RNLI's lifeboat stations. The standard 33ft self-
righter allocated to the station, ordered from Forrest's yard at Limehouse, London, was ready
by July 1867. It was conveyed from London to Stromness on board vessels belonging to two
Scottish shipping firms: the Aberdeen Steam Navigation Company and the Edinburgh, Leith
& Clyde Shipping Company. As was common practice at this time, the lifeboat was carried
free of charge. It reached Stromness in August 1867 and, on the fifteenth of the month, was
taken afloat for the first time, under the command of Capt. Ward.

Once the decision had been made to go ahead with the station, a suitable site for the lifeboat house was found to the south of Stromness at the Ness. In July 1867, Robertson and Smith tendered £149 10s to build the house and £48 for a slipway, but while this tender had been accepted it appears that work did not begin immediately and when it did progress was slow. The house had not been completed by the time the lifeboat arrived, so the boat had to be kept under a tarpaulin sheet in a secure compound at Stromness until the following year. In June 1868 the Inspector reported that the house had been completed at a cost of £144 19s 6d. A special launching carriage, built for almost £100, was supplied for the lifeboat, which itself had cost £280, bringing the total outlay for the establishment of the station to well over £500, a considerable sum at the time.

The first lifeboat, named *Saltaire* (ON.286), had been provided out of a gift from Titus Salt, the former Member of Parliament for Bradford. The boat's first service launch took place on 6 October 1868 when she went to the aid of the schooner *Victor* of Grimsby, which was riding heavily at anchor in rough seas in a dangerous position in Hoy Sound. With the help of the lifeboatmen, the schooner was brought safely into Stromness harbour. After this first service, *Saltaire* performed only two other rescues during almost a quarter of a century on station at Stromness. In October 1875 she went to the aid of the Russian brig *Frichell*, which had run aground in rough seas, but her services were not required. The third and final service by *Saltaire* took place on 8 March 1884, almost a decade since she had last been called on, when she launched to a fishing vessel reported missing. Facing extremely bad weather, the crew found this a particularly arduous service. Heavy snow accompanied the heavy seas and severe gale, but the lifeboatmen searched throughout the night, taking their boat as far north as Birsay looking for the missing craft, but without success. They returned to station having suffered considerably after many hours exposed to appalling conditions.

The first Stromness lifeboat Saltaire *(ON.286) being launched on 8 March 1884 to search for a missing fishing boat.* Saltaire, *a 33ft self-righting type, was on station from 1867 to 1891, during which time she only performed three effective services. (By courtesy of RNLI Stromness)*

Saltaire being hauled out of the water on 8 March 1884 after searching for a missing fishing boat. Carried out in extremely bad weather, this service proved to be a particularly arduous one for the crew. An idea is given in this photograph of the exposed nature of the launching site at the Ness, to the south of Stromness, where almost no shelter was available to protect men or boat during a launch. (By courtesy of RNLI Stromness)

Early lifeboat operations at Stromness proved both difficult and dangerous as the strong tidal currents in the Pentland Firth meant that a lifeboat powered by oars was almost useless. In some instances just getting the boat afloat was often an extremely difficult task given the exposed situation of the lifeboat house. The severity of the conditions encountered around Stromness meant that oars and sail were usually insufficient to enable the lifeboat to perform rescues in the area. That the first lifeboat only launched three times on service in almost twenty-five years on station proves the point. *The Lifeboat* (the quarterly journal of the RNLI first published in 1852) of 1 August 1873 described the kind of work for which the lifeboat was used and hints at the difficulties:

> The lifeboat *Saltaire* has to contend with strong tides, a rocky coast, and deep water. She is intended to be useful mainly in removing the crews of ships which, drifted down on that rocky coast, are unable to reach port, but which, perhaps, can be reached before they come into actual collision with the gigantic cliffs which everywhere look out towards the Atlantic; or, again, to rescue the crews of vessels which have brought up to their anchors in perilous positions, well knowing that unless aid arrives in time cables will part, and ship and crew instantly be dashed to pieces.

While the lifeboat itself was often unable to cope with the conditions, the position of her boathouse did not help. The house at the Ness, a headland to the south of Stromness, although within easy reach of the main shipping lane, was extremely exposed, particularly in westerly winds. During the early years of the station, some attempts had been made to improve the situation. In 1873, when the slipway was found to be too short and hindered launching, the RNLI's Committee of Management had to fund its lengthening. Apart from the physical difficulties faced, the station was not being run smoothly and, in 1879, the RNLI's District Inspector reported that the station was 'very disorganised'.

Launching the lifeboat from the boathouse at the Ness could be an extremely difficult and arduous procedure if the conditions were unfavourable, and they usually were when the lifeboat was needed. The problem was highlighted on 4 March 1890 when the Institution's Deputy Chief Inspector, Cdr Vincent Nepean, RN, and the Northern District Inspector of Lifeboats, Lt K.H. Foote, attended a routine exercise launch of the lifeboat. They witnessed the lifeboat crew struggling to launch the boat in the north-westerly gale and heavy seas, with the low tide also hampering attempts to get afloat. After more than an hour of struggling the boat was finally got away, but she could not beat to windward against the gale.

This incident, which proved to be the catalyst for major changes at the station, as it showed that improvements to the launching procedure were clearly needed. Not only did strong winds and high seas hamper the launching of the small 33ft lifeboat, getting it afloat two hours either side of low water was also extremely difficult. Some of the crew advocated mooring the lifeboat in a partly sheltered cove inside Breakness Point but the Deputy Chief Inspector stated this was untenable. The only practical way forward was to replace the small 33ft self-righter with a much larger boat, a self-righter equipped with drop keels and water ballast, and keep it moored in the harbour all year round. As this large lifeboat would always be afloat, the problem of launching would be lessened, while the drop keels and water ballast would enable her to sail out of the harbour in severe weather more easily. However, the problem of beating out of Hoy Sound against a flood tide in a north-westerly gale would remain in spite of her greater size and power.

The RNLI Committee of Management, at its meeting on 13 April 1890, agreed that this was the way forward for the station and allocated a 42ft self-righting lifeboat, built by MacAlister's yard at Dumbarton, to the station. Just over a year later, the new lifeboat was ready and, on 16 May 1891, she was taken to Greenock for her naming ceremony. The new boat had been provided through funds raised by the Loyal Order of Ancient Shepherds Friendly Society. In front of a crowd of 3,000 she was formally handed over to the RNLI by George Cromar. A service of dedication followed, conducted by the Revd John Barclay, after which Mrs Cromar christened the boat *Good Shepherd* (ON.299). The lifeboat was then launched into the James Watt Dock for the benefit of the crowd. On 5 June she was sent north to her station and, ten days later, arrived at Stromness where she was placed at a mooring in the harbour.

The decision to station a larger lifeboat at Stromness was vindicated by the number of services she performed – almost four times as many as her predecessor during eighteen years on station, and she is credited with saving eighteen lives. The first effective service performed by *Good Shepherd* took place on 17 November 1893 when she went to the aid of three local boats which had been fishing in Hoy Sound and caught out in a sudden north-easterly gale and torrential rain. The lifeboat put out at 11.30 a.m. but the three fishing boats managed to reach Graemsay safely where they were found by the lifeboatmen. The fishermen were taken aboard the lifeboat and brought back to Stromness. Less than a year later, on 4 November 1894, *Good Shepherd* put out to the schooner *Industry*, of Peterhead, which was dragging her anchors and drifting towards Peter Skerry Shoal. The lifeboatmen assisted the schooner to anchor safely and then brought its crew ashore. These casualties were typical of the kind to which the *Good Shepherd* lifeboat was called. Schooners, trawlers, steam trawlers and fishing boats all frequented the seas off Orkney and were often caught out in bad weather.

The first two lifeboats at Stromness, both pulling and sailing, offered little in the way of protection for their crews. As Ernest W. Marwick pointed out in his centenary history of the station, these boats 'gave opportunities for feats of endurance and heroism that have not been surpassed.' In the severe conditions off Orkney, lifeboat crews suffered on most services, but on 7 December 1898 they were to face particularly harsh weather. *Good Shepherd* was launched in extremely difficult conditions – it was bitterly cold, a severe north-westerly gale was blowing and the seas were exceptionally heavy. She went to the aid of the trawler *Shark*, reported in difficulties to the west of Hoy, and she was away for the whole night. As her services were ultimately not required, at 7 a.m. the following morning she was brought ashore at Graemsay. The crew had suffered terribly in the heavy weather and one of the lifeboatmen, James Linklater, had been injured by an enormous a wave which swept over the lifeboat. After an hour's rest, the lifeboatmen left Graemsay to eventually return to the Stromness at 12 p.m. after one of the most testing services they had carried out.

Following this arduous service, two of the lifeboatmen continued to suffer as a result of their exposure that night one, James Linklater, required medical attention, for which the RNLI paid £3 6*s* 6*d*, and also received a grant of £5 from the Institution. For the other member of the crew, George Campbell, the service proved fatal. Campbell caught a severe cold that night and never properly recovered. In January 1902 he died, leaving a wife and three young children 'in a state of destitution'. The RNLI awarded a grant of £15 to his dependents, but clearly the work of life-saving had taken its toll on the lifeboatmen of Stromness.

Not only was exposure a problem for the crew but upkeep of the lifeboat was proving difficult as it was suffering from being permanently afloat. Lifeboats were only kept afloat during the nineteenth and early twentieth centuries as a last resort. Anti-fouling paints were fairly ineffective, and maintaining a lifeboat on a mooring was more difficult and expensive than if it was kept in a boathouse. In 1899 a small room in Stromness was obtained for use as a store room in place of the rough shelter that had been used hitherto. But, the District Inspector

The lifeboat house built at the Ness in 1868 and used until the early twentieth century. This photograph shows the house in 2006 in a semi-derelict state, having been used at one time as a store for the local golf club. (Nicholas Leach)

The lifeboat house and slipway, built in the harbour in 1901, made launching easier and quicker. (From an old postcard in the author's collection)

and local committee argued that a boathouse with a launching slipway was needed to improve matters. During 1900 efforts were made to find a suitable site on the waterfront at Stromness for such a building. After discussions with the harbour board and Board of Trade, a site was found, backing onto Dundas Street and, in September 1900, it was purchased. A building was already on the site, so this was utilised as part of the new house. A timber slipway almost 100ft in length was constructed, giving a direct launch into the harbour, and a winch house added to the building. In November 1901, the coxswain and crew gave their approval to the new building, which had cost £1,250, and soon afterwards they moved in.

From her new boathouse, *Good Shepherd* continued to give good service to shipping in the area. On 22 April 1902 she saved the three-strong crew of a lobster boat caught in a south-easterly gale. On 4 June 1903 she went to the Aberdeen steam trawler *Star of Peace* which had run aground and was breaking up. The lifeboat was taken alongside and saved the trawler's crew of nine. On 23 May 1905, after the Wick steam drifter *Sonnet* ran aground on Braga Skerry, *Good Shepherd* was launched to her aid. Although five of the drifter's crew were rescued by another drifter, the lifeboat was able to save the remaining three men. Shortly after the rescue had been completed, the drifter was washed off the rocks and sank. What proved to be the last service by *Good Shepherd* was also the most notable.

On the morning of 11 December 1907, the trawler *Shakespeare*, of Hull, bound for her home port from the fishing grounds, went ashore in very heavy seas near Breckness. The Stromness fishermen were gathered around the harbour when the request to launch *Good Shepherd* was received. The farmer at Breckness, David Clouston, had galloped on horseback to say that the trawler was wrecked on the Point of Spoil and in extreme danger. At 7.25 a.m. the lifeboat was quickly launched – 'the swiftest that Stromness had ever seen' according to Marwick – and she was soon past Ness Point and Wharbeth, reaching the casualty whose desperate situation was soon obvious to the lifeboatmen. Her hull, which lay about fifty yards from the shore, was entirely submerged with head to the sea. The sea was constantly breaking over the vessel which was surrounded by broken water. Only her masts and part of her funnel were in sight. Two men were clinging to the foremast and another was hanging onto the funnel. Four men had already been drowned: two had been washed away and two had fallen exhausted from the mizzen mast, one when the lifeboat was in sight.

Coxswain Robert Greig quickly made up his mind. He anchored some way ahead of the trawler and, with outstanding teamwork from his crew, slowly manoeuvred the lifeboat into the lee of the wreck until it was only twelve yards away. From there, with the lifeboat being thrown about in the heavy surf and with rocks an ever present danger, the bowman threw a grapnel to the trawler. It took hold on the fore-rigging and a lifebuoy was then passed to the men clinging to the mast. Using the line, the two men were safely brought on board the lifeboat. A line was then thrown to the man on the funnel, who was saved with extreme difficulty as the line jammed and he was so exhausted he had problems holding onto it. The three men on the mizzen mast were taken ashore by the Rocket Brigade Team, which had

Good Shepherd *(ON.299), the second lifeboat to serve at Stromness, putting out on exercise. A large 42ft self-righter with drop keels and water ballast she was designed primarily for sailing. (Orkney Photographic Archives)*

Good Shepherd *launching down the slipway into the harbour for a practice in 1907. (From the George Ellison collection, courtesy of Orkney Photographic Archives)*

Good Shepherd *leaving Stromness Harbour on exercise in 1907 under tow by the South Isles steamer* Hoy Head, *owned at that time by Robert Garden. (From the George Ellison collection, courtesy of Orkney Photographic Archives)*

arrived about the same time as the lifeboat. The team fired a line across the wreck and then set up the breeches buoy to bring the remaining survivors to safety. Tom Wishart, who served for forty-three years on four different Stromness lifeboats, recalls the events:

> In my mind's eye I can still see the shuddering masts of the doomed trawler, and the black figures perched so precariously in the rigging, with the waves frequently washing over them. [Once ashore] the survivors were quickly undressed and massaged by rough but efficient

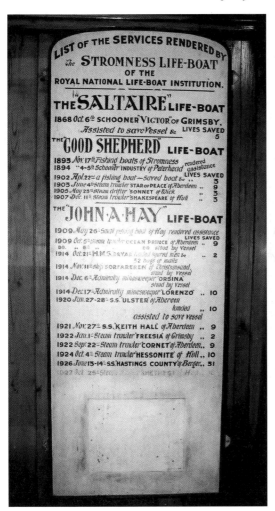

Left: The service board recording the services performed by the pulling and sailing lifeboats of Stromness. The board is on display in the old lifeboat house backing onto Dundas Street which is now owned by Scapa Scuba diving company.

Opposite: Dickinson Edleston, *the first Longhope lifeboat, served the station from 1874 to 1891. This picture was probably taken at her builder's yard at Shadwell in London. (By courtesy of the RNLI)*

hands. Rum was rubbed into the men's arms and legs to bring them some warmth and to restore circulation.

This truly outstanding rescue, performed in an open lifeboat, in conditions difficult to imagine, resulted in Coxswain Greig being awarded the RNLI's Silver medal in recognition of his outstanding seamanship and courage. According to Marwick, 'everything depended on his [Coxswain Greig's] superb seamanship', and Greig was later described as 'the most capable man who ever held a tiller.' Less than eighteen months after this rescue, the station had a new lifeboat, one of the first motor-powered lifeboats in the RNLI's fleet.

A Lifeboat for the Pentland Firth

Hoy, which means 'high island' from the Old Norse 'Haey', is the second largest of the islands that make up Orkney. At its southern end is South Walls, which is almost a separate island linked to the rest of Hoy only by a narrow 'aith'. The eastern shores of Hoy are low-lying and green, much like the rest of Orkney, but along the island's southern and western edges runs an almost unbroken line of cliffs. The eastern side offers many sheltered bays and inlets, and most of the settlements are to be found here including Longhope, which lies on the southern shore of Longhope Bay at the south-eastern corner of the island. The Bay became the rendezvous point for many Baltic convoys during the Napoleonic wars and two Martello towers were built in 1815 to protect the sheltered anchorage provided by the Bay.

During the latter half of the nineteenth century, a gradual increase in the amount of shipping transiting the treacherous waters of the Pentland Firth, described in August 1876 as 'about the stormiest and most dangerous in the world', inevitably brought about an increase in shipwrecks. The need for a lifeboat on Hoy to guard the Firth was brought to the RNLI's attention in 1874 when local residents wrote to the Institution asking for a lifeboat. Soon afterwards, on 5 February 1874, the Inspector of Lifeboats, Capt. John Ward, visited the island to discuss the matter and reported favourably on the proposal to the RNLI in London. As

a result, a decision was made at a meeting of the RNLI's Committee of Management on 5 March 1874 to form a lifeboat station at Longhope at the southern end of the island. The station was to be manned from the village with the lifeboat ready to assist ships in the Firth. *The Lifeboat* of 2 August 1875 recorded the station's foundation:

> The National Lifeboat Institution has formed a lifeboat station at Longhope, on the south side of Hoy, where a lamentable shipwreck, with loss of life, took place some little time since, and from which place it was thought the boat might render service to the crews of vessels in distress in that part of the Pentland Firth.

A 'substantial and commodious' lifeboat house, built on 'a convenient site' provided by local landowner J. Moodie Heddle at the southern end of the neck of land which connects South Walls to the North, was constructed by J. Charleson at a cost of £228. Heddle was instrumental in getting the station established and provided a generous annual subscription of £30 towards its upkeep. The boathouse had doors at both ends so that the lifeboat could be launched directly into Aith Hope through the east doors or, in adverse weather, through the west doors into the North Bay to head out via Scapa Flow. The beach over which the lifeboat launched was 'rough and steep', according to the Inspector, and the lifeboats that used this first boathouse were dragged over wooden skids as no launching carriage was supplied, although it seems that some kind of permanent slipway was needed. Launching was helped by a hauling-off warp which was anchored offshore and used by the crew to pull the lifeboat out through the heavy surf and into open water.

The station's first lifeboat was funded from a legacy of £800 left to the RNLI by Dickinson Edleston, of Sowerby Bridge in Yorkshire. The boat was a large self-righter, 37ft in length and 9ft 2in in beam, with twelve oars, intended principally for sailing and clench-built of larch by the London boatbuilder Woolfe & Son. On 16 September 1874 she was sent to her station, coming by train as far north as Thurso where she was launched. Then, on 23 September 1874, the steamer *Express* towed her to Stromness and then to the entrance of Longhope Bay, from where she was sailed to her new station. She was formally christened *Dickinson Edleston*, after her donor, two days later and the station was officially inaugurated. Heddle became chairman of the Longhope Branch, Edward Corrigall took on the role of honorary secretary, and the station's first coxswain was Benjamin Stout.

Dickinson Edleston was launched just four times on service and during seventeen years on station did not save any lives. Her first launch took place on 24 December 1876 when she went to the barque *Energie*, of Memel, but on this occasion her services were not needed. She went out to vessels reported in distress on 16 November 1877 and again on 30 November 1880 but was not needed on either occasion. Her only effective service came on 20 January 1884 when she launched at 11.30 a.m. at the height of a violent storm to the steamship *Ben Avon*, of Aberdeen, bound from Liverpool to Dundee in ballast. Having lost a propeller, the steamer dropped anchor but in a dangerous position. When the lifeboat arrived the master requested that a telegram be sent to Thurso asking for the help of a steam tug. So *Dickinson Edleston* returned to station and a steam tug was called to tow the steamer to safety.

In June 1887 the self-righting ability of the lifeboat was questioned and three years later she was found to be suffering from rot. In August 1890, when she did not right herself fast enough during capsize trials, she was condemned. A new lifeboat was ordered but, before it was ready, a temporary reserve lifeboat was sent to the station. This reserve boat was involved in an outstanding service on 3 March 1891 to the 1,960-ton steamship *Victoria*, of Sunderland, bound from Hamburg to New York with a general cargo. The steamer was seen flying signals of distress about five miles north of Dunnet Head lighthouse in a violent north-westerly gale with extremely heavy seas and snow showers. The lifeboat found the vessel sinking and that the fires to heat her boiler had been extinguished. Coxswain Benjamin Stout manoeuvred the lifeboat alongside the casualty with great skill so that all twenty-two of its crew could be taken on board. The lifeboat was slightly damaged as she effected the rescue, having been smashed

The second lifeboat to serve Longhope, Samyntas Stannah *(ON.307), was on station from 1891 to 1904. She is credited with saving fifty-two lives in just four service launches. (Orkney Photographic Archives)*

against the side of the steamer by the heavy seas, but she got clear safely. Coxswain Stout then set course for Widewall in South Ronaldsay where the rescued men were landed at midnight. Returning to Longhope was impossible because of the heavy seas and strong tides and the lifeboatmen were forced to stay at Widewall Bay until 5 March, when they were able to return and rehouse the lifeboat.

For this outstanding service, the Silver medal was awarded to Coxswain Benjamin Stout in recognition of his gallantry and courage. Furthermore, extra monetary awards were made to the rest of the crew. Eleven of the rescued crew were German and the Emperor of Germany presented, through the Foreign Office, a gold watch to the Coxswain with monetary awards totalling £24 to the lifeboat crew. The following letter was published in *The Shipping Gazette* a few days after the service:

Sir,– We the undersigned, on behalf of the whole crew of the steamer Victoria, of Sunderland, desire publicly to convey our heartfelt thanks to the fourteen men who, on the afternoon of the 3rd instant, put off from Longhope in the Life-boat, in the most terrible weather and rescued us from our vessel, when she was not only sinking, but as circumstances subsequently proved, was fast driving ashore near Dunnet Head, where we are sure there was not the faintest hope of rescue. Their timely and gallant aid was attended with the utmost danger, for which no thanks can fully express our gratitude. Yours &c, James Harrison, Master; J.R. Scarborough, Mate; M. Woodward, Steward; David Ranken, Second Engineer.

Soon after this dramatic rescue the new lifeboat arrived on station. Completed in February 1891, she was a 39ft twelve-oared self-righter, built by Forrest, at Limehouse in London, incorporating all the latest lifeboat technology including fore and aft sliding keels, two masts and sails. The cost of £637 came from the legacy of the late Mrs E.M. Stannah, of Balham, Surrey, and the boat was named *Samyntas Stannah* in accordance with the donor's wishes. Her first service launch took place on 6 September 1897 when she went to the assistance of the schooner *Wild Wave*, of Dublin. However, her services were not required and she returned to station at 8.30 p.m.

The most outstanding service performed by the Longhope lifeboatmen in *Samyntas Stannah* took place on 31 October 1898 after the 5,900-ton steamship *Manchester City* got into difficulty while making her way through the Pentland Firth on her maiden voyage, en route from the Tyne to Montreal. In a fierce north-westerly gale with very heavy seas her steering gear failed so her crew dropped anchor off Dunnet Head to signal for help. The lifeboat launched at 5 p.m. and soon reached the casualty to find both its anchor chains had parted. At the request of the captain, one of the lifeboatmen went aboard the vessel, which had at crew of fifty-two and was now adrift. With the Longhope lifeboat in attendance, as well as lifeboats from nearby Thurso and Huna, the vessel was allowed to drift with the flood tide through the Pentland Firth despite the dangers of running aground on either the island of Skoma or the Pentland Skerries. Several times she had to go full ahead or full astern on her engines to keep clear of the rocks, but with the local knowledge provided by the lifeboatmen, the steamer safely cleared the Firth and then headed south for Wick, where she anchored. The three lifeboats returned to their respective stations with *Samyntas Stannah* being rehoused at 2 p.m. on 1 November. *Manchester City* eventually reached the river Tyne on 7 November, having gone ashore in the Moray Firth but been pulled clear by steam tugs during her passage south. The Longhope lifeboatman, who had helped pilot the vessel through the Pentland Firth, was still on board and did not return home until several days later.

This incident was the only effective service performed by the *Samyntas Stannah* lifeboat during her time on station. She did perform a couple more services but none had a positive outcome. Her last call out was to investigate the sighting of rockets on 11 August 1902 but this turned out to be people celebrating King Edward VII's coronation and the lifeboat returned to her station at 11 p.m. Two years later she was withdrawn from service after concerns had been expressed regarding her handling and seaworthiness. She was sent to the RNLI storeyard in London, where she was condemned after it was found repairs were not worthwhile. While a new lifeboat was under construction, the Reserve No.3 lifeboat, a 39ft self-righter built as *Christopher North Graham* (ON.291) for Thorpeness in Suffolk, was sent to Longhope and stayed for two years.

The Reserve No.3 lifeboat's only two effective services took place in January 1905. On 6 January, she went to the South Shields schooner *Brazilian,* and its crew of eight, which had got into difficulty bound from the Tyne to Stornoway with a cargo of coal. In very heavy seas and a north-westerly gale the vessel's sails and spars had been carried away and, as she drifted into the Pentland Firth, her crew had no choice but to signal for assistance. The lifeboat launched from Longhope at 2 p.m. but the seas were too rough for Coxswain John Swanson to take the lifeboat alongside the ship, so it was guided with the lifeboat acting as pilot to South Ronaldsay where it was beached. This arduous service was carried out in very cold weather and snow storms, and the lifeboatmen were at sea for twenty-four hours. Just two days after returning to station, on 9 January, the Longhope lifeboatmen were again in action taking the reserve lifeboat to the steamer *Domino*, of Liverpool. When off Dunnet Head in a north-westerly gale, while bound from her home port to Copenhagen, the steamer's rudderhead was carried away. The lifeboat launched at 10.15 a.m. and escorted the vessel to a safe anchorage in Longhope Bay.

Performing two services in such quick succession must have been extremely demanding on the Longhope crew who deserved credit for their efforts. Both the *Samyntas Stannah* and Reserve No.3 lifeboats were relatively large lifeboats designed primarily for sailing and their size and weight meant launching off the beach involved a considerable amount of effort.

The lifeboat house of 1874 was built at a cost of £228 on 'a convenient site' provided by the local landowner at the southern end of the neck of land which connects South Walls to the North. This photograph, dating from 2004, shows the isolated location of this house and the beach over which the lifeboat was launched. (Nicholas Leach)

The old lifeboat house at Longhope, built in 1874 and used for the lifeboat until 1906, used in the 1990s by local fishermen as a packing station for shellfish. (Nicholas Leach)

Most of the RNLI's 39ft lifeboats were launched down some kind of slipway but dragging *Samyntas Stannah*, which weighed almost seven tons, across the beach was both time and energy consuming. Since the stationing of *Samyntas Stannah* at Longhope in the early 1890s the lifeboat was kept on a mooring during the winter months so that launching was easier and quicker, and did not require a team of shore helpers. To assist in recovering the boat after a launch, a winch was supplied in May 1896.

Although keeping the boat at moorings meant that putting to sea in bad weather was easier, the practice was not an effective solution to the problems of launching and, on several occasions, the lifeboat was damaged after breaking from her moorings. The first time, in December 1898, resulted in severe damage to the boat, which was repaired by a local boatbuilder. On the second occasion, in 1900, she was driven ashore and damaged during a heavy northerly gale on 15 and 16 February, with repairs effected by a Stromness boatbuilder. In December 1900, while being launched from the boathouse to take up her moorings for the winter, she was again damaged with repairs to an 8in hole in the port bow undertaken locally. These incidents served to emphasise the inadequacy of the launching arrangements, and showed that a more effective way of launching was urgently needed.

A New Station and a New Lifeboat

The problems of launching were further compounded during the months of July, August and September when the lifeboat was hauled out of the water effectively putting her out of action. Although forming a crew was not a problem, getting sufficient men to launch the boat was very difficult as many were away fishing during the summer. Once these problems had been highlighted, steps towards improving the station's efficiency were taken in 1903. The District Inspector suggested that a slipway be constructed to speed up the launch and recommended a site, called Outer Haven, about a mile and a half along the western shore of Aith Hope. At

Longhope's last sailing lifeboat was the 43ft Watson Anne Miles *(ON.550), on station from 1906 until 1926. This photograph was probably taken on the day of her inauguration service as she is dressed overall. (Orkney Photographic Archives)*

this point a slipway could be built down which the boat would launch into deep water. He justified the investment in a house and slipway as housing the boat would greatly reduce the cost of repairs needed as a result of keeping the lifeboat afloat and exposed to the elements.

In May 1904, the District Inspector visited the station and discussed the situation with Coxswain John Swanson, who had taken over the post in 1900, former Coxswain Ben Stout and the local committee. He concluded that the station was 'far from efficient although there was an excellent crew and no signs of there being any dearth of men.' The building of a new boathouse and slipway also came a step closer as the District Inspector selected a suitable spot on the west side of Aith Hope, subject to a lease being obtained. In October 1904, plans for the new boathouse were produced and early in 1905 tenders for the construction of the new building acquired. In April 1905 a lease was obtained for the site and tenders were accepted for the construction work. Several builders tendered but the successful contractor was Mr Fasey, of London, who had built the lifeboat house and slipway at Tenby, in South Wales.

As well as a new boathouse and slipway, the station was also allocated a new lifeboat, which was completed by Thames Ironworks, in London, in December 1905. Named *Anne Miles* (ON.550) after her London donor, she was the largest lifeboat stationed at Longhope hitherto, measuring 43ft in length by 12ft 6in in beam and pulling ten oars. The new boat was a Watson class non-self-righting lifeboat, designed primarily for sailing, of the type specifically requested by the crew. Although they had also expressed the desire for a motor to be fitted, the RNLI's Committee of Management asked them to wait until the experimental motor lifeboat, then undergoing its initial trials, had been proven. The crew decided upon a Watson sailing lifeboat rather than wait until a motor lifeboat was available. The Watson type, regarded at the time as the most up-to-date design, was intended to be a long-range lifeboat with greater endurance and seakindliness than the self-righters built in great numbers by the RNLI since the 1850s.

Designed by and named after George Lennox Watson, the RNLI's consulting naval architect, the design was broader than the self-righting types and offered much better stability. For a station such as Longhope, where large sea areas had to be covered, it was ideal.

Anne Miles left London on 7 April 1906 and was sailed north to her new station under the command of Capt. Stannard. She encountered very severe weather during the passage but 'behaved admirably', according to Stannard, and arrived on station later in the month to be initially kept at moorings until the new boathouse was ready. She was taken out for an exercise in the Pentland Firth on 26 April and 'thoroughly tried under canvas' to the satisfaction of both her coxswain and crew.

The new lifeboat station and roller slipway were completed in August 1906 and, situated approximately half way out on the Brims side of Aith Hope, enabled the lifeboat to be launched at all states of the tide. The honorary secretary, Capt. John Menzies, reported that the first launch of the new boat down the slipway was 'most satisfactory' and expressed 'the gratitude of the local committee for the splendid equipment for life-saving which had been placed at the station at such a large expense.' Further improvements were effected during the latter part of 1906 with the construction of an access road to the new boathouse. This house and slipway, which cost £2,975 1s 9d, remained in use for more than ninety years, accommodating lifeboats right up to the end of the twentieth century.

With a new boat and boathouse, the efficiency of the Longhope station was vastly improved with *Anne Miles* serving for twenty years during which time she launched on service seven times and saved eight lives. She had to wait more than six years before her services were first required and then, on 8 May 1912, when she went to the IJmuiden trawler *Dubbleman*, no effective service was carried out. Her first service took place more than four years later, on 15 October 1916, when she was called to the schooner *Fulton*, of Marstal, in difficulties in heavy seas during a northerly gale in the Pentland Firth. On reaching the vessel, the lifeboatmen

Anne Miles at moorings off Longhope. This photograph shows the fine lines of the Watson type lifeboat, a broad-beamed type designed to cover large distances under sail.

found that she had been taken in tow by a patrol boat, so the lifeboat escorted both vessels until they were in safe waters.

Anne Miles was involved in another service on 15 April 1922 which had no positive outcome but which proved to be extremely testing. During the afternoon, a message was relayed by Wick wireless station from the steamship *Pretoria* saying that the vessel had broken adrift from the two tugs which had been towing her and assistance was required. She was about thirty-five miles west of Thurso so the message went to both Thurso and Longhope lifeboat stations. *Anne Miles* launched at 4.12 p.m. and her crew began a journey of almost fifty miles in heavy, broken seas, a full northerly gale and torrential rain. The Thurso lifeboat *Sarah Austin* put out at 4.30 p.m. and proceeded under storm canvas towards the steamship's reported position. She reached the casualty at 8 p.m. and sailed around her several times burning flares. Receiving no response she made for Loch Eriboll where the lifeboatmen found out that the steamer's crew had been rescued by a tug. The lifeboat returned to Thurso after fourteen hours at sea, having sailed over seventy miles. Meanwhile, the Longhope lifeboat arrived off Loch Eriboll at 8.45 p.m. and, despite a thorough search of the area, found no trace of the steamer so returned to station. They arrived back at Longhope at 5 a.m. on 16 April having been at sea for thirteen hours and sailed almost 100 miles. In recognition of their efforts during this arduous service the crews of both lifeboats received additional money rewards from the RNLI.

On 12 September 1923 *Anne Miles* performed the most notable service of her career. She went to the aid of the Helsingsborg steamer *Citos*, which had lost her propeller and was adrift in the Pentland Firth in a westerly gale. The lifeboatmen found the casualty lying on her side on the west side of Stroma with a destroyer standing by. The destroyer had rescued nine of fifteen crew who had taken to the ship's boats and attempted to get ashore, although six had been lost in the heavy seas. The remaining eight crew on the steamer were then rescued by

Anne Miles *under oars off Longhope with her crew kitted out in cork life jackets and, somewhat unusually, her masts lowered. (Orkney Photographic Archives)*

The lifeboat house and roller slipway built in 1906 on the Brims side of Aith Hope for Anne Miles, *to make launching easier and faster than it had been hitherto. The house incorporated a landing gangway on the lee side of the slip for the use of the fishermen and this was funded by Mr Middlemore, owner of the site. (From an old postcard in the author's collection)*

Anne Miles which went alongside to save them. These eight men were then landed at St Mary's Village on Holm at 3 p.m., after which the lifeboat returned to station. Just over two weeks later Second Coxswain William Mowat, who had been in command during this service, and the lifeboat crew were invited to go on board HMS *Coventry*, which was moored in Scapa Flow, to be presented with an envelope containing £50 and congratulated for their 'excellent service'. The envelope also contained a message which read: 'Presented to the Coxswain and crew of the Longhope Lifeboat, from the Officers and men of HM Fleet at Scapa, as a token of appreciation for the excellent work performed on 12th September 1923.'

The last service performed by *Anne Miles* took place on 26 November 1924 when she was launched to assist the Hamburg-registered steamship *Curslack*. On arrival at the scene her assistance was not required so she returned to station at 6 p.m. At the time of this service a new motor lifeboat was under construction for Longhope. When this new boat arrived in September 1926, *Anne Miles* left the station. Although she did not save many lives, she was very highly thought of by her crew who regarded her as a superb sea boat. She was also very fast and two trawler skippers told of her travelling at between fifteen and seventeen knots when going out during the *Citos* service in September 1923. After leaving Longhope, she served at Howth, in Ireland, from November 1926 to 1930 and then for a further six years was stationed at New Brighton as the No.1 lifeboat covering the river Mersey. She was sold out of service in October 1936 and was converted into the auxiliary ketch *Zlata*, registered in Portsmouth and fitted with Ford petrol engines. In 1960 she was renamed *Westering* but, since the 1990s, details of her whereabouts have been unknown.

CHAPTER THREE

Motor Lifeboat Pioneers

The pulling and sailing lifeboats in Orkney performed only a relatively small number of services, a high proportion of which did not result in effective rescues, as the strong tides and heavy seas experienced around the islands were often too much for them. But, with the advent of the motor lifeboat during the early twentieth century, and the greater power it provided, Orkney's lifeboat stations were to realise their potential. The introduction of the internal combustion engine by the RNLI was a significant advance as a powered lifeboat had distinct advantages over one relying on sails and oars. Although many technical problems had to be overcome to effectively operate an engine on board a lifeboat, trials of the first motor lifeboat, a converted pulling boat, proved so successful that in July 1904 the RNLI's Committee of Management ordered three engines to be used to convert a further three lifeboats to power.

The initial difficulties were solved during the first year of trials, and the RNLI then felt confident enough that the new lifeboats 'for Fishguard, Stronsay, Stromness and Thurso should be specially designed as motor Life-boats', as *The Lifeboat* of November 1905 explained, adding that, 'fitting these lifeboats for motors entails considerable structural alterations, which have occupied a considerable time in carrying out, but as soon as all is completed, and the engines installed, a very interesting series of trials is anticipated.' The lifeboats had already been ordered from the London boatyard of Thames Ironworks. Although the Thurso boat, *Sarah Austin* (ON.585), was not in the end fitted with an engine 'owing to local difficulties being seen in the future', the two boats allocated to the Orkney stations were both powered.

The new Stromness lifeboat was a self-righting type, 42ft in length, similar to the station's pulling lifeboat but fitted with a Tylor four-cylinder engine of 30bhp which weighed approximately 10cwt. She was named after her donor, the late Mr John A. Hay of Cheltenham, whose legacy of £4,770 2s 11d bequeathed to the RNLI was used to fund five lifeboats of which the Stromness boat was the only one to be motor powered. During her trials *John A. Hay* (ON.561) reached a speed of almost seven knots at which rate she consumed twenty-one pints of petrol an hour. The boat for Stronsay was a Watson type, 43ft in length, and powered by a Blake four-cylinder engine which produced 40bhp and weighed approximately 15cwt. Named *John Ryburn*, she reached a speed of just over seven knots during her trials and consumed twenty-five pints of petrol in an hour.

An Epic Voyage North

The stationing of a motor lifeboat at Stromness had been discussed almost as soon as the first lifeboat had been motorised as it was realised that the station would benefit greatly from having a powered lifeboat. That two motor lifeboats were sent to stations in Orkney suggests a far-sightedness in realising that motor lifeboats would be particularly effective in the area, and be markedly more efficient at rescue work than pulling boats. *John Ryburn* and *John A. Hay*, together with the Thurso pulling lifeboat, left London Docks at 8.50 a.m. on 15 April 1909 and began their journey north by sea, an epic voyage described in detail in *The Lifeboat* of 2 August 1909. Until then, new lifeboats had usually been delivered to their station as cargo on board a steamship or by railway. Such a journey as the three boats were about to embark upon was a major undertaking and probably intended as a proving test of the new motor lifeboats,

The flotilla of lifeboats at Thurso nearing the end of their epic journey north from London. The Stromness lifeboat John A. Hay *(ON.561) is on the left, nearest the quayside, with the Stronsay boat* John Ryburn *(ON.565) in the middle. On the outside is the Thurso boat* Sarah Austin *(ON.585), a twelve-oared Watson sailing type. (RNLI)*

which were somewhat mistrusted by the crews who were to man them. Commander Howard F.J. Rowley, RN, the Inspector of the Northern District, was in charge of the flotilla, and each boat was manned by a crew of five local fishermen. Also included in the crews were Mr Small, the Institution's motor surveyor, and two motor mechanics, who were to assess the engines' performance during the passage.

The first stop for the boats was Harwich, a distance of seventy-three miles, and this was accomplished in just under twelve hours. The Stromness boat led the convoy, with the Stronsay boat next towing the Thurso boat. This order was maintained throughout the voyage until the boats reached the Pentland Firth. After the overnight stop at Harwich, the boats travelled sixty miles to Gorleston, covering the distance at an average speed of a little over seven knots. On Saturday 17 April, the flotilla left Gorleston at 4.10 a.m. aiming for Grimsby but, having had a comparatively smooth journey hitherto, during this third leg of the journey problems with the engines began. Two unscheduled stops had to be made with the result that the tide in the Humber was missed and Grimsby Dock not reached until late in the evening. By the time the boats had been berthed, the crews had been on duty for twenty-four hours.

After a rest day at Grimsby, the boats left at 7 a.m. on 19 April heading for Scarborough, sixty miles away, where they arrived at 4.15 p.m. The next day they made for Hartlepool and on 21 April reached Tynemouth. The engines had given some trouble on the passage to Hartlepool, and leaving Tynemouth one broke down completely and took three days to repair. The next stop was at Blyth, just ten miles from Tynemouth, by when the boats had been travelling for a week. Although 25 April was a Sunday, it was decided that, because of the delay at Tynemouth, the flotilla needed to press on especially as the weather was favourable. The Tay was reached at 7.30 p.m. and the boats moored in Dundee Docks after covering 111 miles in a creditable eighteen and a half hours. From Dundee they set out for Aberdeen, sixty miles north, but arrived within ten miles of Aberdeen as the wind was increasing. An Aberdeen harbour tug was required to assist them, 'plucking the boats into the harbour.'

The boats left Aberdeen on Wednesday 28 April, again receiving 'further valuable help in towing given by the Harbour tug, which accompanied the lifeboats for ten miles.' They reached Fraserburgh at 3 p.m. and, after an overnight stop, made an early start the following morning to cross the Moray Firth. Having to contend with strong winds and squalls of snow and hail the flotilla did not reach its next destination, Wick, until 10.30 p.m. Despite being tired after such a long day, the crews set out early on Friday 30 April for Thurso, thirty miles north. They had to contend with the full force of an ebb tide in the Pentland Firth but reached their destination in the early afternoon. After handing over the Thurso boat at Scrabster, the two remaining boats began the final leg of their voyage north. However, after considerable trouble with the Stronsay boat's engine, she had to return to Scrabster although the Stromness boat reached her station that evening. The Stronsay boat was repaired at Thurso and eventually reached Stromness on Saturday 1 May, after being towed by the steamship St Ola, subsequently proceeding to her station under her own power.

During the epic journey which had taken seventeen days, the new Stromness lifeboat covered 768 miles and arrived at her new station at 8 p.m. on Friday 30 April, while the Stronsay boat covered 808 miles. Throughout, according to *The Lifeboat's* detailed account, 'the flotilla had caused some excitement all along the coast from London,' and 'the lifeboatmen received much kindness.' The account concluded that 'the experiences . . . will prove most useful not only to all on board the three lifeboats, but also to the Institution. The crews were of opinion that the boats behaved wonderfully, and they stated that they could not have credited lifeboats with such remarkable powers.' These highly favourable comments are somewhat at odds with the fact that the motors broke down on a number of occasions – off Grimsby, at Tynemouth, and when leaving Thurso, while at Aberdeen assistance from the harbour tug was required. Undoubtedly the journey had been a considerable test for the new motor lifeboats, but the positive interpretation of events in the official report was no doubt intended to show that the motor lifeboat represented the future of life-saving.

What the RNLI's upbeat accounts of the motor lifeboats' passage failed to mention was the dispute that the timing of the journey caused at Stromness, resulting in the lifeboat crew going on strike. The dispute came about after the date for the passage originally selected, February 1909, was postponed by the RNLI due to poor weather. The Stromness committee selected a crew to travel to London and man the boat during the voyage north but, when the RNLI moved the date to April, the selected crew was no longer available because it was then the lobster fishing season and the men had to be fishing. The station's honorary secretary, G.L. Thompson, wrote to the RNLI asking to postpone the passage until June, but the Institution was not prepared to do this as both Stronsay and Thurso boats were ready and the Inspector had arranged to take all three boats north together.

The assumption was made at Stromness that a crew from London would bring her north but, unbeknownst to the Stromness committee and crew, the RNLI had asked men from Stronsay to crew both boats, their own and that for Stromness. Although a new crew had been selected at Stromness and was ready to go to London, the arrangements already made by the RNLI remained in place and the boats departed on their journey north. When it was discovered at Stromness what had happened, this perceived snub outraged some of the Stromness lifeboatmen. As *The Orcadian* for 5 May 1909 stated, 'Stronsay men to fetch the Stromness lifeboat? The thing was absurd! The Stromness crew were very indignant at this seeming slight and hastily met and discussed the matter amongst themselves.'

When *John A. Hay* arrived at Stromness, as described above, she was initially shunned by many of the crew and forced to berth at the south side of the Warehouse Pier. According to

The 42ft self-righting motor lifeboat John A. Hay *(ON.561) approaching Stromness. This pioneering craft was one of the RNLI's very first motor-powered lifeboats and served in Orkney for almost twenty years. The high end boxes provided the self-righting capability and, because she only had a single engine, she carried auxiliary sails consisting of a modified No.1 rig. In this photograph her main mast has been lowered and the sail rigged as a temporary shelter. (Orkney Photographic Archives)*

The Orcadian, 'unlike the receptions she received at all ports of call en route, she was received here with an ominous silence.' The crew immediately refused to man the new lifeboat and Commander Rowley was handed a letter by Second Coxswain William Gunn asking for an explanation as to why a Stromness crew had not been sent for. A meeting was hastily convened at the Stromness Hotel and Rowley, supported by the honorary secretary and local committee, explained that no slight was intended and 'regret was expressed that the Stromness men did not bring their own boat home'. This, however, was not good enough for the three men representing the striking crew, Second Coxswain William Gunn, John Sinclair and William Laughton, who blamed the Coxswain, Robert Greig, and demanded he be removed form his position. Greig seems to have been made the main scapegoat and both he and the members of the local committee were blamed for the dispute.

The meeting failed to resolve the matter and the arrival of the Stronsay boat *John Ryburn* at Stromness during the evening of Saturday 1 May, having been towed into port by *St Ola*, was the spark for further confrontational scenes. According to *The Orcadian's* account, the ringleader of the disgruntled lifeboatmen was arrested, causing an angry mob to confront the two local policemen while 'the more rowdy members of the mob vented their venom by the reprehensible conduct of stone-throwing, [as] the officers exhibited a praiseworthy coolness'. Despite the hot-headedness of some of the crew, matters calmed down over the next few days. Coxswain Greig offered his resignation, but this was declined by both the Inspector and the local committee, and he remained in his post during the first years of the motor lifeboat's service. The matter must have been resolved as no further reports appeared in the local newspapers and in June the honorary secretary reported to the RNLI that 'the trouble was over and the boat has been out on service'.

On a somewhat more practical level, housing the new motor lifeboat at Stromness proved problematic. On her arrival *John A. Hay* was moored overnight and taken the next day to the

The motor lifeboat John A. Hay *alongside the slipway at Stromness, possibly after arriving on station. This view shows the boat's open layout which provided virtually no shelter for her crew who, on many occasions, performed long and arduous services in dreadful weather. (Orkney Photographic Archives)*

boathouse. The old lifeboat, *Good Shepherd*, was launched and towed to the north end of the harbour where she was moored and, subsequently, broken up. Meanwhile, it was found that *John A. Hay* could not be housed as she did not fit the slipway. Alterations were soon carried out, with rollers fitted to the slipway to ease the boat's passage into and out of the house, and eventually the new boat was ready for service.

The first launch by the new motor lifeboat took place on 26 May 1909. She put out at 10.30 a.m. to go to the assistance of several lobster boats caught out by a sudden south-easterly gale. Two of the lobster boats reached harbour as the lifeboat was putting out, another also reached the shore safely without help and the last was towed in by the lifeboat. Unusually, the station's honorary secretary, George Thompson, was in charge of the lifeboat during this service with the harbour master helping to make up the crew as the coxswain and most of the regular crew were fishing. A few months later, *John A. Hay* was involved in another service to a casualty close to port. On the morning of 5 October 1909 the Aberdeen trawler *Ocean Prince*, with a crew of nine, ran aground on the Ness in fine weather. The crew was in no immediate danger and remained on board but efforts to refloat the trawler failed. During the evening, the weather worsened, a south-westerly gale blew up, and the lifeboat was launched to help. She was taken close enough to the trawler to rescue all nine men, but heavy seas repeatedly swept both boats and the service was completed with difficulty. By midnight the weather had improved so the lifeboat took the crew back to the trawler. When further attempts to refloat the stranded trawler failed, the trawler's crew were landed at Stromness by the lifeboat in the early hours of 6 October.

No further services were undertaken until 1914, by when the First World War had broken out. The first casualty to which *John A. Hay* launched during the war years was HMS *Dryad*, which had gone ashore near Stromness on 21 October 1914. By the time the lifeboat had

Above: *The Stromness lifeboat crew on board*
John A. Hay *soon after she arrived on station.*
Robert Greig, Coxswain until 1915, is at the
wheel with the station's first mechanic, known
initially as the 'motor man', John Baikie, sitting
in the middle of the front row with his arms
folded. The elderly man sitting at the back is
William Leslie, Coxswain of the Stronsay
lifeboat. (Orkney Photographic Archives)

Right: *Coxswain Robert Greig at the wheel*
of John A. Hay. *Greig served as Stromness*
Coxswain from May 1898 until February 1915
and was at the centre of the controversy when
the motor lifeboat first arrived on station. (From
the George Ellison collection, by courtesy of
Orkney Photographic Archives)

John A. Hay putting out from her station in about 1913, passing a steamer at moorings in the bay. *(George Ellison collection, courtesy of Orkney Photographic Archives)*

reached the casualty the warship had refloated undamaged, although two of her crew had been injured and so they were taken ashore by the lifeboat. On 11 November 1914, *John A. Hay* stood by the ship *Sorfareren*, of Christiania, which was in difficulties in heavy seas near Peter Skerry. The lifeboat stayed with the casualty for three hours, until a steam tug and steam trawler arrived to take the vessel in tow. In December 1914 *John A. Hay* was launched twice to assist minesweepers. On the afternoon of 6 December, in very heavy seas and a south-easterly gale, the RN Minesweeper *Orsina* ran aground off Hoy. Once the lifeboat had reached the scene some of the lifeboatmen boarded the stranded vessel which was eventually refloated. On 17 December, the minesweeper *Lorenzo* ran aground in Hoy Sound and, despite heavy seas and a near gale-force wind, the lifeboat succeeded in getting alongside to save ten of the ship's crew.

The rescues during the latter months of 1914 were, perhaps surprisingly, the only wartime services performed by the Stromness lifeboat. The lack of demand for the lifeboat's services was due to changes in the composition of shipping in the area during period. Not only did fewer cargo and fishing vessels visit the area, but the number of naval vessels significantly increased as Scapa Flow became an important base for the Royal Navy. Naval craft were unlikely to request lifeboat assistance should they get into difficulty, something that was to prove catastrophic in June 1916. On the morning of 6 June, the cruiser HMS *Hampshire*, with War Minister Lord Kitchener and his staff on board, was leaving Scapa Flow when, shortly after 8 a.m., she struck a mine about two miles off Marwick Head and sunk. Severe weather had prevented the usual mine-sweeping operations either on the eastern side of Orkney or the more sheltered westerly route, which HMS *Hampshire* took, yet intelligence had suggested that a German minelaying submarine was operating in the area. Matters were made worse by the failure of the naval authorities to organise a rescue operation. The lifeboat crew at Stromness was not informed of the sinking so the lifeboat was not launched. The local expertise of the crew would undoubtedly have helped save lives and operating in the heavy seas would have not been a problem. On the scene, launching the ship's lifeboats in the difficult sea conditions proved impossible and, in the end, only twelve men from the cruiser reached the shore alive. Over 650 of the her complement were drowned, none of Lord Kitchener's party survived, and yet the tragic loss of so many lives could have been avoided.

After the end of the war, *John A. Hay* performed a couple of routine services as life returned to normal. She launched on 27 January 1920 to the steam trawler *Ulster*, of Aberdeen, which had run aground in extremely rough seas and a severe gale. The trawler was in a very dangerous position, but the lifeboat rescued her crew of ten and landed them at Stromness. At midnight, the lifeboat launched again to take the crew back to their the trawler which, eventually, was refloated. On 27 November 1921 *John A. Hay* launched to a vessel aground at Birsay, eighteen miles north of Stromness. In dense fog and heavy seas she reached the casualty, the steam drifter *Keith Hall*, of Aberdeen, at 9.50 p.m. and found nine of the crew in one of the drifter's boats. One man had been lost while this boat was being launched from the stricken vessel, but the nine survivors were landed safely at Stromness.

On 1 January 1922 *John A. Hay* was involved in an outstanding service which, according to the RNLI's Annual Report of 1922, 'illustrates very clearly the value of motor-power.' At 9.15 a.m. news from Birsay reached Stromness that a vessel was in distress off Costa Head, over twenty miles round the coast. Within twenty-five minutes the lifeboat had been launched under the command of Coxswain William Johnston and was heading north towards the casualty in heavy seas and strong winds. While the lifeboat was on its way, honorary secretary George Thomson went to Birsay by car to provide what assistance he could from land. When he reached the scene, he found that the vessel, the trawler *Fresia* homeward bound to Grimsby with a large catch of fish, had already sunk. Her crew had been seen on a small raft drifting towards the islands off Eynhallow. Thomson placed signalmen round the cliffs to guide the lifeboat when she arrived, but, fearing that she would be too late, appealed for shore-boats to put out. Two set out from Evie and one from Rousay, but the heavy seas forced them back and, despite considerable efforts, they had to abandon their attempts as they were unable to compete with the gale force conditions. The men from Evie did succeed in landing on Eynhallow, however, and were ready to provide help should the raft be driven ashore. By about 1 p.m. *John A. Hay* had reached the scene of the wreck. Guided by the signalmen, she found the raft which consisted of little more than a few planks, and rescued two men who were totally exhausted and, a few minutes later, would have died. They proved to be the only survivors of a crew of eleven. The lifeboat transferred them to one of the shore-boats, which immediately took them to Evie, and then started the return journey to Stromness. On the way to her station, she picked up the bodies of two of the *Fresia's* crew but the twenty-five mile journey through rough seas back to her station, which was reached at 6.30 p.m., was a severe test of endurance for the crew.

Throughout the nine hour service, Coxswain Johnston had remained at the wheel. The lifeboat had travelled fifty miles, been continually swept by the waves and the crew blinded at times by the rain, wet to the skin, and faced by extreme cold. Moreover, the actual rescue had been performed in a channel made dangerous by a number of reefs. In recognition of the skill with which the lifeboat was handled, and the extreme exposure suffered by the crew, Coxswain Johnston was awarded the Bronze medal while Letters of Thanks were presented to the eleven other crew members, two signalmen, as well as honorary secretary George Thomson in recognition of his efforts. Extra monetary rewards were given to the crew and signalmen as well as to the fourteen men who went out in shore-boats from Evie and Rousay.

More Power for Stromness

The decision to station in Orkney two of the first ever motor lifeboats was made because they would be particularly advantageous to the crews when faced with the powerful tidal races and strong winds typical of the seas off the north coast of Scotland. With difficult sea conditions to contend with, the lifeboat at Stromness was often called upon to perform rescues that involved travelling significant distances to reach a casualty and thus the range of the lifeboat was important. By the early 1920s, when the Stromness committee was notified that a more powerful motor lifeboat was to be supplied to the station, a new 60ft twin-engined type had just been built to the design of James Barnett, the RNLI's Consulting Naval Architect and it was suggested that one of these boats would be built for the station.

The new 60ft boat, allocated to the New Brighton station on the Mersey, was larger than any built hitherto and, with two engines, represented a massive leap forward in terms of motor lifeboat design. Named *William and Kate Johnston* (ON.682), she undertook a circumnavigation of the British Isles in 1923 during which she covered 2,000 miles in just over two months, travelling up the east coast then around the northern tip of Scotland before coming down the west coast. She visited Stromness during her tour and was taken to sea by members of the Stromness committee and crew in a gale. As well as the 60ft design, the honorary secretary, coxswain and second coxswain also looked at the smaller 45ft Watson motor type which had been built for Tenby.

After assessing both types, the large New Brighton boat seemed to be most suitable for Stromness. But whilst the 60ft type was an impressive boat, its displacement of around forty-four tons meant it was too large and heavy to fit inside the boathouse and would have to be kept afloat, yet the committee and crew at Stromness felt that their boat should be

The 51ft Barnett J.J.K.S.W. (ON.702) arriving at Stromness in March 1928 and being recovered up the slipway, with the boat she replaced, John A. Hay, alongside the slipway. The difference in size and design is clearly shown in this photograph, with the new lifeboat having a much greater range, carrying capacity and more powerful engines. She left her builder's yard at Cowes on 15 February 1928 and spent five days on display at Guernsey before heading north covering over 1,000 miles during a passage which consisted of 125 hours at sea. (Orkney Photographic Archives)

The 51ft Barnett J.J.K.S.W. (O.N.702), Stromness' second motor lifeboat, alongside the pier in the harbour shortly after she had arrived on station in March 1928. This powerful vessel was twin-engined and the first 51ft motor lifeboat to be designed and built. The class took the name 'Stromness' after the station at which the first boat served. (Orkney Photographic Archives)

housed. The station's honorary secretary, Mr G.L. Thomson, went to London with the crew's description of their ideal lifeboat: as well as being housed, it should be around 50ft long with twin engines, a speed of not less than nine knots, have increased sheer, a higher bow and more flare. In addition, protection for the crew should be provided in a forward cockpit and a low foot rail should be fitted below the railings on deck. These matters were discussed with Barnett, the RNLI's Naval Architect responsible for new designs, and many of the new ideas were incorporated in the end product.

The new type, developed specifically for the station, had an operating range of 100 miles at cruising speed and was compact enough to fit inside a boathouse. It became known as the 51ft Barnett 'Stromness' class and was much lighter, with a displacement of 26.5 tons, than the 60ft Barnett. The boat's hull was divided into eight watertight compartments and fitted 160 air cases; the cabin had seating for ten people and cockpits forward and aft, fitted with shelters which had space for a further twelve. Built from mahogany, teak, Canadian rock-elm and English oak, the 51ft Barnett was fitted with two six-cylinder 60hp Weyburn petrol engines contained within a watertight compartment. Each engine was itself watertight, so would continue to run even if the engine room was flooded and the engines themselves submerged, as the air-intakes were located above the waterline. The exhausts were carried up a funnel amidships. The boat's maximum speed was almost nine knots, at which it could travel more than 120 miles.

The new lifeboat undertook her harbour trial at the Cornubia Yard of S.E. Saunders Ltd at East Cowes on 4 January 1928. She left Cowes on 15 February 1928 and, having spent five days at Guernsey where she was on show to the public, arrived at Stromness on 3 March. During the passage north, the new lifeboat spent 125 hours at sea, and travelled a total of 1,007 miles, averaging 8.5 knots. A week later the veteran *John A. Hay* left for Belfast after almost twenty years of service. The new lifeboat was first called upon two weeks after arriving in

51ft Barnett 'Stromness' type J.J.K.S.W. (O.N.702) on the slipway at Stromness dressed overall for her naming ceremony. (By courtesy of John Harrop)

The scene at Stromness waterfront during the ceremony of J.J.K.S.W. at the lifeboat station on 6 June 1928 with people crowded round every vantage point to witness HRH Prince George perform the christening.

Orkney, on 19 March, when she went to the assistance of the steam trawler *Lord Davenport*, of Hull, wrecked on St Johns Head, Hoy. Before the lifeboat arrived on scene two members of he trawler's crew were drowned. The lifeboat was in time to save six survivors using the new line throwing gun which fired a line across to the exhausted survivors. Marwick's centenary history of Stromness records that the lifeboat's 'excellent behaviour in dangerous conditions greatly impressed the lifeboatmen.'

As to the new lifeboat was so much larger than her predecessor, a new lifeboat house and slipway were needed. Built on the site of the existing house, the new building provided much larger and more substantial accomodation. The contract for the construction work was awarded on 3 October 1925 to Melville, Dundas and Whitsun, of Glasgow, and the new house was completed in 1926 at a cost of £10,660. This house was used for the station's lifeboats until 1984 and remained under RNLI ownership until being sold in 2001 (see Appendix 2).

Named *J.J.K.S.W.*, the new lifeboat served at Stromness for more than twenty-five years during which time she is credited with saving 139 lives. She was funded from the combination of five legacies received from Miss J. Moody, Derby; Mr J.P. Traill, London; Mr W.M. Aitken, Edinburgh; Mrs E.J. Hanson, Belper; and Mr W.M. Notting, Bush Hill Park, Middlesex. The initials represented the somewhat cumbersome full title of *John and Ann Moody, J.P. Traill, Kate MacFarlane Aitken, Sam Wood* and *William Notting*. At a ceremony on 6 June 1928 at Stromness, she was christened by HRH Prince George, KG GCVO RN. After the service of dedication conducted by the Revd James Christie and a special lunch at Stromness, Prince George was taken in the new lifeboat, with Coxswain William Johnston at the helm, to Longhope where he christened that station's new lifeboat. The passage across to Hoy was the first time the Royal Standard had been flown from a lifeboat.

In February 1929 Coxswain Johnston was awarded a second bronze medal for another outstanding service. At about 4 a.m. on the morning of 14 February, news reached Stromness that the trawler *Carmania II*, of Grimsby, had gone ashore on the Kirk Rocks, Hoy Sound. The trawler was returning home from Iceland with a large catch of fish when, passing through Hoy Sound at about 3.30 a.m., her steering gear jammed with a strong breeze blowing, a heavy sea running and bitterly cold weather. *J.J.K.S.W.* put out and reached the scene at about 5 a.m. but had no hope of approaching the trawler from seaward, as the seas were breaking 100 to 150 yards up to the casualty, while between her and the shore were reefs and shallow water over which the lifeboat could not pass until the tide rose. The coxswain stood by for three hours until daylight and then decided to attempt a rescue.

Prince George meets the lifeboat crew during the naming of J.J.K.S.W. *(Orkney Photographic Archives)*

HRH Prince George leaving Stromness on board J.J.K.S.W. *after the naming at Stromness on 6 June 1928. The new lifeboat took him to Longhope for the inauguration service there and, during the crossing to Hoy, flew the Royal Standard, becoming the first lifeboat ever to do so. (By courtesy of John Harrop)*

As the tide turned the seas grew heavier, but the lifeboat was manoeuvred through the foaming breakers, dropped anchor, and established communication with the casualty by means of the line-throwing gun. By this time, a huge wave had lifted the trawler on to the top of the reef, swinging her round at the same time. A life-buoy was then sent to the wreck and the lifeboat herself was veered in through the surf, nearer and nearer as the tide on rose. One by one the trawler's crew were drawn through the surf to the lifeboat, until five had been rescued. Then a tremendous wave caught the lifeboat causing the wire anchor cable to snap. The Coxswain, with fine judgment, brought the lifeboat under control and drove her ahead and among the reefs, until she was in the lee of the wreck. He then shouted to the remaining seven of the trawler's crew to get aboard their small boat, which was floating under the trawler's lee having been swept off the deck. This was hauled to the lifeboat and a further five men were rescued, but the small boat's rope parted and the boat, with two men still in it, was swept away. The coxswain immediately took the lifeboat between wreck and shore, caught up with the ship's boat and the last two men were rescued.

For this fine service, witnessed by spectators on the beach, Coxswain William Johnston was awarded a Second Service Clasp to the Bronze medal which he already held. Additional monetary rewards were made to each member of the lifeboat's crew. On hearing the details of this rescue Prince George, who had named the lifeboat the previous year, sent a telegraph to the whole crew congratulating them on their bravery and for undertaking such an outstanding rescue. Coxswain Johnston, not one to enjoy publicity, had to travel to Scrabster for a presentation during which he received his medal from the Duchess of Portland.

Soon after this rescue, during which the new 51ft Barnett lifeboat had proved her worth, *J.J.K.S.W* was involved in yet another long service during which her range, and the endurance of her crew, were tested to the extreme in one of the most tragic incidents to take place in the Northern Isles. On the night of 28 March 1930 the Aberdeen trawler *Ben Doran* ran aground

51ft Barnett 'Stromness' type J.J.K.S.W. *approaches the slipway at Stromness to be recovered, with her mast already folded. (Orkney Photographic Archives)*

J.J.K.S.W. *saving the crew of the trawler* Carmania II, *of Grimsby, in February 1929, a service for which Coxswain William Johnston was awarded the Bronze medal. (By courtesy of John Harrop)*

on the Ve Skerries, to the west of Papa Stour. The vessel was not spotted until the following morning when attempts were made to assist her. But in the gale force winds and heavy seas nothing could be done. The Lerwick Lifesaving Company was called out and several local motor boats put to sea but none was able to get close to the wreck. The nearest lifeboat station was at Stromness and so, late on the afternoon of 30 March, *J.J.K.S.W.* was called to help. She put an out at 4.45 p.m. with Second Coxswain William Linklater in command and fought her way north through the heavy seas and south-easterly gale.

The lifeboat headed first for Scalloway, 134 miles from Stromness, to where a telegram was sent asking for food, fuel and a local pilot to be ready when the lifeboat arrived. She

J.J.K.S.W. is hauled up the slipway at Stromness. The two ships are Northern Lighthouse Board (NLB) tenders with, on the right, NLS Pharos, *the sixth ship to bear that name, and NLS* Pole Star *on the left. Both vessels were regular callers at Stromness where the NLB maintained a depot. (Orkney Photographic Archives)*

Stromness lifeboat crew with J.J.K.S.W. at the head of he shipway. (Orkney Photographic Archives)

reached the port at 7.30 a.m. on 31 March after a passage of almost fifteen hours in the worst conditions. The lifeboat was refuelled and, after a hot meal, the crew set out with the pilot on board to try to save the trawler's crew. They left Scalloway at 9 a.m. and headed for Ve Skerries, twenty-five miles to the north-west. Upon reaching the scene, only the top of the trawler's mast could be seen above the waves but despite a thorough search of the area, no survivors were found. The lifeboat returned to Scalloway at 5 p.m. and, after a few hours sleep, left at 6.30 a.m. on 1 April. She headed south into a southerly gale toward Orkney. After a return journey of just over sixteen hours she reached her station at 11 p.m. The lifeboat and her crew had been away from station for over fifty-five hours and had travelled nearly 260 miles which was, according to the RNLI's account, 'the longest journey on service which has been made by any Motor Lifeboat.' By an unfortunate twist of fate, the RNLI had announced in March 1930 plans for establishing a lifeboat station at Lerwick, the Shetland capital, and if *Ben Doran* had been wrecked a year later her crew would probably have been saved.

The Barnett lifeboat and her crew had been severely tested during the ultimately unsuccessful trip to Shetland, but they were called on to perform another long service just over a week later and again had to travel to Shetland. The Coastguard informed the honorary secretary, G.L. Thomson, that the mail steamer Sunniva had gone ashore on Mousa, a small island on the eastern side of Shetland. *J.J.K.S.W.* put out at 5.30 a.m. on 10 April with Coxswain Johnston at the helm, and headed north into moderate seas and thick fog. Four hours later another message was received at Stromness reporting that all the steamer's passengers and crew had been brought safely ashore in the ship's boats. However, as the lifeboat was not fitted with a radio set she could not be recalled and continued on her voyage. She reached Sunniva at 6 p.m. only to find everyone was safely ashore, and so she made for Lerwick where she arrived at 7.30 p.m. Coxswain Johnston initially decided to remain overnight but, when the fog lifted just before midnight, the lifeboat set off on her journey south. She reached Stromness at 2 p.m. on 11 April having been away from station for thirty-six hours and travelled 240 miles.

The services to Shetland highlighted two deficiencies in the lifeboat service, both of which were rectified soon afterwards. Firstly, the lack of lifeboat cover for Shetland and, secondly, the inadequate methods of communication between shore and boat. The situation in Shetland was remedied when the 51ft Barnett *Lady Jane and Martha Ryland* (ON.731) was sent to a newly-established station at Lerwick in July 1930, while developments in radio communication began to impact on lifeboat operations. The problems of communicating with a lifeboat at sea had been highlighted at stations such as Stromness and Longhope where new motor lifeboats, with a much greater range than any previous lifeboats, often travelled many miles from their stations. Maintaining communications with them had always been difficult and unreliable. Prior to the installation of a wireless set in the Stromness lifeboat, Mr Thomson, the honorary secretary, and his two assistants, John Rae and J.G. Sinclair, always endeavoured to keep in touch with the lifeboat when she was at sea by means of Morse signals or, in event of recall, by Very pistol and later by small rocket. A wireless set was first fitted into a lifeboat in 1927 when the new Rosslare Harbour lifeboat *K.E.C.F.* (ON.700) was equipped with a receiving and transmitting set. The wireless was housed in a watertight case, had a range of over eighty miles, and a certified operator had to be taken on board each time the boat went out. Gradually, wireless sets were fitted into all of the RNLI's motor lifeboats, and radio communication became commonplace.

The benefits of radio communication were demonstrated on 15 January 1931 when *J.J.K.S.W.* was launched to search for one of the local fishing vessels, which had failed to

J.J.K.S.W. outside the lifeboat house at the top of the slipway. This photograph shows the layout of the 51ft Barnett with the small aft cabin housing the engine controls, the shelter forward and the tunnels at the stern in which the propellers were housed. (Orkney Photographic Archives)

return to port in westerly gales and very rough sea. The lifeboat searched for the vessel, but was informed by radio at 1.30 a.m. the following morning she was sheltering off Seago, on Hoy. The missing boat was then quickly located and her cold, wet and exhausted crew were taken aboard the lifeboat and given hot drinks. At dawn, the fishermen were put back on board their boat which was escorted by the lifeboat to Lyness. The radio equipment again proved useful on 25 June 1933 after the trawler *Cape Sable*, of Hull, had gone aground, in very dense fog, in the early morning. *J.J.K.S.W.* launched at 4 a.m. and the lifeboatmen were informed by radio that the trawler was near Hoy Head, not in the position reported initially. The lifeboat then succeeded in pulling the vessel clear of the rocks at high tide and escorted her to Stromness.

During the 1930s *J.J.K.S.W.* undertook a number of services to steam drifters and motor fishing vessels, such as those described above. Most were of a fairly routine nature but that on 15 March 1936 proved to be rather more testing for the Stromness lifeboatmen. At 5.35 a.m. on 16 March 1936, just twenty minutes after news had been received that a vessel was ashore on Hoy, *J.J.K.S.W.* was launched and headed out of Stromness harbour into rough seas, a strong westerly wind and torrential rain. The trawler *Siberite*, of Hull, had gone aground at Rora Head, was rolling heavily and bumping on the rocks. Under Coxswain William Linklater, the lifeboat reached the scene and was taken alongside the trawler three times enabling all eleven of the casualty's crew to jump to safety. Although the lifeboat sustained some damage when she struck the rocks, she safely got clear to land the rescued men at Stromness. This was an excellent service for which the RNLI sent a Letter of Thanks to Coxswain Linklater, while the Board of Trade's formal Court of Enquiry held into the trawler's loss praised the lifeboatmen: 'Owing to the speedy actions of the Stromness lifeboat's crew in answering the SOS, all the trawler's crew were saved, in a very dangerous place. The Court wish to place on record their commendation of this excellently performed work of rescue.'

Having a large area to cover often meant that the Stromness lifeboatmen undertook long and arduous services, some of which did not even result in a rescue being effected. Such was the case on 2 November 1938 when *J.J.K.S.W.* launched at 12.50 p.m. to the Danish schooner *Nordstjernen*, of Marstal, which had been dismasted in very heavy seas and a westerly gale, and was drifting ten miles north of Noup Head on Westray, forty miles from Stromness. The lifeboat reached the reported position at 6 p.m., but her crew could see no sign of the casualty so began a search. At 2 a.m. a message from Wick Radio reported that the schooner had been taken in tow by a trawler and the two vessels were making for Pierowall on Westray. Conditions were absolutely appalling so the lifeboat sheltered in the lee of Papa Westray until dawn, eventually returning to station at 1.30 p.m. after almost twenty-four hours at sea. Following this long and demanding service, the RNLI sent a Letter of Appreciation to Coxswain Robert Greig and his crew in recognition of their efforts. The mechanic, Walter Cursiter, who had spent much of the time at sea operating the wireless, received a special mention and the Danish Government also sent a Letter of Thanks to the RNLI in appreciation of the lifeboatmen's work.

Another long service was performed by the Stromness lifeboatmen on 1 November 1939 after a vessel had been reported ashore on North Ronaldsay, sixty miles from Stromness. In rough seas and a very strong south-easterly wind, *J.J.K.S.W.* battled her way north finding the casualty, the Norwegian steamer *Mim*, at 7 a.m. aground on Reef Dyke. Eleven of the steamer's crew were taken off by a local motor boat, and then the lifeboat went alongside to rescue the remaining twenty-two. While taking off the eleven men, the local boat was damaged and had

On 19 August 1935, the 1930-built Swedish motorship Gunnaren *was stranded in thick fog on the west side of Swona. She was on passage from New York to Gothenburg with general cargo. No lifeboat service was needed but a large salvage operation was undertaken. As the vessel's bow was stuck fast, she was cut in two and the stern section, pictured here, was towed away afloat and undamaged. This section then drifted ashore about a quarter of a mile from the bow, an event photographed by Tom Rosie, a Swona resident. Salvage operations yielded hundreds of apples and pears which were sold locally, and the salvage workers were paid a shilling an hour. (Orkney Photographic Archives)*

J.J.K.S.W. approaching the slipway at Stromness with survivors from the wrecked trawler Leicester City *in March 1953. The trawler got into difficulties to the west of Hoy in heavy fog and was wrecked close to Braebuater Point. (Orkney Photographic Archives)*

to be beached so the lifeboat then took the eleven men and landed all thirty-three survivors at Kirkwall, before returning to her station at 2.45 p.m. on 3 November. Because of wartime restrictions then in force, this rescue had to be undertaken without the aid of the usual coastal navigation lights and the RNLI granted additional monetary rewards to each of the crew.

This early wartime launch proved to be the first of only two effective services performed during the Second World War. The other took place on 15 August 1942 when *J.J.K.S.W.* brought in the motor fishing boat *Excelsior* which had been reported missing in strong winds and torrential rain. But despite the intense naval activity in Orkney during the 1939-45 conflict, the lifeboat was not called out again until the war had ended. Apart from naval craft, the number of vessels in and around Orkney was limited and no doubt many avoided the area because the coastal lights and navigation aids had been removed. The danger of German U-boats was another factor and these craft inflicted severe losses on vessels heading to or leaving Kirkwall during 1940. On 12 January 1940 the Danish motor tanker *Danmark*, of 10,517 tons, was torpedoed while at anchor just to the east of Kirkwall and just over two weeks later, the Norwegian steamer *Faro* became another U-boat victim.

The lack of calls could also be attributed to wartime censorship regulations which ensured that details of Royal Navy ships in difficulties were rarely reported and assistance thus never requested. HM Drifter *Imbat* sank off Lyness on 4 February 1941 after being involved in a collision, details of the other ship involved are lacking and information about casualties is likewise scant. Another incident about which little is know involved HM Trawler *Alberic*, which reportedly sank 'in the Pentland Firth' with the loss of thirteen of twenty-three crew after colliding with the destroyer HMS *St Albans*. Few records of other incidents involving smaller RN craft during the Second World War have survived and the withholding of information about casualties in the area contributed to the Stromness lifeboat's inactivity.

AUNCHING THE LIFEBOAT STROMNESS

Two photographs showing J.J.K.S.W. *on exercise.* Above: *Being launched down the slipway into the harbour, with the* NLS Pole Star *in attendance.* Below: *Then, afterwards, being recovered stern first. (By courtesy of John Harrop)*

*J.J.K.S.W. afloat
in the harbour
at Stromness,
possibly during
a lifeboat day
demonstration,
with the
boathouse and
slipway visible in
the background.
(Orkney
Photographic
Archives)*

The next effective service undertaken by *J.J.K.S.W.* came on 7 September 1946, more than a year after the end of the war, when she refloated a motor launch that had had run aground 100 yards north of the Ness Beacon. During 1947 she performed three routine services, assisting a fishing boat, a motor boat and a tanker. The last of these rescues, on 24 August 1947, involved *J.J.K.S.W.* working with the Longhope lifeboat after the Norwegian tanker *Gundine* has gone ashore on Berry Head, Hoy. The tanker's crew pumped 2,000 tons of crude oil overboard to lighten her so that she would refloat. This action covered both lifeboats in thick oil and when *J.J.K.S.W.* returned to station at 1.15 p.m. the local fire brigade were called out to help clean the boat.

A long service was performed on 18 January 1951 after the 5,000-ton motor vessel *Tatra*, of Tonsberg, with forty-one people on board, was reported to have broken down twenty-three miles north-west of Mull Head, on Papa Westray. *J.J.K.S.W.* launched at 1.35 p.m. and reached the area where the vessel had last been seen at 6 p.m. but could find no trace of it. The lifeboatmen searched until 4.45 a.m. and then headed for Kirkwall to refuel and get a hot meal. The lifeboat put to sea again at 10.40 a.m. and the motor vessel was eventually found being escorted by an Icelandic trawler. One of the lifeboatmen went aboard *Tatra* which, escorted by the lifeboat, made for Kirkwall harbour. *J.J.K.S.W.* returned to her station at 6.30 p.m., seventeen hours after leaving.

In March 1953 *J.J.K.S.W.* was involved in a very fine service. Together with the Thurso lifeboat *H.C.J.* (ON.708), she launched in the early hours of 22 March to the Grimsby trawler *Leicester City* in distress to the west of Hoy. Dense fog made conditions difficult but Coxswain William Sinclair negotiated the lifeboat out of Hoy Sound. As the fog lifted, albeit momentarily, a light was seen from the trawler which had been wrecked close to Braebuater Point, but the fog quickly came down again before the lifeboat could get close. The lifeboat's engines were then stopped so her crew could listen and, after a faint shouting was heard, a life raft was found with four men on board. They were all so exhausted that Mechanic John McLeod and Assistant Mechanic Edward Wilson had to stand at the bottom of the lifeboat's scrambling net to help them aboard. In view of their condition, Coxswain Sinclair decided to return to station immediately and the lifeboat reached Stromness at 4 a.m. by when visibility was down to almost nothing. Sadly, one of the rescued men died just before they reached Stromness but the other three were landed safely. The lifeboat put to sea again at 4.30 a.m. to search for further survivors. Ten of the trawler's crew who had managed to get ashore on Hoy by life raft were taken aboard *J.J.K.S.W.* and landed at Stromness, although two later died. The search continued for further survivors but of the remaining men only bodies were picked up by the two lifeboats and *J.J.K.S.W.* eventually returned to station at 11 p.m. For their fine work during this prolonged and demanding service, the Thanks on Vellum was accorded to Coxswain Sinclair and also to Coxswain Angus Macintosh of Thurso. Additional monetary awards were made to Mechanic McLeod and Assistant Mechanic Wilson.

A fine picture of J.J.K.S.W. *showing the layout of the 51ft Barnett type with the cockpit aft, the small shelter forward, and the funnel exhaust amidships. (From a photograph loaned by a Shoreline member)*

J.J.K.S.W. *with Thurso lifeboat* H.C.J. *(ON.708), nearest camera, alongside the slipway on Stromness waterfront. (Orkney Photographic Archives)*

J.J.K.S.W. landing a sick woman at Scapa Pier in January 1955 for transport to Balfour Hospital. The roads between Stromness and Kirkwall had been blocked by heavy snow and the lifeboat was called into action for several consecutive days after the snow brought transport in Orkney to a standstill and cut off many of the small communities. (Orkney Photographic Archives)

What proved to be the final services undertaken by *J.J.K.S.W.* at Stromness took place in January 1955. Heavy snow brought transport in Orkney to a standstill and cut off many of the archipelago's isolated communities with vehicles stranded in snow up to their roofs. The lifeboat was called into action taking provisions, medical supplies and transferring sick people in need of hospital treatment. On 14 January she took the wife of one of the Graemsay lighthouse keepers, together with her husband and a doctor, to Scapa Pier, where an ambulance was waiting to convey her to Kirkwall hospital. Four days later, she set out at 11.15 a.m. in rough seas to take urgently needed food to the people around Skaill, arriving there at 1.30 p.m. and returning to Stromness in the afternoon. The following day, she took a sick woman to Scapa Pier as the road between Stromness and Kirkwall was still blocked by snow. She arrived at Scapa Pier at 12.50 p.m. where an ambulance was waiting. Four people, who were trying to get back to Stromness, were then taken on board the lifeboat, which returned to station at 3.45 p.m. The following afternoon, the lifeboat took a doctor and nurse to Hoy to attend an elderly lady who had pneumonia.

A Motor Lifeboat for Longhope

Longhope's first motor lifeboat, a 45ft 6in Watson type, was sent to the station in September 1926. Built by S.E. Saunders at Cowes, she left the Isle of Wight on 1 September and arrived at Longhope on 9 September having covered, at an average speed of 7.5 knots, 663 miles during eighty-five hours at sea. The new boat was fitted with a single 80bhp Weyburn DE.6 petrol engine which gave a maximum speed of just over eight knots and a range of sixty-two nautical miles at full speed. She had cost £8,330 1s 1d to build and was funded from the amalgamation of legacies left to the RNLI by Mr William G. King, Mr J. Turnbull, Mr M. Jesset and Mrs S.H. Sandford. The initials of the donors were used to make up the name *K.T.J.S.*

The new lifeboat was formally christened on 6 June 1928 as part of a unique double celebration. During the morning HRH Prince George, later HRH The Duke of Kent, named the new Stromness lifeboat *J.J.K.S.W.*, described above, and then after lunch at Stromness was brought in the newly-christened boat to Longhope for the naming of *K.T.J.S.* He was met at Longhope by the president of the Branch, William Marwick, with the Kirkwall City Pipe Band and Kirkwall Town Band present. The new boat was dedicated by the Revd J.D. Anderson, of Hoy. Introduced by Sir Robert Hamilton, the Prince named the new lifeboat. After presenting long service certificates to various members of the crew, he then boarded the new boat and was taken for a short trip, before retuning by launch to HMS Nelson, the flagship of the Atlantic Fleet, at moorings in Scapa Flow. The first effective service by *K.T.J.S.* took place on 21 March 1929 after the three-masted schooner *J.H. Barrow*, of Lancaster; with a crew of four; had got into difficulty on the eastern side of Swona while on her way from Liverpool to Cockenzie with a cargo of rock salt. The lifeboatmen were able to secure a tow to the schooner, which was then brought to Longhope.

The first motor lifeboat at Longhope, K.T.J.S., dressed overall for her naming ceremony on 6 June 1926. She was named by HRH Prince George, who named the Stromness lifeboat J.J.K.S.W. in the morning, coming to Hoy in the afternoon for the ceremony at Longhope. (Orkney Photographic Archives)

HRH Prince George outside the Longhope lifeboat house after the naming ceremony of K.T.J.S. *in June 1926. (Orkney Photographic Archives)*

The Longhope lifeboatmen were called on to perform a number of difficult rescues during the years between the two wars, and they rose magnificently to the challenges. One of the most outstanding rescues in which *K.T.J.S.* was involved took place in January 1930. In the early hours of 5 January, the steam trawler *Braconmoor*, of Aberdeen, outward bound for the fishing grounds, went ashore on Tor Ness Point, just over three miles from Longhope. The stranded crew fired distress flares and at 2 a.m. the lifeboat was launched into a south easterly wind and heavy rain. An hour after launching, the lifeboat reached the wreck which was lying close to dangerous rocks in very heavy surf. The coxswain took the lifeboat as near as possible to the wreck, anchored, and then veered down towards the casualty. Owing to the strong tide, however, the lifeboat was swept past and had to be hauled back out to her anchor to make another attempt. The manoeuvre was repeated twice more before the coxswain was able to get the lifeboat sufficiently close for the line-throwing gun to be used. A line was fired across the bridge of the trawler and a rope and lifebuoy passed to the stranded crew. One by one, the trawler's crew of nine men were hauled through the surf using the breeches buoy, and all made it to the lifeboat except for the skipper. When he reached the lifeboat, he was found to be dead. It was realised afterwards that he suffered from a weak heart, so it is likely he had died of shock when he went into the surf during the rescue.

For this difficult rescue, which had been carried out with skill and gallantry that resulted in the saving of the steam trawler's crew of nine, Coxswain John Swanson was awarded the Silver medal. The Thanks Inscribed on Vellum was accorded to the other members of the crew, Second Coxswain William Mowat, Bowman Thomas Gunn, Motor Mechanic Robert Johnstone, Assistant Motor Mechanic Charles Mowat, and crew members William Dass, George Johnstone, Sinclair Mowat and Jackie Norquoy. A Letter of Appreciation was sent to honorary secretary William Sutherland, who went to the crags above the scene of the wreck with torches to help ensure a successful outcome, 'for his zeal on this occasion'.

K.T.J.S. on the slipway ready to be launched. She was the first 45ft 6in Watson motor lifeboat to be built, and one of only two of this class powered by a single engine. During her short career at Longhope she had rope fenders, which can just be made out, but these were replaced during a refit in early 1933 before she was sent to Aith. (J.W. Sinclair, courtesy of Orkney Photographic Archives)

Just over two years later, on 9 January 1932, *K.T.J.S.* and the Longhope lifeboatmen were involved in another dramatic and courageous rescue. The trawler *Dorbie*, of Hull, had been wrecked at Tor Ness, at the south-west end of Hoy, in a south-south-easterly gale. Conditions were made more hostile by rain and sleet squalls, severe cold and heavy seas. At 7.30 p.m. *K.T.J.S.* was launched under the command of Coxswain John Swanson, and was taken round Tor Ness in the pitch black to search for the casualty. The lifeboat searched along the shore for the wreck using the searchlight and from time to time burning white flares, but nothing could be seen. Visibility was made worse by the rain and sleet, the lifeboat was continuously enveloped in spray as the heavy seas washed over her, and the crew were also blinded by the glare of the searchlight on the water. Those on board the trawler could do nothing to help themselves, as all lights had been extinguished when the vessel struck the rocks and all flares burnt. Failing to find any sign of the wreck, Coxswain Swanson decided to search offshore as the vessel may have become free from the rocks and be drifting in the Pentland Firth.

Meanwhile, William Sutherland, the honorary secretary, and Mr W. Marwick, the chairman, had arrived at Tor Ness, where they found Mr R. Cutt, a branch committee member who lived two miles away and had telegraphed details of the wreck to the station. They could not see the wreck but, using torches, carried on searching and found the man who had been washed off *Dorbie* and lifted onto the rocks by the heavy seas. They grabbed him and pulled him to safety while two other men, who had both jumped overboard, were also washed ashore and dragged from the waves, alive, but injured, and in a state of exhaustion.

By now, the lifeboat had moved offshore to search for the trawler. Failing to find any sign of the casualty, she had approached Dunnet Head Shore signal station on the other side of the Pentland Firth, and communicated her position using Morse code. This was relayed by telephone, via Kirkwall and Longhope, to the honorary secretary who had telephoned the

K.T.J.S. served Longhope for six years until 1933, when she was replaced by the twin-engined 45ft 6in Watson motor lifeboat Thomas McCunn *(ON.759). This sequence of pictures show her launching down the slipway at Brims. (Orkney Photographic Archives)*

K.T.J.S. being launched down the slipway with another lifeboat moored alongside the slipway, probably the Wick lifeboat Frederick and Emma *(ON.659), a 45ft Watson motor type. (Orkney Photographic Archives)*

The Longhope lifeboat house at Brims with two lifeboats in the Aith, K.T.J.S. and probably Wick lifeboat Frederick and Emma, *and a tug just visible in the background. The occasion for this gathering is not known. (Orkney Photographic Archives)*

Longhope lifeboat crew in the 1920s. Back row, left to right: *A. Barnett snr, W. Nicolson, S. Mowat, G. Johnstone, J. Johnstone.* Front row, left to right: *J. Robertson, A. Johnstone, William Mowat (mechanic), John Swanson (coxswain) and D. Mackay. (Orkney Photographic Archives)*

Coastguard, anxious to ascertain the lifeboat's location. Sutherland immediately sent a message to Dunnet Head requesting that the lifeboat be signalled to return, if possible, to Tor Ness. Despite being very tired from his considerable exertions that night, he then made his way several miles over heather and peat bogs to Melsetter. With several other men he collected bundles of straw and hurried back to Tor Ness where, with casks washed up from Dorbie, a bonfire was made to light up the wreck and guide the lifeboat. By this time the weather had cleared, the wind was only a moderate gale and the strong flood tide had also eased.

The lifeboat reached the scene at 10.45 p.m. and, guided by the bonfire, Coxswain Swanson took the boat towards the wreck. The trawler was about 150ft from the cliff, lying on her port side at an angle of seventy degrees, with seas sweeping over her. Coxswain Swanson anchored to windward, but attempts to veer down on the port side proved impossible. The rocks and mast sticking out prevented the lifeboat getting close so she was anchored in a different position to veer down on the casualty's starboard side. After being guided down a channel so narrow that it was little wider than the boat itself, she was able to get alongside the wreck and the remaining eight men of the trawler's crew, including the captain, were hauled aboard. The men, who had been clinging to the wreck for five hours, were exhausted by their ordeal. The actual rescue took only five minutes and, once the men were safe, the lifeboat was hauled clear and set course for Hoy where the rescued men were made comfortable at Longhope Hotel.

For this outstanding rescue, in which eight fishermen had been saved from the trawler, the Silver Second-Service Clasp was awarded to Coxswain Swanson in recognition of his skilful handling of the lifeboat. Mechanic Robert Johnstone was singled out for special praise for signalling to the Dunnet Head signal station and was presented with inscribed binoculars. The Thanks Inscribed on Vellum was accorded to the coxswain, mechanic and each of the other seven members of the crew. An inscribed barometer was also awarded to William Sutherland, honorary secretary, 'in recognition of his energy and initiative in directing operations in the service to the Dorbie, from the land', as *The Lifeboat* of June 1932 explained.

The lifeboat house and roller slipway built in 1906 at Aith Hope, pictured in the inter-war years by which time it was housing the station's motor lifeboats. (Orkney Photographic Archives)

During the early 1930s a decision was made to supply a new twin-engined lifeboat to Longhope to replace the single-engined *K.T.J.S.* As the station was deemed important enough to warrant the deployment of such a vessel that would be more manoeuvrable, and have the added security of two engines, in 1932 a new motor lifeboat was ordered. Built at the Cowes boatyard of well-known lifeboat builder Groves & Guttridge, the new boat was a 45ft 6in Watson cabin motor type, powered by twin Weyburn CE4 petrol engines, each of 40bhp. During trials the boat achieved a maximum speed of 8.48 knots, and had a cruising speed of 7.5 knots at which her radius of action was almost 100 nautical miles. Completed at a cost of £7119 18s 5d, she was funded from the legacy of Mr William McCunn of Largs and named *Thomas McCunn*. She arrived at Longhope on 11 January 1933 and two days later was taken around to the slipway at Brims where *K.T.J.S.* was launched for the last time to make way for the new boat. The replaced boat was then taken to Stromness in the afternoon where she was met by a crew from Lerwick who took her to Shetland. *K.T.J.S.* was refitted at Hay & Co., Lerwick, having her shelter extended, a new fender fitted, and automatic cowls added to improve air circulation. She was then placed on station at the new Shetland station of Aith in May 1933. She later served at Arranmore and was sold out of service in May 1952.

Thomas McCunn was formally christened at a ceremony held at Longhope Pier on 15 September 1933, during which she was named by Mrs Balkie, wife of the Lord Lieutenant of Orkney. The first service performed by *Thomas McCunn* took place on 25 February 1933, before her official naming. In rough seas and very strong winds, she went to the aid of the Grimsby trawler *Silanion* which had gone aground on Tor Ness. In heavy snow, the lifeboat was taken alongside the stranded vessel and rescued all thirteen members of its crew. Nine months later, on 19 November 1933, another trawler, *Geysir* of Iceland, went aground on Tor Ness. Thomas McCunn was launched at 9 p.m. in very heavy seas and a south-easterly gale. She was taken alongside the trawler, at considerable risk as many hidden rocks in the area made the task of approaching the stricken vessel very difficult, but the lifeboatmen succeeded in saving all sixteen crew as well as two passengers.

In February 1936 the Longhope lifeboatmen were involved in three services. The first took place on 19 February when *Thomas McCunn* launched, under the command of Coxswain William Dass, in very heavy seas and gale force winds to a trawler aground on the Little Skerry. Unfortunately, the trawler's crew drowned before they could be helped. As the conditions were so bad, when the lifeboat returned she could not be rehoused up the slipway, and so was moored at Longhope Pier to await an improvement in the weather. But she was called on again, on 21 February, when a resident of Heckness requested help in getting his son to Scapa for an appendicitis operation as conditions were too bad for an ordinary boat to make the trip. *Thomas McCunn* left the pier and put off with the patient at noon, returning at 3.30 p.m.

Later on the same day, with the severe weather continuing and frequent snow showers falling, the lifeboat was called upon again. At 7.20 p.m. a large trawler was seen ashore at Brims Ness near the entrance of the Aith in which the lifeboat house is situated, but, the lifeboat was at Longhope Pier, eight miles away by sea. The maroons were fired, the crew were fetched by car and, just twenty minutes after the wreck had been seen, the lifeboat cast off. She went into the Pentland Firth and then west towards Brims Ness, keeping close inshore to avoid the spring flood tide which was running. In the strong south-easterly wind, blowing against the tide making a rough sea, the lifeboat reached Brims Ness at 9 p.m. Using the searchlight, the crew found the French trawler *Neptunia*, of Le Havre, only a few yards off rocks known as the Tails of Brims. The wind and sea were on her port beam and she had a heavy list to port. She had launched one of her boats, but it had been stove in and washed away. The Coastguard's life-saving rocket apparatus had been assembled but, although the wreck was near the shore, it was impossible to rescue the stranded crew using the apparatus as the seas around the rocks were too heavy.

Thomas McCunn *(ON.759) at sea with her auxiliary sails raised. Built in 1933, she was a 45ft 6in Watson motor lifeboat powered by twin 40hp Weyburn engines which gave her a maximum speed of 8.48 knots.*

Thomas McCunn *at the head of the slipway outside the lifeboat house. In this photograph the tunnels which housed the propellers can be seen, as well as the single rudder mounted at the stern. (Orkney Photographic Archives)*

It was also difficult for the lifeboat to get alongside the wreck as rocks ran out from the cliffs at the trawler's bow and stern, so the lifeboat anchored to windward and was veered down until twenty-five yards from the casualty. The line-throwing gun was then fired, a heavy line was passed to the wreck, and the casualty's crew told to take it to the bow and ease the lifeboat alongside so that she should not approach the wreck stern first and risk damaging the rudder. Unfortunately, the trawler's crew did not understand English and instead of helping the lifeboat alongside they launched a boat of their own. This craft, 25ft long with air cases, was launched on the lee side of the wreck, brought round to the weather side, and made fast with the lifeboat's rope at one end and the trawler's own rope at the other. It was then hauled to and from the lifeboat five times, enabling the trawler's crew to reach safety before being cut adrift allowing the lifeboat to make for the open sea with forty-one survivors on board. *Thomas McCunn* arrived at Longhope Pier at 11.15 p.m. having completed her third service in sixty hours, the last of which had been skilfully and courageously carried out in conditions made more difficult by intense darkness with the searchlight in use the whole time. The Bronze medal was awarded to Coxswain Dass and each member of the crew received additional monetary rewards. The French Government later awarded its Silver medal to Coxswain Dass and Bronze medals to each of the crew for their part in this service.

During the First World War, the Longhope lifeboat was the most active of Orkney's lifeboats, answering twenty-three calls which resulted in a total of eighty-six lives saved. The first call came on 7 September 1939, just three days after war had been declared, when the Hull trawler *Commander Nasmith* ran aground on the north side of Stroma in rough seas and a gale. *Thomas McCunn* launched into darkness and torrential rain to stand by the trawler until the vessel refloated on the high tide and the lifeboat returned to her station the following morning. On 24 September 1941, *Thomas McCunn* launched to the motor boat *Runda* which was in difficulty a mile north-west of Duncansby Head. The vessel had escaped from Norway with twenty-four people on board and had reached Lerwick safely where fourteen were landed. She then headed south for Buckie but ran out of fuel so the lifeboat took her in tow while the lifeboatmen opened the emergency rations for the escapees.

During the night of 5 August 1944, the Longhope lifeboatmen assisted the American steamer *Charles D. McIver*, of Wilmington, which, carrying urgently needed war materials and with a crew of seventy-five on board, had got into difficulty. The lifeboat launched at 9.45 p.m. in dense fog, found the vessel four miles north-west of Stroma at 10.15 p.m. and stood by until a tug arrived to help the disabled vessel. The lifeboat returned to Longhope at 3 a.m. but was

Right: *William Stewart Dass, coxswain from 1935 to 1946, wearing his oilskins and kapok lifejacket. He was awarded the Bronze medal for the service on 21 February 1936 to the French trawler* Neptunia *from which more than forty lives were saved. (Orkney Photographic Archives)*

Below: Thomas McCunn *inside the lifeboat house from which she operated for almost thirty years.*

called out again at 10.40 a.m. on 6 August after *Charles D. McIver* got into difficulty two miles north of Dunnet Head. Thick fog was still hanging over the area but the lifeboatmen managed to find the steamer, which had drifted with the tide, although there was no sign of the tug. At the request of the Admiralty Salvage Officer, who had been put aboard the steamer from the tug, Coxswain Dass boarded the steamer, set course for Scrabster and, escorted by the lifeboat, the steamer reached harbour safely.

The last service of the war, undertaken in January 1945, was the first of three services performed during the year. On 13 January, *Thomas McCunn* launched at 2.15 a.m. to a High-Speed Naval Launch which was aground on Stroma. Seven members of her crew had been rescued by a local boat from Stroma, so the lifeboat stood by until the Launch refloated on the high tide. The other services of 1945 both took place in June. The first, on 21 June, was

Thomas McCunn *at the head of the slipway outside the lifeboat house. She is one of the most famous Longhope lifeboats and saved more than 300 lives during her outstanding career at the station. (Orkney Photographic Archives)*

Thomas McCunn *on exercise off the famous Old Man of Hoy, on the west side of the island. (By courtesy of John Harrop)*

Above: *The spectacular sight of* Thomas McCunn *launching down the slipway at Brims. (By courtesy of John Budge)*

Right: *Longhope lifeboat crew in front of* Thomas McCunn. Back row left to right: *R. Johnstone, E. Mowat, S. McFadyen, John Norquoy (second coxswain), James Johnstone, F. Johnstone jnr;* front row left to right: *R. Johnstone (mechanic) and Alfred Johnston (coxswain). (Orkney Photographic Archives)*

to the steamship *Fort La Prairie*, of London, which went aground on the Little Skerry. After standing by to see if the vessel would refloat at high tide, the lifeboat was called alongside once the captain had decided to abandon ship and saved all fifty-two crew. Almost exactly forty-eight hours after returning to Longhope, *Thomas McCunn* was called out again, to stand by HM Minesweeper *Ring Dove*, aground on South Ronaldsay. The minesweeper floated clear unaided, and the lifeboat returned to station at 5 a.m. to conclude a busy period for the Longhope crew.

CHAPTER FOUR
Stronsay: Serving the Fishing Fleet

The small island of Stronsay lies to the north-east of Orkney mainland. Although the island's main village, Whitehall, was one of Scotland's major herring ports in the nineteenth century, the fishing industry started to decline in the 1930s and eventually it totally disappeared from Stronsay's shores. But before this, during the 1800s, hundreds of men, women and children were employed in the herring curing stations that lined the small harbour. In its heyday, the harbour's skyline was a mass of masts with up to 300 boats moored there. On a Sunday, when the fleet was in harbour, it was claimed to be possible to walk from Whitehall to the small island opposite, Papa Stronsay, across the decks of the anchored vessels. Today, the island relies on farming and tourism, with the ferry to Orkney mainland providing an important link for the local people.

The decision to place a lifeboat at Stronsay was taken by the RNLI in July 1904 when the Institution's Committee of Management resolved to form a station following a visit to the island by Lt Charles Cunninghame-Graham, RN, the Deputy Chief Inspector of Lifeboats. He visited Kirkwall, Orkney's capital, 'to strengthen the lifeboat service in the Orkney Islands', raise the profile of the RNLI, and ascertain the level of support for a new lifeboat station at Stronsay. A station was deemed necessary there as a result of the growth of the fishing industry and to provide cover for the northern part of the archipelago. The enthusiastic response of

The 43ft Watson motor lifeboat John Ryburn *(ON.565) in Kirkwall Bay dressed overall for her naming ceremony on 28 September 1909. (Orkney Photographic Archives)*

A crowd of well-wishers admire the new motor lifeboat John Ryburn *alongside at the Old Harbour, Kirkwall.*
She visited Orkney's capital for her naming ceremony in September 1909, when she was formally christened by
Mrs Balfour. (Orkney Photographic Archives)

local people resulted in the formation of the Kirkwall and North Isles Branch, the committee
of which was made up of representatives from each of Orkney's North Isles.

The first lifeboat to serve Stronsay was *John Ryburn* (ON.565), one of the early Watson
motor lifeboats, 43ft in length, and built by Thames Ironworks at a cost of £2,770 9s 5d .
She was fitted with a single 40hp Blake petrol engine, which itself cost £375. On trials, she
reached a maximum speed of 7.2 knots with the engine running at 612rpm, while her cruising
speed was 6.4 knots. She was provided from the legacy of Mr William McCunn, of Largs, who
bequeathed the RNLI enough money for two lifeboats. The new lifeboat arrived at Stromness
on 1 May 1909 after the epic journey from the Isle of Wight described in Chapter Three.
Although the intention was to formally christen the new lifeboat at Kirkwall more or less as
soon as she arrived in Orkney, according to *The Orcadian* for 17 April 1909 it was 'decided to
postpone the ceremony, as it is considered that the lifeboat after her passage north will hardly
be presentable, and will first require to be painted.'

John Ryburn remained in Stromness until the middle of May, presumably having her
machinery repaired, and not until the evening of 19 May did she eventually get to Stronsay.
The following day she was handed over to the local committee by Commander Rowley, and
was accepted on behalf of the local committee by Dr Rosie to become Stronsay's first lifeboat.
The Orcadian for 22 May 1909 described the new boat as 'a very handsome and efficient one
fitted up with all the latest approved appliances, and up to date in every way. The motor . . .
has been most severely tried on the passage north, and with the exception of a little heating
of the bushes on two occasions wrought beautifully.' She was initially anchored in Papa Sound,
the channel between Stronsay and Papa Stronsay, until a new lifeboat house and roller slipway
were ready in 1911.

John Ryburn was not formally christened until 28 September. The naming ceremony took
place in Kirkwall Harbour, with members of the newly-formed Kirkwall and North Isles

John Ryburn puts out from the Old Harbour, Kirkwall, at the end of her naming ceremony for a short trip round the Bay with the special guests. (Orkney Photographic Archives)

Branch present and ex-Provost Sclater opening the proceedings. The lifeboat was presented by Lt Charles H. Forbes, the RNLI's representative, who described the suitability of the motor lifeboat to the local conditions, before handing over to the president of the Branch, Col. Balfour of Balfour and Trenabie. The Colonel spoke of the lifeboat as being:

> the specimen of the greatest modern improvements possible in lifeboats' before praising 'those gallant men who have been selected as the crew . . . I think no words sufficiently describe or tell them how greatly we admire their bravery and gallantry . . . [while] around the crew will gather . . . a record of bravery and heroism which will be lasting and live to be handed down to posterity.

The Revd John Rutherford led the service of dedication, after which Mrs Balfour was invited to name the new lifeboat, which she did by breaking a bottle of wine over the bows. The boat then proceeded to sea for a short cruise and in the afternoon returned to Stronsay.

Despite the pride shown by members of the Kirkwall and North Isles Branch when naming the new lifeboat, she had a rather inauspicious start with the somewhat questionable reliability of her motor highlighted by an incident in October 1909. The full-rigged ship *Edenmore*, of Greenock, 1,726 gross tons, on passage from Hamburg to Sydney, ran ashore shortly before midnight on 7 October, grounding on the Rhone off the south-east point of Papa Stronsay. Distress flares were fired, but the lifeboat was in Kirkwall under repair at the time and the local fishing boats were too small to carry all the survivors in the heavy swell. A rescue was effected, albeit with some difficulty, when the RNLI boarding boat was manned by some of the lifeboat crew and succeeded in getting alongside *Edenmore*. Eventually, using the ship's own boat as well, twenty-five survivors reached the safety of Whitehall harbour. Great credit was given to the lifeboat crew for completing the rescue in difficult circumstances. Over the next three weeks, a considerable amount of cargo was recovered from *Edenmore* including Chinaware, much of which was retained by the locals as souvenirs of the wreck.

John Ryburn returned to station from Kirkwall with repairs complete. In 1911 she was taken off the mooring and placed in the new lifeboat house, built at a cost of £3,050 to the east of Whitehall, the island's main village, close to the Fishing Station. The boathouse had a roller slipway to ensure a speedy launch and was built to the standard design of the time with piled concrete pillars supporting a corrugated iron structure. In 1912 a cottage was built for the mechanic at a cost of £300 and named 'Ryburn' in honour of the lifeboat. This house remains standing today.

During what proved to be a short career at Stronsay, *John Ryburn* performed only three effective services, the first of which took place on 3 March 1911. She launched at 10.45 a.m. to the ketch *Haldon*, of Kirkwall, which was bringing coal from Kirkwall to Stronsay. The ketch had become stranded on Ingal Skerry and, although in no immediate danger, her crew of five were landed as a precaution as the weather was threatening to get worse. Two days later the weather moderated and a steamer was able to save the vessel. The next service took place on 10 February 1912. During the early hours of the morning, a vessel stranded on the Holm of Ayre, a small uninhabited island off the north side of Sanday. The lifeboat was immediately launched into the heavy seas and travelled through the night, which was 'cold, thick, and intensely dark', according to *The Lifeboat* of November 1912. The account continued:

> The lifeboat had a long distance to go through narrow, dangerous channels, with rapid tides and treacherous rocks, and no lights to guide the crew . . . The brave men, however, never hesitated for a moment, but felt their way, chiefly by the breakers on the shore, and reached the stranded vessel at 5 o'clock. It was still very dark, and the coxswain ventured as near as he considered safe to get an idea of the position of the vessel. There was a heavy swell, and considerable difficulty was experienced in saving the boat from damage as the tide was low. The boat manoeuvred towards the trawler and a rope was made fast. By this means the lifeboat was held in a position until the four men on board were saved.

The wrecked vessel was the steam fishing boat *Crimond*, of Aberdeen, bound for the fishing grounds off Shetland. Before the lifeboat had arrived, five of the fishing boat's crew of eight had got into the small ship's boat but this broke adrift and was smashed on the rocks, drowning four of those on board. The fifth man was saved by the others on the wreck and, although

The lifeboat house and slipway, built in 1911 to the east of Whitehall, the island's main village, was only used until 1915 when John Ryburn was withdrawn. (Orkney Photographic Archives)

John Ryburn *inside the lifeboat house during her brief time at Stronsay. (Orkney Photographic Archives)*

An unusual image of Whitehall village with John Ryburn *pulled up on the foreshore, possibly to enable repairs to be effected. Behind the lifeboat, to the left, can be seen the fishing boats which, at this time, were numerous, as Whitehall was one of the major herring ports in Scotland. (From an old postcard in the author's collection)*

in a critical condition, was saved by the lifeboat, along with the other three. The journey back to Stronsay in daylight was easier and *John Ryburn* safely reached her station, with the shipwrecked men cared for in the village.

The final service of *John Ryburn* at Stronsay took place on 27 January 1913. At 9 p.m. a messenger reported a vessel ashore on a dangerous reef at Rothesholm Head. The lifeboat was launched into a gale and found the steam ketch *Commander*, of Aberdeen. As the vessel was striking the shore heavily, the skipper asked the lifeboat to stand by in case his craft was holed. The lifeboat remained until high water when the ketch floated off the rocks. Despite some damage to her propeller, the vessel succeeded in reaching Kirkwall under her own steam.

Although a new house and new boat had been built, the station was temporarily closed in 1915 because an insufficient number of men were available to form a crew as a result of conscription for the First World War. *John Ryburn* was moved to Peterhead in June 1915 having been launched eleven times on service and saved four lives while at Stronsay. Although the closure in 1915 was intended only as a temporary measure, the station was not in fact reopened at the end of the war as intended. When the situation was reviewed in the early 1920s, a crew was still unavailable and in July 1930 the station was officially closed. The boathouse and slipway were surrendered to the local landowner in 1938. The house was dismantled during the late 1940s when two local farmers purchased it, presumably for use as a shed elsewhere on the island, with the rollers used for land rolling. However, the concrete substructure of the slipway and boathouse support piles remain intact.

The Station Reopened

The lifeboat station at Stronsay seemed to have had its day and the idea of a lifeboat based in Orkney's Northern Isles lay dormant for more than two decades. However, in 1952, following the tragic loss of *Eyfur Dingur*, an Icelandic boat loaded with scrap metal, and her entire crew while on passage through Lashy Sound in the North Isles of Orkney, a decision was made to re-establish the station, a proposal that received strong local backing. Capt. E.H. Clements was appointed as the station's new honorary secretary and the reserve 45ft 6in Watson motor lifeboat *Edward Z. Dresden* (ON.707) was placed on temporary duty while a new lifeboat for the station was under construction. This reserve lifeboat, built in 1928 for Clacton-on-Sea, served at Stronsay from October 1952 until 1955 and is credited with eleven service launches. During this second operational period of the station, the lifeboat was kept afloat at 'three-leg' moorings in the harbour at Whitehall.

The first service launch of *Edward Z. Dresden* took place in May 1953. During the evening of 22 May, Kirkwall Coastguard rang up the lifeboat station to report that three men who had left Walls, Shetland, the previous evening for Kirkwall in the 30ft motor boat *Vaila* had not arrived. The lifeboat was not immediately called out, but went to Sanday for the island's lifeboat flag day with the honorary secretary, Capt. E.H. Clements DSC, on board. The Coastguard kept in touch in case the lifeboat was needed. Aircraft carried out a search for the missing vessel and early in the afternoon reported unidentified wreckage forty-one miles east by south off Tresness, Sanday. The Coastguard rang Capt. Clements at Sanday, and at 2.30 p.m. the lifeboat put to sea with the secretary on board. She searched extensively, but found nothing and returned to Stronsay for fuel, arriving in the early hours of 24 May. A Danish motor vessel eventually found the motor boat fifteen miles off Auskerry and towed her to the entrance to Stronsay harbour. The lifeboat then towed *Vaila* in, securing her at Stronsay pier.

This routine service was followed by three more during the course of the eighteen months. On 6 October 1953 *Edward Z. Dresden* escorted the steamship *Polyana*, of Christiansand, to

Kirkwall bay after the steamer had radioed she was taking water and needed help. On 11 June 1954 the lifeboat was requested to go to North Ronaldsay to pick up a woman who was about to have a baby. As no other boat was available, *Edward Z. Dresden* set off at 1.20 p.m. and took the expectant mother to Kirkwall where an ambulance was waiting. The final service by *Edward Z. Dresden* at Stronsay took place on 20 September 1954 when she went to the assistance of the motor vessel *Iona*, of Kirkwall, a passenger boat of fifteen tons bound for Shapinsay from Stronsay with five people on board. The vessel had been reported as overdue, but the lifeboat found her and escorted her through Spurness Sound to Eday Gruna buoy.

By the time of this service, a new 52ft Barnett motor lifeboat was under construction for the station. Powered by twin 60hp diesel engines, she was built at the East Cowes boatyard of J.S. White, and was sent north to her station in February 1955. *The Orcadian* of 10 February 1955 described her attributes:

> Her engine room is a watertight compartment and each engine is itself watertight so that it could continue running even if the engine room flooded. The speed is nine knots and she carries enough fuel to travel 216 miles at full speed without refuelling. She carries a crew of eight and in rough weather can take 100 people on board. She has a deck cabin with a paraffin pressure cooker and below decks a second cabin with electric fans for ventilating it. She is fitted with radio telephony for which there is a separate compartment in the deck cabin, a loud hailer and an oil spray . . . She carries a line-throwing pistol and an electric searchlight.

Named *John Gellatly Hyndman* (ON.923), she was funded from the legacy of Miss Elise Amelia Hyndman of Greenock, and saved forty-seven lives during her seventeen years at Stronsay. Her passage north took her from Cowes via Torbay, Newlyn, Fishguard, Holyhead, Donaghadee and Troon, with Cdr Hill, RNR, the Divisional Inspector, and two mechanics, Gerald Gregan

The station was closed in 1915, but reopened in 1952 and the 1928-built 45ft 6in Watson motor Edward Z. Dresden (ON.707) was placed on station on 23 October 1952. This photograph was taken in 1952, probably soon after she arrived on station, with her new crew on board wearing kapok life-jackets. (Orkney Photographic Archives)

The Watson motor lifeboat Edward Z. Dresden *at moorings in Whitehall. She served at Stronsay from 1952 to February 1955 and launched eleven times on service. (Orkney Photographic Archives)*

and Alexander Cursiter, on board. Stronsay's own mechanic, Sydney Swanney, was unable to travel but Coxswain Tom Carter and two crew, John Work and William Rendall, were on board to complete the passage crew. She escorted the new Troon lifeboat *James and Barbara Aitken* (ON.909) to her station and then proceeded via the Crinan and Caledonian Canals, reaching Inverness on 20 February and arriving at Stronsay on 26 February 1955. During the passage from Cowes to Newlyn, conditions were good but from there to Troon she encountered heavy seas and was forced to shelter a day at Holyhead. The last leg of the trip, from Troon to Stronsay was undertaken in excellent weather.

Once the new lifeboat was placed on station, *Edward Z. Dresden* went to the Clyde and was placed in the Reserve Fleet, in which she served with distinction until 1968. Meanwhile, the inaugural ceremony for *John Gellatly Hyndman* took place on 24 August 1955 at the West Pier, Stronsay. The new lifeboat was dedicated by the Revd E.P.G. Fox, chairman of Stronsay Branch and minister of Moncur Memorial Church and, after a vote of thanks to those involved, she was christened by Mrs Joseph Grimond, wife of the MP for Orkney and Shetland. The first service performed by *John Gellatly Hyndman* took place on 15 December 1955 and was a routine affair. At 1.56 p.m. the new lifeboat put out to the local lobster boat *Fulmar*, which was at anchor in Huip Sound but in danger of sinking in very rough seas and the easterly gale. The lifeboat crew found the boat in danger of being blown ashore, and so two members of the crew boarded the boat, which was then towed by the lifeboat to an anchorage in the lee of Linksness.

While many services were performed in difficult and testing conditions, the lifeboat was never called upon to undertake any spectacular rescues. However, because of the long distances often involved in reaching a casualty, and because she regularly took survivors to Kirkwall, many services were long, testing the crew's endurance. The boat's second service proved to be such a test, and took place less than a month after the first. On 7 January 1956 at 5.35 p.m., the lifeboat put out to assist two men marooned on an old wreck close inshore in Inganess Bay. In a rough sea with a moderate gale blowing, the lifeboat took more than two hours to reach the wreck but once there she soon rescued the men and then took them to Kirkwall. The journey back to her station was a long one and it was not until the early hours of the following day that she arrived home.

During the early afternoon of 12 May 1956, Kirkwall Coastguard reported a Norwegian fishing vessel ashore at Vasa Skerry while another fishing vessel, in attempting to help her, had also run aground. *John Gellatly Hyndman* was launched at 1.40 p.m. in a rough sea and found the motor fishing vessels *Astor* and *Leidulf*, each with a crew of seven. They were in no immediate danger but had requested help at high water. The lifeboat therefore put in to Kirkwall before returning to the vessels in the evening. On reaching them again she found that the crew of the *Leidulf* had landed on the Skerry. There was a strong tide and five attempts had to be made before the lifeboat could be manoeuvred close enough to the shore for the crew to be taken on board. The coxswain then proceeded to assist *Astor*'s crew, so he dropped the lifeboat's anchor and veered down to the bow of the fishing vessel. When all the men and their belongings were aboard, the lifeboat proceeded to Kirkwall where the crews were landed. The lifeboat then returned to her station, arriving at 2.30 a.m. on 13 May.

At times, not only did the lifeboat crew have to go through severe sea conditions, but they also faced harsh weather in the form of rain, snow and ice. On 25 February 1957, the lifeboat put out in a moderate sea to go to the aid of the motor vessel *Finvoy*, of Belfast, which was in danger of being driven ashore east of Horse of Copinsay. The passage to the casualty was undertaken through frequent snow squalls. When the lifeboat reached the motor vessel, the vessel's master asked the lifeboat to stand by until the arrival of the steamship *Earl Thorfinn*, one of Orkney's ferries, which was being sent from Kirkwall. *Earl Thorfinn* arrived at 2.15 p.m. and, after she had passed a line aboard *Finvoy*, the lifeboat returned to her station.

Serving in such an remote community, the lifeboat was often called upon to act as a hospital vessel as demonstrated by two services carried out towards the end of 1958. The first, on 11 October, saw *John Gellatly Hyndman* taking a seriously ill child to Kirkwall hospital. The second took place during the afternoon of 16 November after the local doctor informed the station's honorary secretary that a man was seriously ill and needed immediate hospital

52ft Barnett John Gellatly Hyndman *(O.N.923) at the West Pier, Whitehall, for her naming ceremony on 24 August 1952. The crew at the bow are, left to right, Sidney Swanney, Jim Reid, Jim Stout, Jim Work jnr and John Dennison. (Orkney Photographic Archives)*

John Gellatly Hyndman *at her moorings at Whitehall before her cockpit was fitted with a shelter, with the steamer*
Earl Thorfinn *moored at the pier in the background. (Orkney Photographic Archives)*

treatment. As no other suitable boat was available, the lifeboat put out at 5.15 p.m. with the
patient on board, arriving at Kirkwall two hours later.

During 1962 the reserve lifeboat *J.J.K.S.W.* was on temporary duty when the fishing vessel
Maureen, of Kirkwall, with a crew of two, went aground on Torness Point on 17 May. The
reserve lifeboat stood by until the casualty had refloated. *John Gellatly Hyndman* was back on
station on 18 June when a small dinghy was blown out to sea off Noup Head in near gale
force conditions. The lifeboat soon found the dinghy with its single occupant, took him on
board and brought the craft to Pierowall pier. The final service of the year took place on 22
December when the Belgian trawler *Prince de Liége*, of Ostend, went ashore on rocks between
Auskerry and Stronsay. As the trawler was hard and fast on the rocks, the lifeboat could do
nothing except take the vessel's crew of thirteen on board and land them at Kirkwall.

The only service of 1963 took place on 16 September after the 101-ton trawler *Aberdeen
City* went aground at Start Point, Sanday, while on her way to the Faroes fishing grounds
with a crew of thirteen. After leaving her moorings, *John Gellatly Hyndman* soon reached the
casualty and then went alongside to take off nine of the crew, who were landed at Kettletoft
pier. The lifeboat returned to the trawler and, with the help of the trawler *St Giles*, attempted
to tow the casualty off the rocks. In the considerable swell, the casualty was bumping so badly
that she was holed and flooded so the four crew who had remained on her were taken off
by the lifeboat and landed at Kettletoft pier, after which the lifeboat returned to her station
having been at sea for twelve hours.

The year 1965 proved to be a fairly busy one for the Stronsay lifeboat which carried out
no fewer than eleven services. The first took place on 8 January and involved the Danish
gunboat *Vaedderen* which had onboard the skipper of Grimsby trawler *Northern Chief*, who
was seriously ill. *John Gellatly Hyndman* put out at 11.10 a.m. and reached *Vaedderen* forty-five
minutes later, then awaited the arrival of a helicopter from RAF Lossiemouth. The helicopter
took the sick man to Kirkwall from where he was conveyed by air ambulance to Renfrew. The

HRH Queen Elizabeth II and Prince Philip on board Stronsay lifeboat in 1960, with crew Jim Stout and mechanic Sidney Swanney in attendance. (Orkney Photographic Archives)

majority of the other services involved taking patients from various islands to the mainland. On 27 January, the lifeboat took an emergency patient from Eday to Kirkwall, leaving just after noon and returning to Stronsay at 6.15 p.m. On 9 February, as no other boat was available, she repeated the trip to take a sick man from Eday for hospital treatment. On 20 August, the lifeboat was again involved in a medical case when she was called to Papa Westray where a doctor had a patient with acute appendicitis requiring immediate hospital treatment. *John Gellatly Hyndman* left her station at 5.15 p.m., reached Papa Westray at 7 p.m., picked up the patient and arrived at Kirkwall at 10 p.m. The patient was taken to hospital by ambulance and the lifeboat returned to her station just after midnight.

On 26 October 1966, *John Gellatly Hyndman* went to the aid of a Danish fishing vessel aground on the Broad Shoal, Shapinsay. She left her moorings at 1.25 p.m. in a north-easterly gale force wind and reached the vessel, *Bodeltornby*, an hour and a half later. At about 3.30 p.m. the lifeboatmen had got a line aboard the vessel, which was refloated undamaged and proceeded to Kirkwall under her own steam. The lifeboat was recalled, but at 6 p.m. was informed that flares had been sighted from Westray Pier in line with Read Head, Eday. So she set out again and searched the Calf Sound into North Sound but found nothing. Very heavy seas in North Sound made the search extremely difficult but the coxswain continued until 9.15 p.m. when the lifeboat was recalled to her station.

Further services to fishing vessels followed. On 5 December 1966, *John Gellatly Hyndman* was launched to the motor fishing vessel *Fairy Queen*, which was aground in Odiness Bay, Stronsay. The lifeboat stood by for more than three hours until the fishing boat was refloated. On 4 February 1967, she went to the motor fishing vessel *Girl Mina*, a seine netter, aground at Elsness Holm, Sanday. At 9.25 p.m. the lifeboat reached the stranded vessel and put a line on board to tow the vessel off the rocks. When this failed, the lifeboat stood by until the early hours at which point it was decided to take the crew of two men off the vessel as the weather was deteriorating. They were landed at Sanday Pier at about 6.30 a.m. Another attempt was made to refloat the stranded vessel later in the day, but this was unsuccessful. After seventeen hours at sea, the lifeboat returned to her moorings at 1.40 p.m.

The service to *Girl Mina* proved to be the last life-saving rescue performed by the Stronsay lifeboat before the station was closed. Between 1968 and 1972, the lifeboat was called upon either to assist fishing vessels in difficulty or take medical cases from the outer islands to Kirkwall. The three services performed during 1968 were all to fishing vessels, while during 1969 the lifeboat was used to take medical emergencies from Eday to Kirkwall. On 15 March 1971, with Coxswain James Stout in command, she went to the aid of the 299-ton Danish cargo vessel *N/O Pedersen* with a crew of six, which had a broken down engine and was drifting towards Papa Westray. The ship became disabled four miles north of Noup Head in a north-westerly gale. The lifeboat was called out and, soon after 7 p.m., made contact with the casualty. She took the vessel in tow and made for Pierowall in Westray, arriving at midnight.

During 1971, the final services by the Stronsay lifeboat were performed. On 12 January, the reserve lifeboat *The Princess Royal (Civil Service No.7)* (ON.828), a 46ft Watson type built in 1939 and stationed for much of her career at Hartlepool, made an emergency medical trip when she conveyed George Burgess, a resident of Whitehall village, to hospital in Kirkwall. Mr Burgess was an enrolled member of the lifeboat crew but had not been out on service in the lifeboat for some time, and had collapsed in the village the previous night. On 2 May, the 25ft lobster boat *Duncan* sprang a leak after touching rocks on the east side of the Green Holm on Sunday night. The flares she fired were observed from Eday and the Grimsby trawler *Ross Zebra*, outward bound to the fishing grounds, quickly made for the scene while Stronsay lifeboat also put out. *Ross Zebra* arrived first and found *Duncan* close inshore. Coming in very close, the trawler's crew managed to get a line to the lobster boat and towed it off. The lifeboat subsequently took over the tow, bringing *Duncan* into Kirkwall just after 9.30 p.m. *Duncan's* crew had been baling their vessel for more than three hours before firing the distress flares and continued to bale throughout the tow.

John Gellatly Hyndman *at her moorings after she had been refitted and her cockpit enclosed for better crew protection.* (*Orkney Photographic Archives*)

Above: *Stronsay's last lifeboat,* John Gellatly Hyndman, *approaching the pier at Kirkwall pier after transporting a patient from the North Isles. (Orkney Photographic Archives)*

Left: *Crew of* John Gellatly Hyndman *landing a patient from the North Isles at Kirkwall pier. The transporting of medical cases such as this was a fairly regular occurrence for Stronsay's lifeboat. (Orkney Photographic Archives)*

John Gellatly
Hyndman *moored*
at Kirkwall pier after
landing a patient from
the North Isles. (Orkney
Photographic Archives)

The final service of 1971 took place on 5 November after the 47-ton Aberdeen-registered trawler *Vera Grace* ran aground on a shelf near Whitehall village, close to the lifeboat's moorings, in a northerly gale while leaving Stronsay. *John Gellatly Hyndman* was launched and two fishing boats went to the trawler's assistance. While the lifeboat stood by, *Vera Grace* was towed off undamaged by the seine-netter *Ocean's Gift* and the 50ft stern trawler *Kildinguie*. The casualty then made her way back to Whitehall pier. The lifeboat was taken out by Second Coxswain Archie Reid as the skipper of *Ocean's Gift*, James Stout, also coxswain of the lifeboat, was on his way home from Kirkwall aboard the fishing boat when he came upon the stranded *Vera Grace*.

In April 1972, an announcement was made that the Stronsay station was to be closed. A delegation from the RNLI had visited Stronsay in January 1972 to discuss the situation, taking into account the developments at Kirkwall where the Clyde cruising lifeboat *Grace Paterson Ritchie* (ON.988) was by then operating. Lt-Cdr H. Teare, Inspector of Lifeboats for the North of Scotland, explained the matter: 'We discussed the operational problems and as a result of this and other information that the Institution had from their coast review, the Committee decided that we could withdraw the Stronsay Lifeboat.' The last service by *John Gellatly Hyndman* was reported in *The Orcadian* of 1 June 1972:

> The Stronsay lifeboat carried out her last mission on Sunday before she left the islands for good. It was a mercy trip to Kirkwall with a farmer, Mr Tom Stevenson of Smiddy, who had a suspected fractured skull. He was attended to the Balfour Hospital. The lifeboat has been withdrawn from Stronsay as the 70ft long-range lifeboat *Grace Paterson Ritchie* is now stationed in Kirkwall. The loss of their lifeboat has angered the Stronsay people. They claim that such a boat is all the more needed now since a fishing factory is being established on the island, bringing in more fishing boats.

Despite opposition to the closure from the local community, *John Gellatly Hyndman* was withdrawn on 30 May having gained a fine record of service while at Stronsay, launching 116 times on service and saving forty-seven lives. With her removal in May 1972, the Stronsay station was closed and a permanent lifeboat was stationed at Kirkwall, deemed to provide more effective lifeboat coverage, particularly as the Clyde class cruising lifeboat *Grace Paterson Ritchie* could adequately cover the northern islands including Stronsay. As described in Chapter 7, this lifeboat had been operating from a base in the capital, cruising the islands as an experimental operation since 1968 and had, in fact, worked with the Stronsay lifeboat a number of times.

Stronsay's last two lifeboats were both kept in the harbour at Whitehall, at moorings between the two piers of the harbour, and the gear was stored in premises at the top of the West Pier. The mechanic at that time, Sidney Swanney, on the top floor of this building with the gear stored on the ground floor in what used to be shop premises. This building has changed hands several times, and is today known as Cardinham House. The station's service boards are on display in the community centre.

After leaving Orkney, *John Gellatly Hyndman* was placed in the Relief Fleet and was immediately taken to Shetland. She arrived at Scalloway for her annual overhaul at the beginning of June 1972, but was first sent to Lerwick to act as relief, and remained there until the spring of 1973 when the Lerwick lifeboat *Claude Cecil Staniforth* returned to station. After a lengthy period in the Relief Fleet, *John Gellatly Hyndman* was sold out of service in 1985. Throughout most of the 1990s, she languished at the small Boathaven in Littleport, near Ely, until a change of ownership in 2002 saw her move to Plymouth where she was restored and partly converted internally. Her original name was restored and she was then taken to a permanent berth at Portishead Marina.

CHAPTER FIVE

A New Barnett for Stromness

In 1955, two new 52ft Barnett lifeboats, sister vessels, were built for service in Orkney. *John Gellatly Hyndman* (ON.923), went to Stronsay as described in Chapter One, while the other was allocated to Stromness. The Stromness boat, *Archibald and Alexander M. Paterson* (ON.924), was funded from the gift of Miss Margaret M. Paterson, St Petersburg, Florida, USA, in memory of her brothers Archibald and Alexander Paterson, her uncle, Neil Munro, and her grandfather Hugh Graham, who drowned in the Cook Straits in 1868. The new boat was built by J.S. White, East Cowes, at a cost of £36,919, and powered by twin 60hp Ferry VE6 diesel engines. At her maximum speed of nine knots, she had a radius of action of 118 nautical miles, which increased to 176 when cruising at eight knots.

The boat arrived at her new station on 21 May 1955, after a long journey from Cowes under the command of Lt E.D. Stogden, Northern District Inspector of Lifeboats, with Coxswain James Adam, Mechanic Alan Cursiter, J. McLeod, Peter Simpson and William Sinclair Jnr, making up the crew. She was met in Clestrain Sound by *J.J.K.S.W.*, as described in *The Orcadian* for 26 May 1955: 'The two boats made a colourful sight as they came together, the old leading the new ... The new lifeboat's blue and grey contrasted with the blue and teak of the old. Both made a bonny sight.' *Archibald and Alexander M. Paterson* was then recovered up the slipway for the first time into the boathouse, part of the floor of which had been removed to accommodate the new boat, which was slightly longer than her predecessor. After a successful first launch, she was taken on her first exercise going to the back of the Holms. She returned to the lifeboat slipway to pick up honorary secretary T. Harvey, members of the local

Archibald and Alexander M. Paterson *(ON.924), one of two 52ft Barnetts built for Orkney stations, on trials shortly after being built at East Cowes. (From a photograph loaned by a Shoreline member, by courtesy of Jeff Morris)*

Archibald and Alexander M. Paterson *arrives on station on 21 May 1955 and is hauled up the slipway for the first time, with her predecessor,* J.J.K.S.W., *moored alongside the slipway.*

lifeboat committee and Provost T.N.F. Hourston for a short trip in Hoy Sound. Two days later *J.J.K.S.W.* was taken south, ending an illustrious career at Stromness. She went to Buckie and, after an overhaul there, entered the Reserve Fleet in which she served for a further nine years, undertaking duties at Lerwick, Aberdeen, Aith, Stornoway, Barra Island, Stronsay, Holyhead and New Brighton.

The new lifeboat was christened on 25 August 1955, at a ceremony at Stromness, by Miss Chris McKinnon, the niece of Miss Margaret Paterson, after a service of dedication conducted by the Revd H.C. Ross, minister of the North Church, Stromness. During a long and distinguished career at Stromness, *Archibald and Alexander M. Paterson* saved fifty-two lives and launched 123 times on service. Her first service took place during the evening of 9 December 1955 after the landing craft L405 went ashore at the Ness, near the entrance to the harbour. The lifeboat stood by until, as the tide fell, the landing craft was left high and dry. At 4 a.m. the following day, *Archibald and Alexander M. Paterson* again put out to help and secured a tow line to pull the craft clear. The second coxswain then went aboard to act as pilot as the lifeboat brought the casualty into harbour.

The first life-saving service by *Archibald and Alexander M. Paterson* took place on 10 March 1956. She launched at 4.23 p.m. to the fishing boat *Amber Queen*, with a crew of three, which had broken down two miles off Inganess, near Yescanaby, in rough seas and a southerly gale. The disabled boat was taken in tow and brought safely into Stromness harbour at 7.45 p.m. after a service that was both routine and typical of much of the work *Archibald and Alexander M. Paterson* was called upon to perform during her time at Stromness. Another service to a fishing vessel was performed on 19 September 1963 when *Archibald and Alexander M. Paterson* launched at 9.45 p.m. to the fishing boat *Donside*, of Aberdeen, which was ashore near Nethertown, with a crew of seven. The lifeboatmen succeeded in getting a line aboard

The scene during the naming ceremony of Archibald and Alexander M. Paterson *in the harbour at Stromness on 25 August 1955. (RNLI, by courtesy of Jeff Morris)*

Looking down the slipway into the harbour as Archibald and Alexander M. Paterson *is launched. (Orkney Photographic Archives)*

Archibald and Alexander M. Paterson being launched down the slipway into the harbour. (From a photograph loaned by a Shoreline member)

Archibald and Alexander M. Paterson being prepared for recovery up the slipway shortly after she had been placed on station. (From a photograph loaned by a Shoreline member)

the casualty but initial attempts to get the boat clear failed. When the line parted at the third attempt, Coxswain Sinclair took the lifeboat into deeper water and dropped anchor to try a different approach. The lifeboat was veered down as close as possible to the casualty and a line was fired over the stranded vessel so that another tow line could be rigged. Although this parted, it was reconnected and eventually, with the help of the fishing boat *Kinora*, *Donside* was pulled clear at 11 p.m. and towed into Stromness by the lifeboat.

Late on the morning of 28 May 1966, the Norwegian motor vessel *Kings Star* ran aground on the North Shoal so *Archibald and Alexander M. Paterson* was called out. She reached the

Archibald and Alexander M. Paterson *being launched, possibly for a lifeboat day, as she is crowded with children forward and a large number of other people, all no doubt thrilled at going down the slipway. (Orkney Photographic Archives)*

casualty just after midday to find most of the crew had taken to the ship's boats. The master informed Coxswain Sinclair that a tug was on its way but, as this would not arrive before midnight, asked the lifeboat to stand by. The motor vessel had been holed and so Coxswain Sinclair arranged by radio for several portable pumps to be brought out to the stranded vessel by various local boats. All was proceeding smoothly until, at 2.25 p.m., the motor vessel suddenly slid off the rocks. The lifeboat then put the crew back on board and, with the ship's boats in tow, escorted the motor vessel back to Stromness.

The Stromness lifeboatmen have often been called upon to work in extremely poor weather conditions, such as on the afternoon of 13 February 1970, when they put to sea in a blinding snowstorm, heavy seas and a north-easterly gale to help the fishing boat *Mayflower*, whose crew of three radioed for assistance after dropping anchor in the Bay of Skaill. As *Archibald and Alexander M. Paterson* was away from station to be re-engined with twin 78hp Thornycroft diesels and fitted with radar, the reserve 46ft Watson motor lifeboat *Princess Royal (Civil Service No.7)* (ON.828), on temporary duty, put to sea in the terrible conditions. Visibility was almost zero so Coxswain Sinclair went out in his own motor boat *Evelyn*, which was fitted with radar, keeping very close company with the lifeboat. *Mayflower* was located at 3.30 p.m. and escorted back to Stromness Harbour, without incident, in a little over an hour.

Princess Royal (Civil Service No.7) was called out again on 7 July, putting to sea during the afternoon after the fishing vessel *Welfare*, with a crew of six, had been reported aground on the Kirk Rocks. In choppy seas and a fresh westerly wind, the lifeboat reached the casualty at 4.30 p.m. and the lifeboatmen laid out a kedge anchor from the stranded vessel. As the fishing vessel was in no immediate danger, the lifeboat returned to moorings in the harbour, putting to sea again at 8.30 p.m. to provide further assistance. On the rising tide, the lifeboat was able to pull the vessel clear and then escort her to the harbour.

Stromness crew and the committee of the Stromness Branch of the RNLI, during the 1960s. Back row left to right: *Ivor Donaldson, James Mowatt, William Sinclair, Alfred Sinclair (coxswain), Edward Wilson (Chief Engineer), Jack Leslie, Leslie Halcro and Granville Swanney (winchman).* Front row left to right: *William Halcrow (Honorary Treasurer), Jon Allan (Honorary Secretary), Dr J.W. Cromarty, John Rae (chairman), J.E.P. Robertson, Captain John Hourie and James Wishart. (Orkney Photographic Archives)*

Archibald and Alexander M. Paterson returned to station in August 1970 after re-engining and continued her life-saving work, escorting the motor boat *Victory* to safety on 31 January 1971 and helping the fishing boats *Wilma John, Corilda, Mayflower, Three Boys* and *Merica* on 1 March. She performed a series of routine services in 1971 and 1972, but the final service of 1972, proved to be rather more challenging. On 1 August, the trawler *Glengairn*, of Aberdeen, went ashore on Switha Island and both Stromness and Longhope lifeboats were called out in the early hours to stand by the casualty. Throughout the day various unsuccessful attempts were made to refloat the vessel. Eight of the trawler's crew were landed by the Longhope lifeboat, which returned to the scene at 9 p.m. enabling the Stromness lifeboat to return to station. She put to sea again at 7.45 a.m. on 2 August to relieve the Longhope boat, which had stood by throughout the night, and remained standing by throughout the day, returning to station at 10.45 p.m. having been at sea for thirty-five hours over two days.

Another long service was undertaken on 21 December 1974 when *Archibald and Alexander M. Paterson,* again working with the Longhope lifeboat, went to the trawler *Lans,* of Ostend, which was ashore at Berry Head, Hoy. The Stromness boat put out at 1 a.m. by when the Longhope lifeboatmen had found the trawler hard aground, lying broadside to the rocks, at the foot of 600ft high cliffs. Heavy seas were sweeping the stranded vessel and breaking against the face of the cliffs. Longhope Coxswain John Leslie dropped anchor and veered his lifeboat as close as possible to the casualty so that a rocket line could be fired towards the trawler. When

Archibald and Alexander M. Paterson *being launched, with the Northern Lighthouse Board ship* Pole Star, *the third of that name, dressed overall at her berth alongside the Lighthouse pier. The ship arrived on 22 July 1961 during Stromness Shopping Week (the annual 'fair') and was open to the public during that week, with the lifeboat house also open. These photographs were probably taken at this time. (Orkney Photographic Archives)*

Archibald and Alexander M. Paterson *afloat in Scapa Bay, probably during a locally organised fund-raising day. (Orkney Photographic Archives)*

Reserve lifeboat Princess Royal (Civil Service No.7) *(ON.828) launching for lifeboat day in 1970. Built in 1939, she served at Hartlepool for almost thirty years before entering the Reserve Fleet. During 1970 she was operating in the north with stints at Lerwick, Kirkwall and Stronsay, as well as at Stromness during which she launched on service on two occasions. (Orkney Photographic Archives)*

Archibald and Alexander M. Paterson *being launched down the slipway, probably on exercise. The protective tunnels which housed the propellers can be seen in this fine photograph. (Orkney Photographic Archives)*

this fell short, Coxswain Leslie decided that they would have to wait until the tide turned before making another attempt.

The Stromness lifeboat made the next attempt to reach the trawler. She dropped anchor at 6.45 a.m. and the crew attempted to veer her down from a different angle, but they were also unable to get close enough to effect a rescue. In the very heavy swell, the hydraulically-operated windlass was unable to raise the lifeboat's anchor so the crew switched to manual operation. The lifeboat lifted on a particularly heavy swell, and the full weight of the boat came on the anchor cable, the stop catch on the windlass bent and freed the handle which suddenly spun backwards, catching lifeboatman James Flett and breaking his arm. The anchor was recovered and the lifeboat immediately returned to Stromness to land the injured man. Soon after the Stromness lifeboat had left the scene, with the wind increasing to gale force, a helicopter from RAF Lossiemouth arrived and, with outstanding skill, the pilot manoeuvred the aircraft to within a few feet of the cliff face enabling nine men to be rescued in three trips from the wrecked trawler. The men were put aboard the Longhope lifeboat, which subsequently landed them at Stromness. In recognition of the outstanding skill and courage of the crew of the helicopter, a Letter of Appreciation, signed by the Director of the RNLI, was sent to the Commanding Officer of 202 Squadron, RAF Leaconfield.

During 1982 *Archibald and Alexander M. Paterson* was away for overhaul with the relief lifeboat *John Gellatly Hyndman*, the 52ft Barnett built originally for Stronsay, on temporary duty. She was called out at 1.15 p.m. on 26 January to go to the fishing vessel *Prolific*, with a crew of four, which had a fouled propeller fourteen miles from Stromness off Hoy Sound. Once on scene, the lifeboatmen connected a tow line to the disabled vessel and set course for Stromness. However, in the very rough seas and near gale-force northerly winds, the tow

Archibald and Alexander M. Paterson on exercise with an RAF Whirlwind rescue helicopter in Stromness Bay. *(Orkney Photographic Archives)*

A fine photograph of Stromness waterfront with Archibald and Alexander M. Paterson *being launched down the slipway from the 1926 lifeboat house on some kind of publicity trip. (Orkney Photographic Archives)*

line parted during the journey. It was soon reconnected, enabling the two boats to reach Stromness safely, almost twelve hours after the lifeboat had set out. Less than two months later, with *Archibald and Alexander M. Paterson* back on station, she escorted the motor vessel *Merlin* with a crew of two to safety on the afternoon of 22 March. The vessel was taking in water in Rackwick Bay in extremely heavy seas and hurricane force winds.

Archibald and Alexander M. Paterson was launched for what proved to be the last time on service at Stromness at 11.30 p.m. on 4 June 1984 after a report that red flares had been sighted in Hoy Sound. Despite a thorough search of the area, the lifeboatmen found nothing and returned to station just over two hours after setting off. A week after this service, the lifeboat left the station with an impressive record of fifty-two lives saved. Between June and October 1984, when the station's own new lifeboat arrived, the relief 52ft Barnett lifeboat *John Gellatly Hyndman* was on station, launching twice during that time and saving two lives. *Archibald and Alexander M. Paterson* served in the Relief Fleet at Montrose, Arranmore, Lowestoft and Howth until being sold out of service in May 1989 to a couple in Wadebridge, Cornwall, who renamed her *St Issey*.

Fast Lifeboats Come to Orkney

Following the changes of the 1970s, including the new lifeboat at Longhope and the new station established at Kirkwall (described in the following chapters), Stromness received a fast afloat lifeboat during the early 1980s. The RNLI had been developing faster lifeboats during the 1960s and 1970s and introduced the Arun class in the early 1970s. Capable of approximately eighteen knots, the Arun represented a radical departure in British lifeboat design. The hull was made from glass reinforced plastic and the watertight wheelhouse provided with an

52ft Arun Joseph Rothwell Sykes and Hilda M *(ON. 1099) at William Osborne's yard at Littlehampton, where she was fitted out, on 26 May 1984. The 48ft 6in Oakley* Charles Henry *(ON. 1015), formerly of Selsey, lies outside the Arun after being overhauled and made ready for service at Baltimore. (Jeff Morris)*

inherent self-righting capability. A flying bridge incorporated an upper steering position and a small 'Y' class inflatable was carried on the wheelhouse roof for inshore work. The excellence of the Arun's design was recognised by the Design Council in 1982 when a design award was presented to the RNLI for the type's hull shape and overall design. The prototype Arun, named *Arun* (ON. 1018), visited Orkney during her passage around the coast in July 1971 and called at Stromness on 2 August before going to Shetland. She then returned to Stromness and Scapa, visiting Longhope on 13 August and came round to Kirkwall the following day.

The Arun building programme began in the mid-1970s and, with the design, the type enabled the RNLI, was able to adopt a policy of stationing fast lifeboats throughout the British Isles. An Arun was allocated to Stromness in 1983 after it had been determined that a permanent mooring could be provided in the harbour, for the type was unable to be housed in the boathouse. Built at Littlehampton by William Osborne at a cost of approximately £370,000, the new lifeboat, *Joseph Rothwell Sykes and Hilda M* (ON.1099), arrived on station on 12 October 1984. She was placed on service three days later and served Stromness for fourteen years. Powered by two 485hp Caterpillar 3408TA diesel engines, she had a top speed of eighteen knots, twice that of the previous lifeboat. She arrived from the RNLI depot at Poole having travelled north after a period of training for Coxswain W. Sinclair, Mechanic S. Taylor, Second Mechanic J. Adams and crew members M. Flett and C. McIver, with Lt John Unwin, Divisional Inspector for North of Scotland in command. With the lifeboat moored afloat in the harbour, the now empty boathouse was used as a crew facility until, in 1995, the local council approved a sheltered alongside berth at the South Pier from where the lifeboat could be easily reached by the crew. A temporary crew facility was then established on the pier.

The naming ceremony of the new lifeboat took place at Stromness Harbour on the afternoon of 22 August 1985. At the start of the ceremony, Mrs Stout, chairman of the

Joseph Rothwell Sykes and Hilda M *on speed trials after completion and before going on station, 1984. (RNLI)*

Joseph Rothwell Sykes and Hilda M is put through her paces off Stromness. She served at the station from 1984 to 1998 and is credited with saving eight lives during that time. (By courtesy of RNLI Stromness)

Community Council, presented a Township Plaque to the crew of the lifeboat. The plaque, bearing the Coat of Arms of Stromness, was subsequently fixed to the lifeboat's superstructure. The service of dedication was conducted by the Revd R.S. Whiteford, Moderator of Orkney Presbytery, after which Mrs Mary Milne, sister of the executor of the Sykes Estate, formally christened the lifeboat. With the official guests on board and to the sound of three local pipers, the new lifeboat then went to sea for a short trip. The somewhat unusual name was a combination of two bequests, one from Miss Doris Rothwell, her sister Mrs Nora Sykes and her husband Joseph Sykes, to be used to provide a lifeboat named *Joseph Rothwell Sykes*, and another from Mrs Hilda May Vyvyan to be used for a lifeboat for Orkney named *Hilda* or *Hilda M*. These bequests were combined into the name *Joseph Rothwell Sykes and Hilda M*.

Before the naming ceremony, the new lifeboat had already performed a service. In the early hours of 22 January 1985, she had gone to the fishing vessel *Janeen*, with a crew of six, which was ashore on Outer Holm, off Stromness. In rough seas, a north-easterly gale and heavy, driving snow, the lifeboatmen found that the fishing vessel had refloated and so the lifeboat escorted the casualty into the harbour before returning to her moorings at 4.30 a.m. This proved to be one of many services carried out by *Joseph Rothwell Sykes and Hilda M* to local fishing vessels during her time on station.

On 21 May 1986, she put out during the morning to help two local lobster boats, *Scot* and *Sarah*, each with a crew of two, which had been unable to return to Brims Ness, on Hoy, because of rapidly deteriorating conditions. In rough seas and a south-south-easterly gale, she headed out at full speed, soon reached the two boats in Rackwick Bay and escorted them to safety. Almost exactly a year later, on 19 May 1987, she assisted the fishing vessel *Karen* and her crew of three, who got into difficulties seventeen miles north-west of Brough Head.

The vessel's mast had broken and so, when the lifeboat reached the casualty at 2.25 a.m., two lifeboatmen went aboard to help the fishermen rig temporary stays. The fishing vessel was then towed back to Stromness, with the boats arriving in the harbour at 8.50 a.m.

A different and somewhat unusual incident took place during the morning of 17 August 1991 after the fishing boat *Red Rooster*, with just one man on board, went aground on one of the Churchill Barriers. Although *Joseph Rothwell Sykes and Hilda M* went to the scene soon after the Coastguard's report had been received, she reached the area to find the boat marooned but its occupant in no danger. The lifeboat remained standing by in choppy seas and a fresh westerly wind until the stranded boat was helped from the land by a mobile crane which parked on the road adjacent to the grounded boat and lifted it off the rocks.

A far from routine service for the Stromness lifeboat crew was undertaken on 17 June 1992 after the replica twelfth century Hebridian Birwinn *Aileach* suffered steering failure in moderate seas, a heavy swell and force six north-westerly wind forty miles north of Cape Wrath and about seventy miles south-west of Stromness. The relief Arun lifeboat *Newsbuoy* (ON.1103), on temporary duty, put out at 8.50 a.m. and reached the casualty at 1.15 p.m. after a long passage. Once on scene, the lifeboat's small inflatable boat was used to rescue the crew of nine from the replica vessel. A tow was then rigged but the passage back to Stromness was very slow. Good headway was made until, at 6 p.m., the tow line parted forcing Coxswain Flett to bring the lifeboat round and alongside the casualty to reconnect the tow. Apart from this, the service continued without incident until the two boats reached the safety of Stromness at 8.55 p.m. For this long and demanding service, a Framed Letter of Thanks, signed by the chairman of the RNLI, was awarded to the lifeboat station congratulating Coxswain Flett and each member of the crew.

Joseph Rothwell Sykes and Hilda M *in the harbour for her naming ceremony on 22 August 1985.*
(Orkney Photographic Archives)

The champagne breaks over the bows of Joseph Rothwell Sykes and Hilda M *at the end of her naming ceremony on 22 August 1985. She was named by Mrs Mary Milne, sister of the Executor of the donor's estate. (Orkney Photographic Archives)*

Early on the morning of 21 December 1995, the fishing vessel *Keila*, with a crew of seven, ran aground in Marwick Bay, six miles from Stromness. *Joseph Rothwell Sykes and Hilda M* was soon on scene but, as the lifeboat could not get close to the stranded vessel, the lifeboatmen fired a line across to the vessel which was in very shallow water. A tow line was hauled across but repeated attempts to pull the vessel clear failed, although the vessel was stopped from going further up the beach. During the day, the fishing vessel *Orkney Reiver* took over the tow enabling the lifeboat to return to station to refuel. She returned at 6 p.m. and a tow line was run out to another fishing vessel, but further attempts at high tide failed to pull *Keila* clear. The tug *Erland* then arrived and the lifeboatmen helped to secure a tow line to the stranded vessel before returning to Stromness. At 6.30 a.m. on 22 December, the lifeboat put to sea again and stood by while further attempts were made to refloat *Keila*. This time the efforts were successful and, escorted by the lifeboat, the tug brought the vessel to Stromness Harbour.

On many occasions, Orkney lifeboats have worked with the Sumburgh-based Coastguard rescue helicopter 'Oscar Charlie' and on 2 April 1997 Stromness lifeboat undertook a service in which the helicopter played a part. In rough seas and a south-westerly gale, the fishing vessel *Zenith*, with a crew of five, began taking in water twenty-nine miles north-west of Stromness. As well as *Joseph Rothwell Sykes and Hilda M* launching to assist, the helicopter was also called out and succeeded in lowering two pumps onto the fishing vessel before the lifeboat arrived.

Joseph Rothwell Sykes and Hilda M at moorings in middle of the harbour in April 1995. This mooring was used until 1995 when an alongside berth was established. (Donald Budge)

52ft Arun Joseph Rothwell Sykes and Hilda M at moorings alongside the South Pier in 1997. (Nicholas Leach)

Joseph Rothwell
Sykes and Hilda M
*leaving the harbour on
exercise, August 1997.
(Nicholas Leach)*

Joseph Rothwell
Sykes and Hilda
M *passing Hoy
Low Light as she
sets out on exercise.
(Nicholas Leach)*

Joseph Rothwell
Sykes and Hilda M
*returns to harbour after
an evening exercise
in summer 1997.
(Nicholas Leach)*

View from the South Pier showing Joseph Rothwell Sykes and Hilda M *at moorings and the lifeboat house and slipway of 1926 in the background, centre right, on the waterfront. (Nicholas Leach)*

The helicopter stood by until the lifeboat reached the casualty and then returned to base to refuel. The lifeboat remained on scene for over an hour by when the salvage pumps on *Zenith* had reduced the level of water in the fishing vessel to enable the engine to be restarted.

The last service performed by *Joseph Rothwell Sykes and Hilda M* as Stromness lifeboat took place on 19 July 1998. She put to sea at 7.59 p.m. to go to the aid of the fishing vessel *Incentive*, with a crew of three, which had broken down twenty-five miles west of Hoy Sound. The lifeboat reached the casualty within two hours of launching, secured a tow line and then brought the vessel into Stromness, arriving at the harbour at 2.35 a.m. on 20 July. Three months after this routine service, a new lifeboat arrived in Stromness and the Arun left for the last time. Reallocated to Broughty Ferry, *Joseph Rothwell Sykes and Hilda M* served there until 2001 and in 2002 was sold out of RNLI service to become a lifeboat in Finland.

The new lifeboat at Stromness was one of the new generation of faster all-weather lifeboats being introduced by the RNLI. Two new designs had been developed, the 17m Severn and 14m Trent, each capable of twenty-five knots at full speed and incorporating the latest equipment and technology to make rescue work easier and more efficient. The larger of the two types, the Severn, was ideal for rescue work in Orkney and, in June 1997, the RNLI announced that a new Severn had been allocated to Stromness. The new lifeboat, self-righting by virtue of the inherent buoyancy in the watertight wheelhouse, was moulded in fibre reinforced composite at Green Marine's Lymington boatyard and fitted out by Berthon Boat Company, also at Lymington. Twin Caterpillar 3412 diesel engines, each of 1,250bhp, gave a top speed of twenty-five knots and the latest navigation aids were also fitted.

The new Severn, which had cost £1,580,000 to build, was provided by the late Miss Violet Matton, of Seaford in East Sussex, who donated the residue of her estate to the RNLI, and her two sisters, Dorothy and Kathleen, each of whom also supported the RNLI, through

17m Severn Violet, Dorothy and Kathleen *(ON.1236) moored at the RNLI Depot, Poole, in September 1998 prior to crew training and going on station. (Nicholas Leach)*

Stromness lifeboat crew at Poole on 5 October 1998 during crew training for the new 17m Severn class lifeboat. Left to right: David Wishart, John Banks (Coxswain), Stewart Taylor, Billy Wilson and Alan Banks. (RNLI)

Violet, Dorothy and Kathleen *in heavy seas passing Duncansby Head on her way to Orkney. (Andy Anderson)*

their wills. In memory of her donors, the boat was christened *Violet, Dorothy and Kathleen* at a ceremony on 19 June 1999, in front of a large crowd of supporters and well-wishers determined not to let the rain spoil the event. The proceedings were opened by the chairman of the Stromness Branch, Capt. M. Gunn, and the new lifeboat was handed over by Mr A.M. MacKenzie, Convenor of the Scottish Lifeboat Council. Capt. George Walker, honorary secretary, accepted the new boat and Mrs M. Pirie, President of the Ladies Lifeboat Guild, proposed a vote of thanks. After the Service of Dedication, conducted by the Revd A. Price, Mrs Margaret Kirkpatrick, widow of the late Longhope Coxswain Dan Kirkpatrick, formally christened the lifeboat, after which the guests went out for a short trip.

Before her naming, the new lifeboat had been out on service several times. She arrived at Stromness in October 1998, was placed on service on 22 October and was soon in action. She was called out at 10.36 a.m. on 4 November to the fishing vessel *Yukon Star*, of Kirkwall, which had gone aground twelve miles east of Stromness after a rope had fouled her propeller. Prior to the arrival of the lifeboat at the scene of the grounding, the vessel's skipper, the only person on board, had managed to get ashore unaided. Due to the shallow water in the area, the lifeboat was unable to get close enough to pull the vessel clear and so, as the Scapa Pilot Launch was by then on scene, the lifeboat returned to station. Her first effective service was carried out on 25 March 1999, when she brought in the fishing vessel *Boy Shane* and its crew of four.

During 2000, *Violet, Dorothy and Kathleen* was kept busy assisting a variety of people and craft. On 22 May she towed in the yacht *Carronach* and landed its crew of two. On 6 June she stood by the RN Explosive Device Team's guardship, and on 30 June brought in the fishing vessel *Incentive*. Four days later, on 3 July, the lifeboat crew assisted to save a sick diver on board the diver support craft *Radiant Queen*, which was brought to safety. On 3 October, the lifeboat launched to escort the Fraserburgh-registered *Valhalla*, which was eleven miles west of Brough Head when the propeller became entangled in nets. The lifeboat stood by while a

The naming ceremony of 17m Severn Violet, Dorothy and Kathleen *took place at Stromness harbour on 19 June* *1999. In the rain, she was named by Mrs Margaret Kirkpatrick, widow of the late Coxswain Dan Kirkpatrick who was* *lost when the Longhope lifeboat capsized in March 1969. (Andy Anderson)*

With a piper on the bow, Violet, Dorothy and Kathleen *puts out from the harbour at the end of her naming* *ceremony with invited guests on board for a short trip. (Andy Anderson)*

Violet, Dorothy and Kathleen at moorings alongside the South Pier, 2001, with Stromness' famous waterfront to the left and the harbour buildings, including the lifeboat crew facilities, background centre. (Nicholas Leach)

tow rope was attached between the casualty and the Banff-registered fishing boat *Enterprise*, which towed the casualty to Scrabster harbour.

During 2001, the relief lifeboat *Fraser Flyer (Civil Service No.43)* was on station between June and December and performed a number of services. Her first took place on 4 August when she went to the small motor cruiser *Margeurita* which was having steering difficulties. The lifeboat crew rigged a tow and brought *Margeurita* into Stromness harbour. On 26 August, the relief lifeboat brought in the fishing vessel *Brilliant* and during October helped two more fishing vessels, standing by *Valhalla* on 3 October and escorting *Sunbeam* twelve days later.

In 2002 *Violet, Dorothy and Kathleen* was back on station and undertook perhaps her most notable rescue at Stromness after a Scrabster fishing boat fouled its propeller in severe weather conditions. The lifeboat set out in the early hours of 26 April 2002 after the 17m fishing vessel *Faith Ann* got into difficulties fifty miles west of Orkney. The lifeboat launched with Coxswain Capt. John Banks in command and, on clearing Stromness Harbour, entered Hoy Sound encountering very rough and confused steep seas caused by the strong north-westerly gale force nine winds, producing a ten to twelve metre swell. The sea and weather conditions remained much the same throughout the service with the wind gusting to force ten. In the conditions, the best speed the lifeboat could manage was twelve knots.

Four hours after leaving Stromness, the lifeboat reached the casualty which, although disabled and drifting with a fouled propeller, was in no immediate danger. Coxswain Banks realised he would have to adopt an unorthodox approach to pass a tow and decided to run down sea towards the bow of *Faith Ann*. Once the tow was connected, a course was set for Scrabster, on the mainland, as conditions in Hoy Sound meant returning to Stromness was extremely dangerous if not impossible. The tow was connected via a large tyre to *Faith Ann's* towing bridle but after only twenty minutes it parted when the tyre tore in half. This was

17m Severn Violet, Dorothy and Kathleen *passing through Gorleston harbour entrance in Norfolk, July 2001. She was on passage to Vosper Thorneycroft's boatyard on the Solent, travelling via Dover. (Martin Fish)*

The unusual sight of two Stromness lifeboats at Gorleston in Norfolk. 17m Severn Violet, Dorothy and Kathleen *leads her predecessor at the station, 52ft Arun* Joseph Rothwell Sykes and Hilda M, *out of the harbour in July 2001 while both boats were on passage. (Martin Fish)*

52ft Arun Joseph Rothwell Sykes and Hilda M *passing through Gorleston harbour entrance in Norfolk, July 2001, on her way from Broughty Ferry to Poole to enter the Relief Fleet. (Martin Fish)*

The workshop and changing room at the south end of the harbour close to the South Pier. The facility was converted from a former harbour building in 1999. (Nicholas Leach)

The old Harbour Board office building, near the ferry terminal, which was converted in 2001 into a training room and store for the lifeboat crew and officials. (Nicholas Leach)

The berth for the lifeboat alongside the South Pier with relief 17m Severn The Will *(ON.1201) on duty while* Violet, Dorothy and Kathleen *was away from station undergoing maintenance work. The relief boat was on duty from 11 October to 3 December 2006. (Nicholas Leach)*

the first of six times that the tow parted, even though Coxswain Banks was only towing at six knots. On each occasion the tow was reconnected swiftly with excellent boat handling by Coxswain Banks and good teamwork by the crew.

At 9.20 p.m., Coxswain Banks requested assistance from the Thurso lifeboat and so 52ft Arun *The Queen Mother* (ON.1149) put out from her Scrabster berth with Coxswain William Munro in command. The Stromness lifeboat was twenty-one miles to the west and managing to maintain a speed of six to seven knots towing the casualty. Thurso lifeboat rendezvoused with the Stromness boat and casualty nine miles west of Scrabster. In the intervening time the tow had parted three times so the Thurso lifeboat took over to complete the tow to Scrabster. After two failed attempts, the tow was successfully connected and at 11.20 p.m. The Thurso lifeboat commenced towing *Faith Ann* to Scrabster. Thurso lifeboat was able to reduce the towing speed to three knots and maintain steerage. At 2.30 a.m., the Stromness lifeboat took up position astern of *Faith Ann*, a stern rope was attached to assist entry into harbour, and, half an hour later, the casualty was safely moored in Scrabster harbour.

For this rescue, Coxswain Banks was accorded the Thanks of the Institution on Vellum in recognition of his seamanship and determination during the fourteen hour rescue. A framed Letter of Thanks, signed by the RNLI chairman, was sent to Coxswain Munro of Thurso. Commenting on the service, John Caldwell, Divisional Inspector of Lifeboats Scotland, said, 'This service was carried out in extreme weather conditions. The seamanship displayed by both the coxswains and crews, whose joint efforts led to the successful execution of a fifty-two mile tow in storm force conditions, was exemplary. Both crews are to be commended for their determination and endurance.' Vellum Service Certificates were

The impressive sight of 17m Severn *Violet, Dorothy and Kathleen at full speed on exercise off the west side of Hoy, heading back to Stromness, June 2004. (Nicholas Leach)*

presented to the Stromness crew: Second Coxswain Fred Breck, Mechanic Ronald Taylor, Emergency Mechanic Callum MacIver, and crew members Colin Mowat, David Wishart, Neil McGibbon, Alan MacLeod and David Sutherland. This excellent service typifies the dedication of the Stromness lifeboat crew who, at the oldest of Orkney's lifeboat stations and with the latest all-weather lifeboat, remain ready to go to sea in the worst of weathers whenever required.

CHAPTER SIX

The Post-War Era at Longhope

B y the twentieth century the lifeboat stations at Stromness and Longhope had become well established, and were about to be joined by a third at Stronsay. Motor lifeboats became accepted as the lifeboatman's main tool for the job and, together with advances in equipment, design and continuous improvements in navigation, the seas around Orkney were safer. However, vessels still got wrecked in the treacherous waters around the islands and, in going to their aid, the lifeboatmen of Orkney performed many outstanding and courageous rescues. At the end of the Second World War, both Stromness and Longhope were operating lifeboats of 1920s and 1930s vintage respectively, but these boats, *J.J.K.S.W.* and *Thomas McCunn*, continued to give good service. At Longhope the crews, involved in many notable rescues during the war, performed further remarkable services after 1945 and the station acquired one of the proudest records of service of any in the British Isles.

The first award to be made after the war was presented in 1946 when the Institution's Thanks on Vellum was accorded to Mr William Sutherland following his retirement as honorary secretary, a post he had served since 1922. During those twenty-four years the Longhope lifeboat had rescued 272 lives. In 1932 he had been awarded a pair of inscribed binoculars by the RNLI and in the same year won an inscribed barometer for his energy and

Longhope lifeboat crew in the late 1950s standing in front of Thomas McCunn. *Back row left to right: Dan Kirkpatrick (Coxswain), James Johnstone (Mechanic), R. Johnstone, John Norquoy and R. Kirkpatrick; front row left to right: R. Johnstone, R. Johnston and J. Nicholson. (Orkney Photographic Archives)*

Thomas McCunn *alongside Longhope pier. This photograph clearly shows the layout of the 45ft 6in Watson design, with the aft cockpit, the shelter housing the engine controls operated by the mechanic, the funnel amidships for the exhaust and the small forward cockpit. (Orkney Photographic Archives)*

initiative in directing the service in which the crew of the Hull trawler *Dorbie* was saved. Mr Sutherland was succeeded as honorary secretary by his daughter, Miss M. Sutherland.

During 1949, *Thomas McCunn* performed three routine rescues. The first took place on the evening of 3 March when the lifeboat launched at 10.40 p.m. in choppy seas and torrential rain to the fishing vessel *Mazurka*, of Peterhead, which had engine failure. The boat, with a crew of seven, was towed to Longhope in the early hours of the following morning. On 1 July, *Thomas McCunn* launched at 3.25 a.m. to search for a man reported missing after going out in his boat the previous evening to tend lobster creels. The man was found at 4 a.m., half-a-mile off Tor Ness and taken back to the lifeboat station. The last service of the year took place on 25 August after the Grimsby trawler *St Clair* ran aground north of Tarf lighthouse. *Thomas McCunn* launched and the lifeboatmen found the vessel on her side on the rocks. Her crew of fourteen had managed to get ashore safely in their boat and thirteen were brought back to Longhope by the lifeboat, with one remaining on Swona to keep watch on the trawler.

On 12 April 1951, the Longhope lifeboat was involved in a very long and arduous service after the motor tanker *Oljaren*, of Gothenburg, bound for Stockholm with a cargo of diesel, ran aground on Muckle Skerry. *Thomas McCunn* launched at 1.40 a.m. under the command of Coxswain Alfred Johnston into heavy seas and a south-westerly gale, finding the tanker on the west side of Muckle Skerry. Coxswain Johnston took the lifeboat alongside but the crew, consisting of forty men, decided to remain on board so the lifeboat stood by until 1 p.m., when with conditions worsening, the captain decided to abandon ship. With great difficulty, Coxswain Johnston again took the lifeboat alongside the tanker and, as heavy seas broke over the casualty and crashed onto the lifeboat, rescued twenty-four men. However, the captain and fifteen others decided to remain on board and so, turning the lifeboat round in the confined area between the tanker and the rocks, Coxswain Johnston brought her clear and returned to Longhope. At 5.45 p.m., the captain radioed for further assistance so the lifeboat put to sea again. When she reached the tanker, none of the sixteen men would leave so the lifeboat returned to Longhope once again, arriving back at 11.30 p.m. At 2.35 p.m. on 13 April, the owners of the tanker sent a message to the captain of the vessel, instructing him to abandon ship and so *Thomas McCunn* was launched for a third time, rescued the remaining sixteen men and landed them at Longhope in the late afternoon. For his skill, courage and determination during this prolonged and difficult service, the Bronze medal was awarded to Coxswain Johnston.

In December 1954, Dan Kirkpatrick took over as coxswain of *Thomas McCunn*. Kirkpatrick was to become one of the most decorated of all Scottish lifeboatman, but also one who would go down in history for the tragic end to his career. His first service in charge of the lifeboat took place on 11 April 1955 after the Aberdeen steam trawler *Gava* had gone ashore on Clettack Skerry. The lifeboat saved four of the trawler's thirteen crew after nine had been rescued by another fishing vessel, *Enterprise*, and then took the casualty in tow to Longhope.

In the early morning of 3 February 1956, *Thomas McCunn* was launched to the freighter *Dovrefjell*, of Oslo, aground on the Pentland Skerries. Extremely heavy seas breaking over the stranded vessel prevented either the Longhope lifeboat or the Wick lifeboat, which had also launched, getting close enough to rescue the crew of forty-one. The lifeboats stood by while the stranded men were lifted off their ship by Naval and RAF helicopters and landed at John O'Groat. Once the whole crew was safe, the lifeboats returned to their stations having each been at sea for almost ten hours. Most of the freighter's crew had been made up of Italians and both Norwegian and Italian Governments expressed their thanks for the help of the two lifeboats. King Haakon of Norway subsequently awarded the Norwegian Medal for Heroism to both Coxswain Kirkpatrick and Coxswain Neil Stewart, of Wick.

On 4 February 1959, Kirkpatrick's local knowledge proved essential when he took *Thomas McCunn* to the aid of the 117ft trawler *Strathcoe*, of Aberdeen, ashore in the Pentland Firth in a small cleft in a cliff known locally as the Geo of the Lame. The lifeboat was launched at 3.27 a.m. after Dr S. Peace, the station's honorary secretary, received a message from the Coastguard giving details of the trawler's fate. The Stromness lifeboat *Archibald and Alexander M. Paterson* was also launched as *Strathcoe* was reported to be eight miles from Longhope and eleven from Stromness. After following a course close to the coastline, the Longhope lifeboat found the casualty, in the words of the official report, 'hard ashore, heading east-south-east with a list to starboard of forty-five degrees. The cliffs on either side of the small gully were 500 feet high, and the bottom round the stern of the wreck was rocky with a number of large and dangerous boulders.' The trawler's situation appeared desperate as the seas were breaking over the funnel and the vessel's radio, lights and distress flares were out of action. At 4.50 a.m. the Stromness lifeboat arrived on scene and she stood by to seaward to act as a radio telephone link with the shore. Meanwhile, the Longhope lifeboat approached the casualty.

In the Longhope lifeboat, Coxswain Kirkpatrick let go the anchor and veered down to the starboard quarter of the wreck intending to take the trawler's crew off by breeches buoy. After three attempts, a line was retrieved by the trawler's crew and secured inside the wheelhouse. Attempts to take the men off the trawler began at first light, although the initial efforts proved somewhat hazardous: 'the first man, when being taken off by breeches buoy, grabbed at the securing rope on his way across and as a result was washed out of the buoy. He managed to haul himself along the rope and reached the scrambling net rigged over the lifeboat's side.' Following this, Kirkpatrick realised it was too dangerous to continue to haul the men out of the trawler and so decided to wait until the tide began to turn when conditions would improve. By 7.45 a.m., conditions had eased sufficiently to enable the lifeboatmen to haul the trawler's remaining thirteen crew aboard using the breeches buoy. At just after 8 a.m. all the men were safe and at 8.09 a.m. the lifeboat left the scene.

The poor visibility and heavy ground sea breaking on the cliffs made the rescue a particularly hazardous one, with the lifeboat crew working together throughout, as Kirkpatrick recalled:

> Second Coxswain John Norquoy gave . . . invaluable support, particularly in his handling of the securing ropes. The two mechanics, Robert Johnston and Robert Rattray Johnston, handled the engines faultlessly and mechanic Robert Johnston succeeded in carrying out a minor repair to the radio telephone equipment.

Kirkpatrick was awarded the Silver medal for this outstanding service, and the other members of the crew were also formally recognised. The Thanks of the Institution on Vellum was accorded to Second Coxswain John Norquoy, Bowman James Johnston, Mechanic Robert Johnston, Assistant Mechanic Robert Rattray Johnston; medal service certificates to crew members James Nicholson, Daniel Raymond Kirkpatrick and Robert Johnston. A Letter of Appreciation was sent to the Stromness honorary secretary in recognition of the help given by the Stromness lifeboatmen.

On 6 December 1959, Kirkwall Coastguard informed honorary secretary Dr S. Peace that the trawler *George Robb* was ashore on the Stacks of Duncansby. At 12.10 a.m., *Thomas McCunn* was launched under the command of Coxswain Kirkpatrick. The conditions faced by the lifeboat crew were appalling as the severe gale was raging against the flood tide churning up mountainous seas. The last message received from the trawler stated she was in need of immediate help as she was taking in water very fast. Coxswain Kirkpatrick maintained full speed as the lifeboat ploughed her way through the turbulent waters in the Pentland Firth. At one point during the passage the lifeboat dropped heavily into the trough of a wave and, as water repeatedly swept over her, the wireless was put out of action. The mechanic Robert Johnston tried to carry out repairs but leaving his post at the engine controls proved impossible. The rescuers' attempts were further hindered by the extremely poor visibility – the Duncansby Head lighthouse, with a range of twenty miles, was not seen by the lifeboatman until they were just five miles away. But worse was to come: as the lifeboat was taken across the flood outlet at the east end of the Pentland Firth, *Thomas McCunn* encountered extremely violent, short and steep seas. As one heavy sea struck her, she rolled to starboard and was hit by another wave which rolled her over on to her beam ends. With a wall of water crashing down on to the boat, the lifeboatmen clung on as the lifeboat came upright. She freed herself of the water and the rescuers carried on as the wind increased to hurricane force.

South of Duncansby, Coxswain Kirkpatrick took the lifeboat towards the estimated position of the trawler with a parachute flare burning, but no sign could be seen of the casualty. By 3.30 a.m. it was clear that the trawler would not be found, so the lifeboat returned to Longhope to obtain further information. She arrived at her station, where it was learned that the Coastguard had tried to recall her but because of the damage to the wireless the message had not been received. The crew's efforts during this very arduous search were recognised by the RNLI: the Thanks of the Institution on Vellum was accorded to Coxswain Kirkpatrick, and Vellum service certificates were issued to the remainder of the crew, Second Coxswain James Johnston, Motor Mechanic Robert Johnston, Assistant Mechanic Robert Rattray Johnston and crew members James Swanson, James Nicholson, Robert Johnston and Dr S. Peace.

Naming ceremony of the ill-fated Thurso lifeboat Dunnet Head (Civil Service No.31) *(ON.920) at Scrabster on 18 August 1956 with* Thomas McCunn *from Longhope in attendance. After less than a year at Thurso, this lifeboat, the first 47ft Watson motor type built, was destroyed by fire together with the boathouse at Scrabster on 10 December 1956. (From an old photograph supplied by John Budge)*

During 1960 *Thomas McCunn* performed four further services, all routine in nature, which proved to be her last as the Longhope lifeboat. On 26 March, she escorted the trawler *Little Ouse* to safety and, on 9 June, assisted the trawler *Adolph Hennecke*, of Rostock. On 1 November she took a sick man, who was suffering from pleurisy, from Hoy to the mainland in rough seas and an easterly gale. Her last service took place just over a week later, on 10 November, when she escorted the locally owned fishing yawl *Delightful* from Aith Hope round to Longhope Pier. No effective services were performed during 1961 and in April 1962 a new lifeboat was sent to Longhope. *Thomas McCunn*, which had given sterling service for almost three decades, left with an outstanding record having saved more than 300 lives on over 100 missions. She was reallocated to the Reserve Fleet in which she served until 1972 and was then sold out of service. In private hands, she was re-engined with two 80bhp Mermaid four-cylinder diesels, altered only internally, and maintained much as she was when in service. Initially kept at Walton-on-the-Naze, she was moved to Hampshire during the 1980s and by the 1990s was at Hayling Island, moored at the local Yacht Club. In 2001 she returned to Longhope to become the centrepiece of the local museum, described in Appendix 3.

One of the last duties undertaken by *Thomas McCunn* as Longhope lifeboat was to escort home her replacement, the new lifeboat *T.G.B.*, a 47ft non-self-righting Watson cabin motor type. Built at a cost of £35,500 at the yard of J.S. White, East Cowes, the new boat was powered by twin 60bhp Gardner 6LW diesel engines, which gave a top speed of almost nine knots, and she was funded by an anonymous gift. She was also fitted with the latest electronic equipment, including en echo-sounder, direction finding radio and VHF radio. She arrived at Longhope on 24 April 1962 to be met by the old lifeboat off Swona and escorted to her new station. Coxswain Dan Kirkpatrick was at the wheel of *T.G.B.* having been accompanied on the passage north from Cowes by Mechanic Robert Johnston and two crew members, Ray Kirkpatrick, the Coxswain's son, and Robbie Johnston. The Inspector for the Northern District, Lt-Cdr M. Roden, was also on board together with A. Cursitor, engineer for the District. A small crowd gathered at Longhope Pier as the new boat tied up at 2.50 p.m. for, as The Orcadian put it, 'a quiet, friendly welcome, intimate, rather like a family gathering to see a new baby', an apt description for the close-knit lifeboat community of Longhope. After half an hour at the pier, the new boat was taken round to Brims to be housed for the first time. The boathouse doors had been enlarged and heightened to accommodate the new boat, which was successfully recovered up the slipway before undertaking a first launch from her new home to ensure she fitted the keelway.

Before being officially named, *T.G.B.* had already recorded her first service. On 4 August 1962, the Peterhead motor fishing vessel *Daisy* sprung a leak and foundered forty miles east of Stronsay on her way home from the Shetland fishing grounds. Both the Stronsay and Longhope lifeboats were launched and were joined by Shackleton aircraft and thirty vessels including sixteen Peterhead vessels who sailed out in the gale force winds to help with the search. One of the Shackleton aircraft spotted the life raft, which was being battered in the heavy seas and frequent rain squalls. The fishermen were picked up by the Danish vessel *Mella Dan* at 10 a.m, on 5 August, about fifty miles east-north-east from where *Daisy* had gone down. *T.G.B.* was only fifteen miles away having travelled ninety-five miles. The ten men were transferred from the Danish vessel to the lifeboat which then went to Wick, another 100-mile journey, where

47ft Watson motor lifeboat T.G.B. (ON.962), pictured during trials, was provided from the gift of an anonymous donor. She was one of eighteen boats of the 47ft Watson class built between 1955 and 1963. Unlike her predecessor at Longhope, she had a fully enclosed cockpit and midship steering position and served the station for seven years, during which time she saved twenty-four lives. (From a photograph loaned by a Shoreline member, by courtesy of Jeff Morris)

Thomas McCunn *and the new 47ft Watson* T.G.B. *(ON.962) alongside Longhope pier on 24 April 1962, the day the former was replaced by the latter.* T.G.B. *had travelled from her builder's yard at Cowes and was escorted home by the veteran* Thomas McCunn. *(Orkney Photographic Archives)*

they were landed at 1 a.m. on 6 August. *T.G.B.* returned to Longhope at 5.30 a.m. having covered 240 miles during a service which lasted almost thirty hours, the longest service ever performed by a Longhope lifeboat. Coxswain Dan Kirkpatrick commented afterwards, 'It was a pretty dirty trip with a strong wind and heavy seas. . . it was a straightforward job but long ...We were all very pleased with the performance of the new lifeboat.'

After an impressive start to her life-saving career, *T.G.B.* was formally named on 23 August 1962 at Longhope Pier by the Hon. Mrs Alexander Ramsey. Lord Saltoun, Convenor of the Scottish Lifeboat Council, handed the boat over to the Branch, and she was accepted by Jackie Groat Jnr, the honorary secretary. The Revd D.A. Williams, minister of the parish of Stenness, assisted by Revd Charles Abel, minister of the South Isles, conducted the service of dedication. The Hon Mrs Ramsey then named the lifeboat, after which the guests and supporters retired to the community centre for refreshments and presentations. At 5 p.m., Lord Saltoun and other guests were taken back to Houton Pier by *T.G.B.* from where two special steamer trips had been laid on to return those who had attended the ceremony to mainland.

T.G.B. was involved in a number of outstanding rescues during her time at Longhope. In 1964, with the lifeboat less than two years on station, Coxswain Kirkpatrick's seamanship was put to the test when *T.G.B.* went to the trawler *Ben Barvas* on 3 January. After launching at 10.26 p.m., the lifeboat reached the trawler an hour later to find it stranded on the Little Skerry and being swept by heavy steep seas whipped up by wind and tide. Coxswain Kirkpatrick took the lifeboat across the west end of the Skerry to assess the situation and plan how best to effect a rescue. In the light of parachute flares, the trawler could be seen lying close to the shore upright but rolling in the surf, with reefs close ahead and astern of her. An attempt was made by Coxswain Kirkpatrick to approach the trawler from the south, but when about sixty feet off a huge sea carried the lifeboat broadside to within thirty feet of the wreck and evasive action was necessary. The lifeboat's engines were put astern and she was taken clear, just as a huge sea broke above the trawler's port rail. As getting alongside the trawler was almost impossible, the lifeboat was anchored to the south of the casualty and attempts began to get a line on board it.

Second Coxswain James Johnston fired a rocket line across the trawler's stern, which was used to secure a stronger line between lifeboat and casualty. The heavy seas made handling the rope extremely difficult, but with coxswain and crew working together the lifeboat was held in position about 90ft from the trawler. At 12.15 a.m., the operation to rescue the nine survivors by breeches buoy began, and involved the whole lifeboat crew, as the official RNLI account explained:

> Bowman Ray Kirkpatrick and his brother Jack manned the outhaul forward. The second coxswain and Robbie Johnston manned the inhaul amidships; James Swanson tended the nylon warp, while assistant mechanic Robert R. Johnston attended to the engines and radio.
> The coxswain continued to keep firm control of the situation.

Transferring the men to the lifeboat was an exhausting task as the tide swept each astern, forcing the lifeboat crew to muster all their strength to heave the survivors on board. The situation was made more difficult after the second man had reached the lifeboat because the trawler's fuel tanks fractured, covering the lifeboat's ropes and decks with diesel oil. The deck became very slippery and the rescue work harder. However, with the scrambling net rigged amidships, the coxswain, with the bowman, hauled survivors aboard. At 1.20 a.m. the rescue was completed as the last man to leave the trawler, the skipper, got into the breeches buoy.

The nylon rope was cut, the lifeboat swung away, the deck was cleared of ropes and the lifeboat's gear was secured for the passage home. After she left the casualty, the lifeboat came up with the trawler *Ben Screel*, which had on board five survivors from *Ben Barvas* who had left earlier in an inflatable life raft. These five men were transferred to the lifeboat and all fourteen survivors landed at St Margaret's Hope at 4.30 a.m. Thus ended another remarkable rescue performed by the lifeboatmen of Longhope. The Silver medal awarded to Coxswain Kirkpatrick reflected the leadership, courage and skill he had shown throughout this rescue, and was his second such award. The Thanks of the Institution on Vellum was accorded to Second Coxswain James Johnston, Bowman Ray Kirkpatrick, Mechanic Robert Johnston, Assistant Mechanic Robert Rattray Johnston, and crew members James Swanson, Robbie Johnston and Jack Kirkpatrick for their part in the service.

When Coxswain Kirkpatrick was awarded a third Silver medal, he became the only man alive at the time to hold three such medals marking him out as an exceptional coxswain. The rescue for which he was awarded his third medal began in the early hours of 1 April 1968 after the station's honorary secretary Jackie Groat had been informed by the Coastguard that the trawler *Ross Puma* was ashore on the south-east side of Stroma. By the time *T.G.B.* had launched at 2.56 a.m., a new position for the casualty had been received stating it was two miles north of Torness Point on Hoy. The lifeboat made good progress despite gale force winds and rough seas, with squalls reducing visibility to less than fifty yards. By 3.24 a.m., with the lifeboat off Torness Point the lifeboat crew sighted a red flare to the north. At 3.30 a.m. radio contact was made with the trawler and from then on excellent radio communications were maintained. Fifteen minutes later the lifeboat crew sighted *Ross Puma*, aground on the north side of the Little Rackwick Shoals, which extend about 600 yards out to sea. The vessel was lying only about fifty yards from the shore where the cliffs were over 300ft high.

The trawler was listing about thirty-five degrees to starboard and was rolling and pounding heavily. The crew on the starboard side aft were trying to get some shelter from the deck house but were being swamped by the seas which continually broke over the vessel. With seas rising and falling 15ft to 20ft alongside the casualty, Kirkpatrick decided that the trawler's crew must be taken off immediately as the vessel was in danger of being swung beam on to the sea and rolled over the reef. The lifeboat was taken to the seaward side of the shoals and anchored to windward of the casualty. About eighty fathoms of cable were veered, and the lifeboat came within twenty yards of the trawler's starboard quarter. The lifeboat was rolling and pitching violently in the confused seas and swell inside the shoals. This made it extremely difficult to fire the rocket line with any accuracy, and when a line was fired, it fell short of the trawler.

At this point, the lifeboat crew found that a tide eddy, together with the wind and sea, began to carry the lifeboat closer into the skerries. The lifeboat struck a rock under her port side but Coxswain Kirkpatrick immediately went ahead on the engines and the anchor cable was shortened. The immediate danger was cleared enabling the lifeboat to be positioned about twenty-five yards from the trawler on her starboard quarter. The coxswain decided that the best hope of saving the trawler's crew was to take them off by using one of the casualty's own life rafts rather than with the lifeboat's breeches buoy. He sent a message by radio telephone announcing his intentions, and a rocket line was fired which, this time, fell across the deck of the trawler. The trawler's crew secured the line to one of the life rafts, and a second line was attached on the opposite side of the raft to secure it to the trawler. One by one, the seven members of the casualty's crew jumped from the deck into the life raft. At times, the raft was several feet below deck level and a moment later several feet above it. At one point, one of the crew hesitated and found himself hanging over the side of the trawler but his crew mates managed to haul him back aboard before the next sea broke.

Throughout the operation, Coxswain Kirkpatrick kept the lifeboat in position by skilful use of the engines while the bowman, Ray Kirkpatrick, remained forward tending the anchor cable. The two mechanics controlled the engine and the radio telephone, and the other two crew manned the searchlight. Once the seven men had got aboard the raft, the lifeboat crew hauled in the securing rope while the eight crew of the trawler who remained on board slacked away on their rope. As soon as the raft cleared the slight shelter afforded by the side of the trawler it was swept violently towards the skerries. While the lifeboat crew were trying to heave the raft alongside, a heavy sea struck both the raft and the lifeboat completely filling the lifeboat's after cockpit. The raft shipped about a foot and a half of water and was carried to leeward but, with a great effort, the lifeboat crew hauled it back alongside and helped the seven survivors aboard the lifeboat.

Eight men remained aboard the trawler so the raft was hauled back and the manoeuvre repeated. The eight men jumped into the raft one by one and released the trawler's rope, after which the lifeboat crew pulled the raft alongside their boat and took the eight men on board. The time was 4.35 a.m. and the rescue operation had lasted forty minutes. A message was passed to Wick radio to say that the rescue had been completed, while the survivors were given rum and hot soup. The lifeboat cleared Little Rackwick Shoals and set course for Longhope, reaching Longhope Pier at 6.30 a.m. For this outstanding service, the Silver medal was awarded to Coxswain Kirkpatrick and the Thanks of the Institution on Vellum accorded to the rest of the crew: Second Coxswain James Johnston, Bowman Raymond Kirkpatrick, Mechanic R. Johnston, Assistant Mechanic James Swanson and crewman Robbie Johnston.

In further recognition of his courage and seamanship, Coxswain Kirkpatrick was elected to receive the annual gift of £5 from the Miss Maud Smith endowment for the bravest act of life-saving that year.

Tragedy in the Pentland Firth

Coxswain Daniel Kirkpatrick received further recognition for his medal-winning exploits when he was given a gift from the James Michael Bower Endowment Fund. This fund, established in 1955 by the P&O Steam Navigation Company as a memorial to James Michael Bower, late third officer of the steamship *Stratheden* who lost his life in a disaster, awarded those who receive either the Gold or Silver medal for gallantry. Coxswain Kirkpatrick was never formally presented with his medal for the courageous rescue of the fifteen men from the trawler *Ross Puma*. Indeed, it was the last service of note performed by the lifeboat *T.G.B.* at Longhope as, less than a year later, she capsized on service with the loss of her entire crew of eight including Kirkpatrick in a tragedy unequalled in Orkney lifeboat history. The impact of the tragedy was felt not only by the people of Hoy and Orkney, but also by the RNLI on a national level.

The disaster occurred on 17 March 1969 when *T.G.B.* went to the aid of the Liberian ship *Irene*. The auxiliary Coastguard at Brough Ness contacted honorary secretary Jackie Groat at 7.29 p.m. and informed him that *Irene* was in difficulty. The casualty's position had not been established, but she was believed to be five miles east of Halcro Head, South Ronaldsay. The Coastguard requested that the lifeboat be launched and so, at 7.40 p.m., the maroons were fired. Twenty minutes later, *T.G.B.* was at sea with a crew of eight. The south-easterly gale in

The Liberian steamship Irene *aground on South Ronaldsay in March 1969. (Orkney Photographic Archives)*

the Pentland Firth, estimated at the time at force nine, was accompanied by a very rough sea and heavy swell. Visibility, which HM Coastguard estimated as between half and three miles, was reduced by rain and snow flurries. At 8.40 p.m., *T.G.B.* gave her position as three miles south-east of Cantick Head lighthouse. At 9.07 p.m., she was a mile east of Swona Island. A few minutes later the lookout at Brough Ness Coastguard station stated she was clear of the Lother Rocks. About 9.30 p.m., she was estimated to be half way between Brough Ness and Pentland Skerries heading east. At 9.28 p.m., the last officially recorded signal from the Longhope lifeboat was received by Wick radio. This message acknowledged a signal giving the latest position of *Irene*. Two minutes later the principal keeper saw the lifeboat north of the Cantick Head lighthouse and he last saw her stern light to the eastward, about a mile away about 9.35 p.m.

Shortly after 10 p.m., the Coastguard at Kirkwall asked Wick radio to inform *T.G.B.* that conditions alongside *Irene* were 'almost impossible.' By 10.30 p.m., the Coastguard became concerned about the safety of the Longhope lifeboat as this message had not been acknowledged. Coast rescue emergency parties were sent to vantage points on the east coast of South Ronaldsay. The search was coordinated by the Coastguard, while close contact was maintained with the Inspector of Lifeboats for Scotland, Brian Miles, and the honorary secretary. Meanwhile, the 70ft Clyde lifeboat *Grace Paterson Ritchie*, which was lying at Kirkwall, had put out at the request of the Coastguard. At 9.15 p.m., *Irene* grounded half a mile south of Grim Ness where a Coastguard team had managed to reach her. The first man from the ship was brought ashore by the Coastguard at 12.42 a.m., in the early hours of 18 March, and by 1.30 a.m. all the ship's company had been brought to safety.

Just after 11 p.m. on 17 March, the Kirkwall Coastguard asked *Grace Paterson Ritchie* to make for a position south of *Irene* and rendezvous with *T.G.B. Grace Paterson Ritchie* reached the position at 11.15 p.m. and fired a parachute flare, but no reply was received. Staff Coxswain Ian Ives, in charge of *Grace Paterson Ritchie*, made for a position a mile south-east of Old Head. In the high seas, visibility was very poor and finding the Longhope lifeboat in such conditions was impossible so Kirkwall Coastguard agreed that a search should be conducted at daylight with the help of aircraft. At daybreak, a Shackleton aircraft from RAF Kinloss and helicopter from RNAS Lossiemouth worked with *Grace Paterson Ritchie* and the Stronsay, Thurso and Stromness lifeboats, all of which put out on the morning of 18 March.

Not until 1.40 p.m. on 18 March did the Thurso lifeboat crew spot the Longhope lifeboat, upturned, four miles south-west of Tor Ness. The stricken lifeboat was then towed to Scrabster Harbour, escorted by the Stromness lifeboat. Only seven bodies were recovered, six with lifejackets on. The coxswain, Daniel Kirkpatrick, was not wearing a lifejacket. The door of the port side of the wheelhouse was found open and it is probable that the missing man, James Swanson, was either lost overboard before the capsize or that his body was lost through the open door. The lifeboatmen who gave their lives were: Coxswain Daniel Kirkpatrick, Second Coxswain James Johnston, Bowman Raymond Kirkpatrick, Mechanic Robert Johnston, Assistant Mechanic James Swanson and crew members John Kirkpatrick, Robert Johnston and Eric McFadyen.

The immediate aftermath of the tragedy saw representatives of the RNLI fly to Hoy and attend to the needs of the lost lifeboatmen's families. Margaret Kirkpatrick and Maggie Johnston had both lost a husband and two sons. The Inspector of Lifeboats for Scotland, Brian Miles, who had been involved in the search for the capsized boat, recalled the heartache of that terrible night: 'I looked down the hill, and it struck me like a physical blow. We had taken someone out of virtually every house.' Shortly after the disaster, the Lord Lieutenant of Orkney launched a special appeal for the families of the lost men. Meanwhile, the funeral

Covered by tarpaulin sheeting, T.G.B. *is driven by road out of the RNLI's depot at Boreham Wood after being salvaged following the capsize on 17 March 1969. She was subsequently repaired and put back in service, serving at Arranmore in Co. Donegal from 1970 to 1978. (By courtesy of the RNLI)*

service for the lifeboatmen was held on 22 March at Walls Old Parish Church, Hoy. Among many who attended were the chairman of the RNLI, Admiral Sir Wilfred Woods, the Duke of Atholl, Lord Saltoun, Secretary of the RNLI Stirling Whorlow, and the Chief Inspector of Lifeboats Lt-Cdr W.L.G. Dutton.

Following this terrible tragedy, the Institution carried out a detailed inquiry into the events that led to the lifeboat's capsize. On 10 June 1969, a Procurator Fiscal's inquiry was held at Kirkwall. The jury unanimously found that the seven crew whose bodies had been found in the upturned hull of the lifeboat died from drowning. The body of the eighth man, James Swanson, had not been recovered. The Sheriff stated that no evidence had been heard indicating or implying negligence, nor had any evidence been found that the boat or equipment was other than first class and all precautions and procedures which ought to have been taken had been. The actions of the honorary secretary and the Coastguard were deemed correct, as were those of the staff coxswain in charge of *Grace Paterson Ritchie*. Although nobody was sure exactly what had happened to the lifeboat, the inquiry report stated that she had capsized after being overwhelmed by 'very high seas and maelstrom conditions'.

On 9 August 1970, a statue was unveiled by HRH Queen Elizabeth, the Queen Mother, in Osmondwall Cemetery in memory of the eight Longhope lifeboatmen who died. The statue, in the form of a lifeboatman gazing out to sea, was placed at the head of the graves of the eight men. The RNLI was represented by Sir Wilfred Woods, the Duke of Atholl, Convenor of the Scottish Lifeboat Council, and Commander P.D. Sturdee, Chief Staff Officer (Operation). This fine memorial overlooks the sea as a poignant reminder of the courage and bravery of the lifeboatmen of Hoy.

Above: *HM The Queen Mother in Osmondwall Cemetery, on Hoy, on 9 August 1970, unveiling the 6ft tall bronze memorial, modelled by Ian Scott, to the lifeboatmen lost in the T.G.B. tragedy of March 1969. She flew across the Pentland Firth in a helicopter of the Queen's Flight and was welcomed by Orkney's Lord Lieutenant, Colonel H.W. Scarth, of Breckness, and Mrs Scarth. (By courtesy of the RNLI)*

Right: *The impressive memorial in Osmondwall Cemetery on Hoy to the eight lifeboatmen lost in T.G.B. in March 1969, with a plaque at its base reading 'Greater love hath no man than this, that he lay down his life for his fellow men'. (Nicholas Leach)*

Lifeboats to Challenge the Firth

The tragedy at Longhope affected all connected with the lifeboat service, and criticism of the service followed the disaster with questions about its operation being raised. *T.G.B.* was clearly in the best condition possible, and her construction and maintenance were of the highest order, yet she had still been overwhelmed by the seas of the Pentland Firth. But worse was to come for the RNLI and its volunteer crews. Within a year, on 21 January 1970, the Fraserburgh lifeboat *Duchess of Kent*, a 46ft 9in Watson cabin type, was overwhelmed by an enormous freak wave and capsized with the loss of five of her crew of six while helping the Danish fishing vessel *Opal*. Following the two disasters, much soul-searching took place within the Institution's hierarchy while questions were asked about its efficiency and indeed about the fundamental nature of its operations. It appeared from the outside that lifeboat crews were not being provided with the best lifeboats and, in the late twentieth century, the idea that a lifeboat would capsize and not right itself was inconceivable.

The Longhope and Fraserburgh disasters prompted the RNLI to rethink its entire design and development programme, and launched the Institution into a new era. With regard to the design of lifeboats, the provision of self-righting boats was now a matter of urgency. Non-self-righting boats, although built and maintained to the highest standards, were inevitably vulnerable to capsize, and this vulnerability had resulted in the tragedies at Longhope and Fraserburgh. To overcome this weakness, an air-bag system was developed so that non-self-righting lifeboats, including 47ft Watsons such as *T.G.B.* and the 52ft Barnetts like that at Stromness, had a once-only self-righting ability. In addition, all new lifeboat designs developed since 1969 have been fully self-righting. Indeed, the next lifeboat built for service at Longhope was a self-righter.

On Hoy, in the aftermath of the tragedy, discussions over the future of the station itself were held, but suggestions that it should be closed were rejected as local people were adamant a lifeboat was needed. Margaret Kirkpatrick, whose husband and sons had been lost, when asked whether she would wish her remaining son to join the service, said: 'If he should want to go on the next Longhope lifeboat, I will not stop him or try to.' The people of Hoy were clearly proud of their lifeboat tradition and, while not forgetting the men lost in 1969, wanted to look forward. The honorary secretary Jackie Groat explained a few years later:

> There has to be a lifeboat on Hoy: it's a necessity of life. The Pentland Firth is one of the wildest stretches of water in the kingdom . . . The Firth is also one of busiest shipping channels around the British Isles. The whole island was united in wanting to have a new lifeboat as soon as possible after the disaster . . . I didn't want to be the person who sent people out to their deaths, but how would you feel, sitting here and knowing that there were people in trouble out there on the sea?

To cover the area immediately after the tragedy, the 70ft Clyde class cruising lifeboat *Grace Paterson Ritchie* based at Kirkwall was operated around Scapa Flow. At Longhope, as an interim measure, the 52ft Barnett lifeboat *Hilton Briggs,* a 1952-built reserve craft, was supplied and John Leslie, second coxswain at Stromness for seven years, was appointed full-time Coxswain at Longhope with a staff mechanic to assist. Men came forward to form a new crew and spent many hours training on both *Grace Paterson Ritchie* and *Hilton Briggs*, until the latter was declared operational on 22 May 1970. Following the success of the training programme, the Committee of Management decided that the station would remain open and proceeded to allocate it a new lifeboat. At Fraserburgh, the station was closed in 1970 after the lifeboat disaster and not until 1979 was it reopened.

Meanwhile, *T.G.B.*, the lifeboat in which the Longhope lifeboatmen had died, was taken to the south coast and repaired at William Osborne's yard at Littlehampton while a decision was made about the boat's future and whether she should be allocated to another station or serve in the Institution's Relief Fleet. The boat was relatively undamaged by the capsize and, as the RNLI's finances were not in a particularly healthy state, writing off what was basically a seaworthy boat was not something the organisation could realistically afford. So, modification work was carried out at Osborne's, including making the after-cabin watertight, to make capsize more difficult. Structural changes were also made to the boat to further increase the boat's range of stability, after which she was reallocated to the Arranmore station on Ireland's north-west coast. She served there for eight years and then spent a further six years in the Relief Fleet before being sold to the Scottish Maritime Museum in Irvine. She was placed on display at the Museum, initially outside, before being moved under cover. She forms the centrepiece of a small exhibition about the RNLI and the Longhope station.

Meanwhile, the station returned to near normal with the new crew ready for the next call. The first rescue performed following the events of 17 March 1969 was a somewhat mundane one. On 23 June 1970, *Hilton Briggs* took a sick man off Hoy for urgent hospital treatment on Orkney mainland. She put out at 11.10 p.m. and took the patient to Scapa Pier where an ambulance was waiting, and returned to Longhope in the early hours of the following morning. On 16 October 1970, *Hilton Briggs* was again called into action, going to the motor fishing vessel *Capella*, of Buckie, which had grounded on the east side of South Ronaldsay. Together with *Grace Paterson Ritchie,* at the time based at Scapa, *Hilton Briggs* refloated the fishing vessel which then made for Kirkwall, escorted by the cruising lifeboat. This was first time since the disaster that the maroons had been heard in Longhope and the honorary secretary Jackie Groat was pleased with the service commenting that, 'We are very pleased with the boat and the crew have passed their first real test with flying colours.'

In 1970 a new 48ft 6in Solent lifeboat was placed on station at Longhope. Steel-hulled and self-righting, the new craft was better equipped than any of her predecessors to handle the

The permanent replacement for T.G.B. *was a 48ft 6in Solent self-righter with a steel hull, named* David and Elizabeth King & E.B. *(ON. 1010) and funded from the legacy of Miss Charlotte E. King, of Edinburgh, and an anonymous gift. (From a photograph loaned by a Shoreline member, by courtesy of Jeff Morris)*

*David and Elizabeth King & E.B. alongside Longhope pier for her formal naming and dedication ceremony
on 27 May 1971. She was named by Mrs Marion Thornton, of Edinburgh, in memory of the donor's parents.
(Orkney Photographic Archives)*

ferocious conditions encountered in the Pentland Firth. The Solent was based on a design of
lifeboat developed during the 1960s, the 48ft 6in Oakley, which employed a system of water
ballast transfer to achieve self-righting. However, the Solent dispensed with this system so,
although similar in appearance externally, it was in fact significantly different as self-righting
was achieved by virtue of a fully watertight wheelhouse. The Oakley was wooden hulled, while
the Solent had a steel hull of all welded construction, a cast-iron ballast keel and aluminium
superstructure. Building in steel rather than wood reduced time needed for construction and
thus minimised costs. The steel hull was sub-divided by watertight longitudinal bulkheads into
centre and wing compartments, and further subdivided by four main watertight bulkheads.
The machinery installation consisted of two Gardner 6LX diesel engines, each developing
110bhp at 1,300rpm, giving a speed of nine knots. Controls for the engines were mounted
alongside the steering position in the wheelhouse, giving the Coxswain complete control over
the boat while she was at sea.

The first of the new design to go on station, *R.Hope Roberts*, was placed at Rosslare
Harbour in July 1969. The boat for Longhope, *David and Elizabeth King & E.B.* (ON.1010),
was built at Cowes by Groves & Guttridge at a cost of £58,936. Together with another new
Solent lifeboat destined for Thurso, *The Three Sisters* (ON.1014), she sailed for her station on
5 December 1970 with Commander Teare, the new Divisional Inspector for Scotland, in
charge and a crew of Ian McFadyen, Billy Budge, Jimmy Sutherland and Coxswain Jack Leslie.
She arrived at Longhope on 11 December and was escorted across the Pentland Firth and into
Hoy Sound by *Hilton Briggs* and *Pentland (Civil Service No.31)* (ON.940), the latter boat having

been replaced at Thurso by *The Three Sisters*. About 100 people lined the pier at Longhope to welcome the new lifeboat and, after being refuelled, she went out on her first exercise with Coxswain Leslie in charge. The new Solent performed her first service on 29 December, being called to take a sick woman from Hoy to Scapa Pier where an ambulance was waiting to take the woman to hospital in Kirkwall. After a rather low-key start, *David and Elizabeth King & E.B.* went on to serve the station for almost twenty years.

The new lifeboat was provided out of the legacy of Miss Charlotte E. King, of Edinburgh, together with an anonymous gift, and was named after her donor's parents with the E.B. part of her name coming from the anonymous gift. The naming ceremony took place on 27 May 1971 and was held at Longhope Pier in bright sunshine and a strong south-easterly wind. Approximately 700 people were present, including 200 who had been brought by the motor vessel *Orcadia* from Stromness specially for the occasion. Longhope Branch chairman, Mr Isaac Moar, conducted the proceedings, introducing the various guest speakers. The Duke of Atholl, Convenor of the Scottish Lifeboat Council, accepted the lifeboat from the donor and handed her into the care of the Longhope Branch. She was accepted by Jimmy Groat, Branch Honorary Treasurer, who was acting on behalf of his brother, Jackie Groat, the honorary secretary, who was unable to attend because his wife, Edna, had died three days previously. The Service of Dedication was conducted by the Revd Ewan G.S. Traill, minister of Orkney South Isles, assisted by the Revd Stuart D.B. Picken, Moderator of the Presbytery of Orkney. The lifeboat was then christened by Mrs Marion M. Thornton, an Edinburgh solicitor's wife, whose mother had been close friends with the late Miss King who had left instructions in her will that Mrs Thornton should name any new boat funded by her legacy.

During eighteen years of service, *David and Elizabeth King & E.B.* was involved in some outstanding rescues and is credited with saving thirty-two lives while on station. Her first

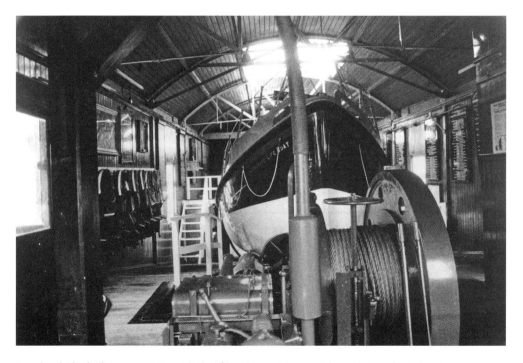

David and Elizabeth King & E.B. *inside the lifeboat house at Brims. (Orkney Photographic Archives)*

effective service came on 11 May 1971 when she went to the local fishing boat *Tussan* (K165), which was disabled in the Pentland Firth three miles north-west of Stroma Light. The fishing boat had a blocked fuel pipe and was drifting rapidly in the ebb stream towards Torness. The lifeboat took the vessel in tow at 4.55 p.m. and brought her safely to Scrabster, then returned to station at 10 p.m.

One of the more dramatic services in which *David and Elizabeth King & E.B.* was involved took place on 1 August 1972, in the early hours of the morning, after the Aberdeen trawler *Glengairn* had gone ashore on Swale Island in the Pentland Firth in moderate seas and a north-westerly wind. The lifeboat put to sea at 4.30 a.m. and, on reaching the casualty, found her on a shelf of rocks with a starboard list of twenty degrees. Stromness lifeboat *Archibald and Alexander M. Paterson* was also called out and the two lifeboats stood by until high tide. The motor vessel *St Clements* arrived at 2 p.m. and, together with the two lifeboats, made several unsuccessful attempts to pull the trawler clear. With the weather steadily worsening, the trawler's skipper asked for eight of his crew to be taken off, leaving four on board. The Longhope lifeboat took the eight men off and landed them at Longhope, then returned to continue standing by the stricken vessel. When she reached the trawler again, the Stromness lifeboat returned to station, leaving *David and Elizabeth King & E.B.* to stand by throughout the night. The Stromness boat returned the following morning to relieve the Longhope boat, which returned to station after almost thirty hours on service.

The most outstanding service in which *David and Elizabeth King & E.B.* was involved took place in February 1973. At 11.54 p.m. on 9 February, word was received at the station that the

David and Elizabeth King & E.B. *at full speed in the Pentland Firth. She served at Longhope from December 1970 until March 1988, during which time she saved thirty-two lives and launched seventy-seven times on service. (Orkney Photographic Archives)*

Longhope lifeboat crew in the mid-1970s with David and Elizabeth King & E.B. *The four standing at the back are,* left to right: *Jackie Groat (honorary secretary), Jack Leslie (coxswain), Isaac Moar, and Jimmy Mowat. Seated at the front,* left to right: *are Ian McFadyen (mechanic), Billy Mowat (second coxswain), John Budge, Billy Budge and Jimmy Swanson (assistant mechanic). (RNLI)*

trawler *Ross Tern* was ashore on Stroma and breaking up. As the lifeboat prepared to launch, Coxswain John Leslie was informed that the casualty, contrary to initial reports, was in fact on the Tarf Tail, Swona Island, and that six men were adrift in a life raft while five remained aboard. The vessel was in imminent danger of breaking up. At 12.17 a.m. on 10 February, *David and Elizabeth & E.B.* set out at full speed to the casualty. The wind was force three and the sea was smooth, with good visibility, although frequent snow showers accompanied the lifeboat as she made for Swona Island. Meanwhile, six of the trawler's crew had got into a life raft and cast themselves adrift from the wreck. At about 1 a.m., *David and Elizabeth & E.B.* was at the west end of Swona and a faint flicker of light was sighted to the south-east. Coxswain Leslie ordered a parachute flair to be fired and, in its light, the canopy of the life raft was seen less than a mile away. The lifeboat was immediately brought alongside the life raft, which was bouncing about dangerously and, with excellent teamwork, the lifeboat crew held the raft steady while the six survivors were taken aboard. The life raft was then cast adrift and Coxswain Leslie turned his attention to the trawler.

In the light of further parachute flares, the crew could see the casualty hard aground, listing heavily to starboard with five survivors clinging to the superstructure. Rocks on both quarters of the casualty prevented the lifeboat from going alongside. The swell and confused sea were producing a rise and fall of about 10ft, but, using parachute flares and the searchlight to illuminate the area, Coxswain Leslie brought the lifeboat's bow against the transom of the stricken vessel. In the restricted channel, with rocks to port and starboard, any error of judgment would have been fatal while the risk of the trawler slipping off or capsizing completely was also ever present. With the lifeboat crew on deck, the operation to snatch the survivors to safety was effected. Holding the lifeboat in position throughout was a difficult task as the combined effects of wind, sea and tide were swinging her stern towards rocks on the east side. The last survivor had to be hastily grabbed and dragged aboard the lifeboat as Coxswain Leslie came astern to try to straighten up the lifeboat and avoid the rocks.

At 1.21 a.m., with all survivors accounted for, the lifeboat made for St Margaret's Hope, where she arrived at 2.30 a.m. to land the rescued men. A doctor had been requested to meet the lifeboat and he tended three of the survivors who were suffering from exposure, while one had hurt his ankle during the rescue. In snow showers and complete darkness, the lifeboat made the return journey to Hoy, arriving back at Longhope at 5.15 a.m. after a difficult and dangerous rescue. In recognition of his outstanding seamanship, skill and courage during this service, Coxswain Leslie was awarded the Bronze medal, and medal service certificates were presented to Acting Second Coxswain Billy Budge, Mechanic Ian McFadyen, Assistant Mechanic Jimmy Swanson and crew members John Budge and Ian Williamson.

The Longhope lifeboatmen were again involved in another notable rescue towards the end of 1974. Shortly before midnight on 20 December, the fishing vessel *Lans*, of Ostend, was reported ashore at Berry Head, on Hoy, and in need of immediate assistance. *David and Elizabeth King & E.B.* was launched at 12.15 a.m. into a strong southerly wind with rough seas. An hour after launching, she reached the fishing vessel which was hard aground, broadside to the rocks, at the foot of 600ft high cliffs, listing to starboard and being swept by heavy seas breaking against the face of the cliffs. By the light of parachute flares, the lifeboatmen realised getting alongside would be impossible so they dropped anchor just outside the line

The unusual sight of three 48ft 6in Solent lifeboats together, pictured at Scrabster harbour. The are, left to right, Thurso lifeboat The Three Sisters *(O.N. 1014), Relief lifeboat* Royal British Legion Jubilee *(O.N. 1013), and Longhope lifeboat* David and Elizabeth King & E.B. *(By courtesy of John Budge)*

of the breakers and Coxswain Leslie began to veer the lifeboat towards the casualty using the engines with the anchor rope holding the lifeboat in position. A rocket line fired to the trawler fell short as the conditions were so bad. However, with *Lans* lying beneath Berry Head and apparently not in immediate danger of either foundering or capsizing, Coxswain Leslie decided to wait until the tide turned before making another attempt to reach her.

With the wind increasing to gale force, the lifeboatmen stood by, hoping the storm would ease. A request was then made for a helicopter to assess the situation from the air, although it was doubted if the aircraft could operate close enough to the cliffs to be able to undertake a rescue. A helicopter took from RAF Lossiemouth reached the fishing vessel shortly after dawn and, with outstanding skill and courage, the pilot took it to within a few feet of the cliff face. In three trips, he plucked all nine men from *Lans* to safety, winching them aboard the Longhope lifeboat which landed them to Stromness. In recognition of the remarkable skill shown by the helicopter pilot and crew in effecting a rescue, a Letter of Appreciation signed by the Director of the RNLI was later sent to the Officer Commanding 202 Squadron, RAF Lossiemouth.

A somewhat routine service was carried out on 18 July 1979 after the motor vessel *Linhav* ran aground on Roan Head during the morning. *David and Elizabeth King & E.B.* was launched at 5.40 a.m. in rough seas and a westerly gale and, an hour later, reached the casualty, which had a hole in her cargo hold, but was not in immediate danger. While the master and two of the crew remained on board, three men were taken off and landed at Flotta Pier after which the lifeboat returned to Longhope Pier. Temporary repairs were made at low water, after which the coaster refloated on the high tide and made her way to Flotta Pier.

Between 1980 and 1986, *David and Elizabeth King & E.B.* launched on service only six times, performing routine rescues. On 2 August 1980, she towed the local lobster boat *Scott*, with two men on board, to Aith Hope in dense fog. On 20 November 1982, she escorted the fishing vessel *Jaseline*, of Inverness, to safety. On 26 March 1983, she towed the 73ft cargo vessel *Kilmany*, with three men on board, to safety at St Margaret's Hope after the vessel had broken down south of South Ronaldsay. Less than two months later, on 22 May, she assisted the Danish cargo vessel *Vibeke Vesta* after the vessel's cargo had shifted. On 15 December 1984, she escorted the cargo vessel *Alsterberg*, of West Germany, which was being towed by the tug *Kinloch*. And on 27 March 1986, she escorted two craft, the fishing vessel *Shalimar* which was towing the converted fishing vessel *Crombie*.

Two services within the space of four days in January 1987 resulted in thirteen lives being saved by *David and Elizabeth King & E.B.* On 17 January, she launched to the Icelandic trawler *Saeborg*, with eleven men on board, which had broken down just over three miles off Brim Ness. In choppy seas, the lifeboat towed the trawler to Lyness Pier before returning to Longhope Pier where she was moored to await an improvement in the weather before being rehoused. On 21 January, just a day after being rehoused, she was again called upon and this time went to the fishing vessel *Shalimar*, with two people on board, which had engine failure off Little Rackwick on the west coast of Hoy. In rough seas and a strong wind, the lifeboat reached the casualty at 11 a.m. and towed her to Stromness before returning to station.

What proved to be the last service launch at Longhope by *David and Elizabeth King & E.B.* took place on the afternoon of 18 January 1988 after a sighting of red flares between Swona Island and John O'Groats. The lifeboat launched at 4 p.m. and, in rough seas and a severe south-easterly gale, searched the area with the assistance of a helicopter but found nothing and returned to Longhope at 7 p.m. Two months later, she was replaced by a new lifeboat after eighteen years of service. A further year in RNLI service operating from Invergordon was followed by sale from the RNLI's fleet in March 1990. Renamed *Island Lass*, she was used as a privately owned pleasure boat at Castletown in the Isle of Man until being sold on again. She was then kept at a number of different ports until, by August 2003, named *Storm*, she was based at the Bowling Canal Basin, near Dumbarton.

The Last Slipway Lifeboat

The new lifeboat placed on station at Longhope on 26 March 1988 was a 47ft Tyne class, steel-hulled, self-righting type built by the Cowes boatyard of Fairey Allday Marine. The Tyne class was designed in the late 1970s to replace the nine-knot Watson, Barnett, Solent and Oakley displacement-hulled lifeboats at stations such as Longhope which employed slipway launching. The boat's semi-planing hull with a shallow draught of 4ft 2in, a long straight keel and a flared bow, allowed speeds of approximately eighteen knots to be reached, roughly twice that of the types it replaced. The propellers were protected by partial tunnels, substantial bilge keels and a straight wide keel extending to the transom and ending in a hauling shoe. The wheelhouse had a low profile to fit into boathouses, with a flying bridge amidships and a separate cabin aft of the upper steering position. The hull plating and internal structure were built from corrosion-resistant steel, with aluminium alloy for the deck and superstructure. Power came from two 425hp General Motors 6V-92 diesel engines. The two main fuel tanks, holding 510 gallons of diesel between them, supplemented by a reserve tank of 102 gallons, gave a range of 238 nautical miles.

The Tyne allocated to Longhope was the twenty-fifth of the class and, built at a cost of £560,000 from the legacy of Mrs Mary Salvesen, was named *Lord Saltoun* (ON.1138) after a past Convenor of the Scottish Lifeboat Council. She made the passage north from Poole, where the crew had undertaken a training course in operating the new vessel, in company with the 1977-built 54ft Arun *City of Bradford IV* (ON.1052) which had been reallocated to Thurso. So an unusual double passage was undertaken with the Arun going to Scrabster and the Tyne continuing to Longhope.

The 47ft Tyne class lifeboat Lord Saltoun *(ON.1138) on speed trials in 1988 shortly after being completed by Fairey Marine, Cowes. (By courtesy of Jeff Morris)*

1. *Stromness. The lifeboat house and roller slipway, built in 1926 on the site of the 1901-2 boathouse, nestles amongst the other buildings on Stromness waterfront. (All colour photos by Nicholas Leach unless stated)*

2. *Stromness. 52ft Arun* **Joseph Rothwell Sykes and Hilda M** *(ON.1099) at moorings alongside the South Pier, south of the Scrabster ferry terminal at which can be seen the P&O ferry* **St Ola.**

3. *Stromness. 52ft Arun* **Joseph Rothwell Sykes and Hilda M** *passing the Ness as she heads out of the harbour on exercise, August 1997.*

4. *Stromness. The scene in the harbour during the naming ceremony of 17m Severn* **Violet, Dorothy and Kathleen** *(ON.1236) on 19 June 1999. The boat was christened by Mrs Margaret Kirkpatrick, widow of the late Coxswain Dan Kirkpatrick of Longhope. (Donald Budge)*

5. Stromness. 17m Severn **Violet, Dorothy and Kathleen** *at moorings alongside the South Pier.*

6. Stromness. Relief 17m Severn **Fraser Flyer** *(Civil Service No.43) (ON.1237) on temporary duty, August 2001.*

7. *Stromness. 17m Severn* Violet, Dorothy and Kathleen *passes the Old Man of Hoy, one of Orkney's best know landmarks, as she heads for Stromness.*

8. *Stromness. 17m Severn* Violet, Dorothy and Kathleen *at full speed in Hoy Sound.*

9. Longhope. The lifeboat house and roller slipway built on the Brims side of Aith Hope in 1906 with 48ft 6in Solent **David and Elizabeth King & E. B.** *(ON.1010) visible at the head of the slipway. (By courtesy of the RNLI)*

10. Longhope. The lifeboat house and slipway at Aith Hope built in 1906 and used until 1999. It has since become the Longhope Lifeboat Museum, housing the station's former lifeboat **Thoms McCunn** *(ON.759) as the main exhibit.*

11. Longhope. 48ft 6in Solent **David and Elizabeth King & E. B.** *served as Longhope lifeboat from December 1970 to March 1988 and saved thirty-two lives. (By courtesy of Longhope RNLI)*

12. Longhope. 47ft Tyne **Lord Saltoun** *(ON.1138) on exercise in Aith Hope, August 1997. She served the station for eleven years and was Longhope's last slipway-launched lifeboat.*

13. *Longhope. 52ft Arun* **Sir Max Aitken II** *(ON.1098) passing Cantick Head lighthouse. Built for Stornoway, she served at Longhope from 1999 to 2004 and was the first lifeboat to be operate from the purpose built afloat berth.*

14. *Longhope. 52ft Aruns* **Sir Max Aitken II** (*right*) *and* **The Queen Mother** *(ON.1149) off Longhope pier in June 2004 as the former was replaced by the latter.*

15. Longhope. Passing the cliffs at Cantick Head, **The Queen Mother** *was sent to Longhope in June 2004 after she had been replaced at Thurso by a new 17m Severn lifeboat.*

16. Longhope. Old meets new in Aith Hope: **The Queen Mother** *off the old lifeboat house with former lifeboat* **Thomas McCunn** *at the head of the slipway.*

17. Longhope. Accompanied by relief 17m Severn **The Will** *(ON.1201) from Stromness, the new 16m Tamar* **Helen Comrie** *(ON.1284) arrives at her Longhope station for the first time, October 2006.*

18. Longhope. **The Queen Mother** *(left) and* **Thomas McCunn** *(right) greet the 16m Tamar* **Helen Comrie** *as she arrives at Longhope for the first time, October 2006.*

19. Longhope. 16m Tamar **Helen Comrie** *is put through her paces off Hoy, October 2006.*

20. Longhope. 16m Tamar **Helen Comrie** *puts out on exercise from Longhope pier, October 2006.*

21. Kirkwall. The impressive 70ft Clyde cruising lifeboat **Grace Paterson Ritchie** *(ON.988) which served in Orkney from the late 1960s until July 1988.*

22. Kirkwall. 52ft Arun **Mickie Salvesen** *(ON.1135) at moorings inside the old harbour. She served at Kirkwall from 1988 to 1998 and saved thirty-five lives.*

23. *Kirkwall. Two relief 52ft Arun lifeboats moored together at Kirkwall in 1994: on the left,* **Edith Emilie** *(ON.1062), on passage to Lerwick, with* **Newsbuoy** *(ON.1103) alongside the pier.* **Newsbuoy** *was on relief duty Kirkwall from April to August 1994 and then went to Stromness, where she stood in for* **Joseph Rothwell Sykes** **Hilda M.** *(Donald Budge)*

24. *Kirkwall. Arrival on station of the new 17m Severn* **Margaret Foster** *(ON.1231) in the snow March 1998, escorted in by 52ft Arun* **Mickie Salvesen.** *The new lifeboat had travelled from Poole, in Dorset, via Dover (27 February), IJmuiden in Netherlands (28 February), Lowestoft (1 March), Grimsby (2 March), Tynemouth (3 March) and Aberdeen (4 March), arriving at her new station on 5 March. (Donald Budge)*

25. *Kirkwall. 17m Severn* **Margaret Foster** *on service in gale force nine winds to a fish farm boat which had broken down and was adrift in Carness Bay on 13 June 2000. The lifeboat took the boat in tow and brought it to Kirkwall harbour less than an hour after launching. (Donald Budge)*

26. *Kirkwall. 17m Severn* **Margaret Foster** *alongside the pontoon berth, installed in 2003 to improve boarding arrangements, adjacent to the crew facility on the West Pier in Kirkwall's old harbour.*

27. Kirkwall. The impressive sight of 17m Severn **Margaret Foster** *at full speed.*

28. Kirkwall. **Margaret Foster** *in Shapinsay Sound passing Heliar Holm lighthouse.*

29. Kirkwall. The unique sight of three 17m Severn class lifeboats together at Kirkwall's Old Harbour, 3 May 2003. From left to right; Kirkwall lifeboat **Margaret Foster***, Islay lifeboat* **Helmut Schroeder of Dunlossit II** *(ON.1219) on passage and relief lifeboat* **Fraser Flyer** *(Civil Service No.43) (ON.1237). (Donald Budge)*

30. Kirkwall. 17m Severn **Margaret Foster** *with relief 52ft Arun* **The Duke of Atholl** *(ON.1160) alongside her in the old harbour in 2001. (Donald Budge)*

31. Kirkwall. 17m Severn **Margaret Foster** *on exercise with the Coastguard rescue helicopter 'Oscar Charlie'. The helicopter is based at Sumburgh in Shetland, but regularly exercises with Orkney's lifeboats.*

The scene at Longhope Pier during the naming ceremony of 47ft Tyne Lord Saltoun *(O.N.1138) on 22 July 1988 when she was named by Lady Saltoun. Also in attendance are lifeboats from Thurso and Stromness as well as former Kirkwall lifeboat* Grace Paterson Ritchie *which had just been replaced at that station by a 52ft Arun and was on her way south. (Andy Anderson)*

Lord Saltoun was formally named and dedicated at a ceremony at Longhope Pier on 22 July 1988 with lifeboats from Stromness, Kirkwall and Thurso present. Despite mist and rain, virtually the whole population of Hoy was in attendance on what was a memorable day for the local community. Brigadier S.P. Robertson opened proceedings: 'We look back on the unforgettable days of Longhope lifeboat with sadness and with happiness, for this is a time for both, but always with gratitude and immense pride.' Honorary secretary Jackie Groat accepted the lifeboat and paid tribute to Lord Saltoun 'for his unfailing support and advice following the lifeboat disaster. He was a pillar of strength to all and will always be remembered with special affection and esteem.' After the service of dedication led by Hoy minister the Revd Graham Monteith, Lady Saltoun, daughter of the late Lord Saltoun, fulfilled a personal dream to see a lifeboat named after her father by christening the new boat.

Thurso's 54ft Arun lifeboat City of Bradford IV *(O.N.1052) on the left with Stromness' 52ft Arun lifeboat* Joseph Rothwell Sykes and Hilda M *(O.N.1099) moored at Longhope Pier for the naming ceremony of* Lord Saltoun *on 22 July 1988. (Andy Anderson)*

Above: Lord Saltoun
*during her naming
ceremony at Longhope
Pier on 22 July 1988
with Thurso and
Stromness lifeboats.
(Andy Anderson)*

*Right: At the end of
her naming ceremony,*
Lord Saltoun *puts
to sea with a piper on
board accompanying
the official guests
for a short trip,
22 July 1988.
(Andy Anderson)*

With such good wishes and support, the new 47ft Tyne began her career at Longhope which, in the end, proved to be rather short lived. During just over a decade at the station, *Lord Saltoun* launched sixty-seven times and saved twenty-seven lives. She was the last lifeboat to operate from the lifeboat house at Brims in Aith Hope and thus Orkney's last housed lifeboat. In 1989, the boathouse was adapted to better accommodate the Tyne with the installation of a new fuel storage tank, the extension of the slipway bilgeways and improvements to the keelway channel. In 1991, a crewroom and toilet facility were constructed in the roof space of the boathouse.

The first effective service by *Lord Saltoun* took place on 17 January 1989. She was launched at 10.06 p.m. after the local doctor had asked for assistance in getting a patient to hospital in Kirkwall. In rough seas and a near gale force wind, the lifeboat took the patient to Houton Pier on the mainland, transferred him to the waiting ambulance, and then returned to Longhope Pier. She was moored there until 11.30 a.m. the following day, when the weather improved sufficiently to enable her to be rehoused. Later the same year, on 2 June, *Lord Saltoun* was launched after the Coastguard had reported the small fishing boat *Shelty*, with one person on board, broken down and drifting off South Ronaldsay. The lifeboat soon reached the casualty, towed it to Widewall Bay where it was moored safely, and then returned to her boathouse.

For much of the 1990s, *Lord Saltoun*'s services were largely of a routine nature, and usually involved towing vessels to safety or conveying sick or injured persons to Orkney mainland. In 1990, she helped the fishing vessel *Invader* on 12 March, conveyed an injured girl to Houton on 16 July and on Christmas Day took out a doctor and conveyed a sick woman to Houton. The following year she was called on to perform similar rescues, saving four from the fishing vessel *Ebenezer* on 25 May and taking injured people to Houton on two occasions. In 1992, on 19 January, she took a sick woman and doctor to Houton and on 23 June towed the Pentland Skerries Lighthouse relief boat, which had broken down at the Skerries, to Burwick. On 3 January 1993, she launched to the fishing vessel *Sharona*, which had broken down and was using her trawl doors as anchors. The lifeboat towed the vessel clear of land and escorted it to Scrabster. On 27 January 1994, after the passenger vessel *Golden Mariana* experienced engine problems, she was towed by the Flotta oil terminal vessel *Graemsay Lass*, and *Lord Saltoun* launched to escort both to Lyness. Less than a month later, on 20 February, the fishing vessel *Green Castle* asked for help after going ashore near the Old Man of Hoy. When the call came, *Lord Saltoun* was on exercise in Scapa Flow with the Coastguard rescue helicopter and Stromness lifeboat, so all units went to the vessel's aid. Despite both lifeboats trying, neither succeeded in pulling it off, and it eventually floated clear next day at high tide.

During the 1990s, the RNLI embarked upon a programme of re-engining Tyne lifeboats with new D-DEC engines, which were more powerful and utilised Detroit Diesel's electronic control system. In May 1996, *Lord Saltoun* was sent to Leggetts boatyard at Grimsby to have

Lord Saltoun *arriving at Wick for the naming ceremony of Wick's new 47ft Tyne lifeboat* Norman Salvesen *(O.N. 1121) on 16 September 1988. (Tony Denton)*

Above: *The scene at Scrabster harbour on 9 August 1989 for the naming of Thurso's new 52ft Arun lifeboat* The Queen Mother *(ON.1149), by HRH Queen Elizabeth the Queen Mother, with* Lord Saltoun *and the Longhope lifeboat crew in attendance. This 52ft Arun became the Longhope lifeboat almost fifteen years later. (Tony Denton)*

Right: Lord Saltoun *leaves Scrabster and passes the P&O ferry* St Ola *after the naming of the new Thurso lifeboat* The Queen Mother *on 9 August 1989. (Tony Denton)*

the new engines installed, with relief Tyne *The Famous Grouse* (ON.1133) arriving on station. The re-engining of *Lord Saltoun* took almost a year and she did not return to station until the middle of April 1997. However, when she did return, problems were encountered with the new system and so, in September 1997, *The Famous Grouse* came back to Longhope while repairs to the new D-DEC engines in *Lord Saltoun* were undertaken at Buckie Boatyard.

The station lifeboat returned in October 1997 but further electrical problems were experienced and she again left station on 12 December 1997 for repairs. With no relief Tynes available, cover was provided by the relief 52ft Arun *Margaret Russell Fraser* (ON.1108), which was kept on moorings off Longhope Pier as she could not use the slipway at Brims. She had a busy few months during her stay at Longhope. Within the space of three days in December she was called out twice: on 15 December, when she saved two fish farm tenders and three people and, on 18 December, when she stood by the cargo vessel *Lass Neptun*. In March 1998, she twice went to the fishing vessel *Challenger*. On 9 March she escorted the craft to safety and three days later she saved the vessel and her three crew.

47ft Tyne Lord Saltoun *launching down the slipway at Brims, August 1997. (Nicholas Leach)*

47ft Tyne Lord Saltoun *putting out on exercise in Aith Hope, August 1997. (Nicholas Leach)*

47ft Tyne Lord Saltoun *is recovered up the slipway of the lifeboat house at Brims, August 1997. (Nicholas Leach)*

Looking up the slipway at 47ft Tyne Lord Saltoun *during recovery into the lifeboat house at Brims. (Nicholas Leach)*

Inside the lifeboat house at Brims with 47ft Tyne Lord Saltoun *being hauled onto the cradle at the top of the slipway. (Nicholas Leach)*

The lifeboat house and slipway built in 1906 at Brims. It was used until 1999 for the station's all-weather lifeboat and was altered several times during this period, latterly in 1989 for a 47ft Tyne class lifeboat when a new fuel storage tank was installed and the slipway bilgeways were extended. In 1991 a new crewroom was constructed in the roof space of the boathouse. (Nicholas Leach)

Margaret Russell Fraser stayed until 21 March 1998, at which point she was replaced by another relief 52ft Arun, *Newsbuoy* (ON.1103), which remained at Longhope until October 1998. *Newsbuoy* performed one service, on 15 May 1998, when she towed in the fishing vessel *Sapphire* and her crew of four. On 6 October 1998, *Lord Saltoun* finally returned to station with new engines ready for service and was involved in a fine service on 19 March 1999 after an engine fire broke out aboard the 102m chemical tanker *Multitank Ascania*, which was carrying 1,750 tonnes of highly flammable vinyl acetate. *Lord Saltoun* launched at 3.21 a.m. with Coxswain Ian McFadyen in command and a Sea King helicopter was scrambled from RAF Lossiemouth. Twenty minutes later it was established that the casualty with fifteen people on board was three miles north-west of Dunnet Head in the Pentland Firth, disabled and drifting north of Scrabster. At 3.55 a.m., Thurso's Arun lifeboat *The Queen Mother* (ON.1149) left her berth at Scrabster with Coxswain William Farquhar in command and eight crew on board. The severe weather conditions with very rough seas, hail showers and a force eight to nine gale, prevented the lifeboat proceeding at full speed. At 4.20 a.m., as she was standing by in violent conditions, *Lord Saltoun* fell off a particularly large wave resulting in mechanic John Budge falling and breaking his leg, with the lifeboat then leaving the scene to land the injured mechanic at Scrabster. Soon afterwards, the helicopter arrived and, despite the tanker's deck heaving in the severe weather, managed to get a line on board to lift off fourteen crew, leaving behind the master, who wished to remain on board.

By this time, the fire was getting worse and the casualty was drifting southwards as the tide forced it into Thurso Bay. The Orkney Harbours tug *Einar* made an attempt to take the casualty in tow, with Thurso lifeboat passing a line between the two vessels. Just after 6 a.m., *Einar* began towing the casualty bow to bow but, half an hour later, the tow line parted and the master of *Einar* reported he could do nothing else. As the tanker drifted ever closer to

Thurso lifeboat The Queen Mother *(ON.1149), on left, and Longhope lifeboat* Lord Saltoun *stand by the tanker* Multitank Ascania *on 19 March 1999. Also on hand are the Orkney Harbours tug* Einar *and a rescue helicopter lifting off the crew. (J. Mathieson, by courtesy of the RNLI)*

Last launch of an operational lifeboat down the slipway of the lifeboat house at Brims, 11 September 1999, with 47ft Tyne Lord Saltoun *hitting the water. (By courtesy of John Budge)*

Dunnet Head, the danger of her going ashore increased, and so Coxswain Farquhar skilfully manoeuvred the Thurso lifeboat near enough to the casualty for his crew to grab the floating mooring rope and establish a tow. In the 6m seas, as the lifeboat pitched and rolled violently with both propellers out of the water at times, Coxswain Farquhar expertly worked the lifeboat's engines, although initially it appeared the lifeboat was making little headway. At one point the casualty was less than 400m from Dunnet Head, but by 7.05 a.m. the lifeboat was slowly but surely pulling it clear of the coast.

Throughout the operation *Lord Saltoun*, which had returned to the scene, stood by in case the master needed to be taken off. Meanwhile, Coxswain Farquhar had requested that two of his crew go aboard the casualty to assist in rigging a tow but the Divisional Inspector advised that no RNLI crew should board the casualty due to the risk of explosion. The master was winched off at 8.19 a.m. and reported the fire was still burning. With all personnel evacuated, the Coastguard declared a two mile exclusion zone. The following day, salvage experts went aboard and found the fire extinguished, so *Multitank Ascania* was then towed to Scapa Flow.

For this service, Coxswain Farquhar from Thurso was awarded the Bronze medal, while the rest of his crew were presented with medal service certificates. Coxswain Ian McFadyen and the Longhope crew received framed letters of appreciation signed by the chairman of the RNLI, as did the captain and crew of RAF helicopter Rescue 137 and the master and crew of the tug *Einar*. The service was summed up by John Caldwell, Divisional Inspector of Lifeboats (Scotland): 'the rescue units involved in this service worked together in an extremely professional manner and it was the teamwork of all involved that resulted in the successful outcome to an incident that could have involved loss of life and a major ecological disaster.'

On 21 July 1999, soon after this rescue, Mechanic John Budge, who had been injured during the operation, and his wife Lesley attended a royal garden party at Buckingham Palace in the presence of Her Majesty The Queen. He was one of thirty-four lifeboatmen, station personnel, fundraisers and RNLI staff, their spouses and children chosen to attend in recognition of their long and devoted service to the Institution. John Budge joined Longhope lifeboat crew in January 1970 and became emergency mechanic in 1971. In 1982, he became assistant mechanic, before taking on the position of full-time motor mechanic in September 1994. He was awarded the RNLI's long service badge, awarded for twenty years' service at a lifeboat station, by HRH The Duke of Kent in 1992.

After the relief Aruns had been operated from moorings, a decision was made to move the lifeboat to the Longhope Pier mooring permanently and dispense with the boathouse and slipway operation at Brims. As a result, the 52ft Arun *Sir Max Aitken II* (ON.1098), which had just been replaced by a new 17m Severn at Stornoway, was allocated to Longhope in 1999. She arrived on 6 August 1999 and, after several days of crew training, was placed on station on 12 August. *Lord Saltoun* remained in the boathouse at Brims until 11 September when, after a special ceremony to mark the end of the slipway era, she launched for the final time in front of a large crowd. During the ceremony, which marked the end of 125 years of lifeboats launching into Aith Hope on South Walls and over ninety years of lifeboat operations from the boathouse at Brims, honorary secretary Dr Tony Trickett spoke of the history of the station while also looking to the future with an afloat lifeboat. *Sir Max Aitken II* was initially kept at the moorings off Longhope Pier utilised by the relief 52ft Arun lifeboats while a portacabin provided rudimentary crew facility. During 2002, a new purpose-built shore facility was constructed at Longhope Pier and this was officially opened on 23 June 2003 by Mrs Norma

52ft Arun Sir Max Aitken II (ON.1098) at moorings off Longhope Pier shortly after she arrived on station in August 1999. She was built in 1984 for the Stornoway station in the Outer Hebrides and served there until February 1999. (Donald Budge)

52ft Arun Sir Max Aitken II *(ON. 1098) alongside the pontoon at the specially constructed mooring berth at Longhope pier, July 2003. (Andrew Cooke)*

Marwick, Vice-Convenor of Scottish Lifeboats. The pier was also extended to provide a sheltered berth for the lifeboat and a new boarding pontoon was installed.

Most of the calls made on *Sir Max Aitken II* during her five year stint at Longhope were to assist vessels and tow them to safety. Her first service involved escorting the bulk carrier *Yeoman Bank* on 4 April 2000. Six months later, on 2 October 2000, when the fishing boat *Challenger* capsized at the back of Brims, the lifeboat stood by ready to assist. The casualty's crew were picked up by *Incentive*, another fishing vessel, and although the lifeboat took the upturned boat in tow, it sank shortly afterwards. On 15 November 2000, *Sir Max Aitken II* and Orkney Harbours tug *Harald* were called to assist the Danish-registered cement vessel *Portland* which was drifting out of control north of Stroma. The 98m vessel, with twelve crew on board, reported engine failure to Pentland Coastguard at around 8 a.m. With no cargo on board, the ship's engine was repaired during the morning but the lifeboat and tug stood by until the vessel left the Pentland Firth. During the evening of 11 March 2003, the Pentland Ferries vessel *Claymore* ran into difficulties approaching St Margaret's Hope. Travelling back to Orkney around 7.45 p.m., the ferry lost power to her bow thruster and began drifting in storm force winds. *Sir Max Aitken II* went to her aid and evacuated twelve passengers who were put ashore at the Hope. Although it was feared *Claymore* would be driven ashore, she came to rest against another vessel and was later safely towed to her berth.

During the early years of the twenty-first century, the RNLI began the phasing-out of Arun class lifeboats with most replaced by 17m Severns and 14m Trents, faster and more modern designs. At some stations, such as Longhope, newer Aruns were sent as a temporary measure to replace older Aruns reaching the end of their service lives. As part of this policy, *Sir Max Aitken II*, built in 1984, was replaced during 2004 by the former Thurso Arun *The Queen Mother*, built in 1989, which had been replaced at Thurso by a new Severn lifeboat. After

Sir Max Aitken II *putting out from the berth at Longhope pier. (Nicholas Leach)*

Sir Max Aitken II *on exercise off Hoy. She served at Longhope from 1999 to 2004 and was launched on service twenty times. (Nicholas Leach)*

52ft Aruns Sir Max Aitken II *and* The Queen Mother *moored together at Longhope Pier during the changeover from the former boat to the latter, June 2004. (Nicholas Leach)*

Longhope lifeboat crew on board The Queen Mother *at Longhope Pier, June 2004.* From left to right: *Kevin Thomson, Robbie Gillespie, John Budge (mechanic), Lorna Helle, Kevin Kirkpatrick (coxswain), Angus Budge (deputy second coxswain), Michael Johnstone, Robert Seatter, Alex Sinclair, Alan Lane. (Nicholas Leach)*

The Queen Mother *approaches the yacht* Dasher *ready to effect a rescue in storm force winds on 27 August 2004 after the yacht had been caught out in the severe weather. (Frank Bradford, by courtesy of RNLI)*

being replaced, *The Queen Mother* left Thurso in April 2004 and went to Buckie for overhaul before coming north to Longhope on 17 June 2004. Funded from the legacy of Miss Sarah Sinclair Gray, Dunoon, and the Institution's funds, this lifeboat was particularly appropriate for Longhope as the station had a long association with the late HRH Queen Mother. She had unveiled the statue in memory of the lifeboatmen lost in the 1969 disaster and had close links with both Thurso and Longhope. The changeover was a low-key affair in mid-June, with *Sir Max Aitken II* remaining at Longhope for crew training purposes until eventually departing for Buckie in August. She achieved a record of twenty launches on service while at the station.

The Queen Mother had been on station for just over two months when she was involved in a very testing rescue. On 27 August 2004, she launched at 10.24 a.m, into storm force ten to twelve winds to help the yacht *Dasher* which had lost her primary anchor and, with three people on board, was being driven towards rocks at Ward Point on Burray. The lifeboat crew established a tow despite ferocious wind and sea conditions and then pulled the yacht clear of the shore to begin the tow back to Hoy. The two vessels reached Longhope at 1.31 p.m. but the wind made it almost impossible to manoeuvre alongside the pier so, with assistance from the Coastguard and around twenty villagers, the yacht was secured on the pier. RNLI Operations Director Michael Vlasto commented that the service was 'carried out in some of the worst conditions that can be encountered off the north coast of Scotland and around Orkney. The Longhope lifeboat crew demonstrated seamanship skills and teamwork of the highest order.' Following this service, Coxswain Kevin Kirkpatrick was accorded the Thanks of the Institution on Vellum and Mechanic John Budge received a framed Letter of Thanks signed by RNLI chairman Sir Jock Slater. The rest of the crew received Vellum Service Certificates.

A year after this service, the RNLI announced that Longhope was to receive a new lifeboat of the Tamar class. Development of the Tamar, originally designated the Fast Slipway

52ft Arun The Queen Mother *putting out on exercise from Longhope. Built in 1989, she served at Thurso for fifteen years until coming to Orkney. Her stationing at Longhope was particularly appropriate as the station had a close affinity with the late HRH The Queen Mother. (Nicholas Leach)*

52ft Arun The Queen Mother *passing the cliffs at Cantick Head while on exercise, June 2004, with Coxswain Kevin Kirkpatrick at the wheel. (Nicholas Leach)*

52ft Arun The Queen Mother *in the Pentland Firth with, nearest camera, Thurso lifeboat* The Taylors *(ON.1273), and Wick lifeboat* Roy Barker II *(ON. 1224) furthest from camera. The large rigid-inflatable visible beyond the Wick lifeboat is the tour guide boat* North Coast Explorer *to the aid of which all three lifeboats went on 27 July 2004, a day after this photograph was taken. The* Queen Mother *launched during the afternoon to the 35ft rigid-inflatable, which had thirteen people on board, which was taking on water in the Pentland Firth. The rescue operation was coordinated by the Aberdeen Coastguard after the vessel raised the alarm to say that its pumps were unable to cope with the intake of water. As well as* The Queen Mother, *lifeboats from Thurso and Wick, together with the fishing vessel* Harmony, *were at the scene within an hour. The passengers were transferred to* The Queen Mother *and the vessel was then towed to John O'Groats. (Kieran Murray)*

Boat 2 (FSB2), started during the late 1990s as a project to design a replacement for the slipway-launched 47ft Tyne class. The FSB2 experimental prototype, ON.1251, was launched in September 2001. After extensive evaluation trials, she was converted into a fully-fledged prototype lifeboat. The FSB2 had a flat keel to enable it to be slipway-launched, but this did not affect the boat's ability to be kept afloat, at stations such as Longhope, with the propellers and rudders protected by a central keel and small side keels. The design was subsequently designated the Tamar class and production of service boats began. DML shipyard, Devonport, Plymouth, fitted out the composite hull and deck structure which was manufactured by Green Marine of Lymington. The Tamar was equipped with twin 1,015bhp Cat C18 marine diesel engines, which gave a sufficient power-to-weight performance to reach the intended speed of twenty-five knots. New technology incorporated into the design included the innovative systems and information management system (SIMS). This integrated the electronic systems, such as navigation, communications, engine management and radar, enabling the crew to obtain information from one screen and manage most of the lifeboat's functions remotely, reducing the need for crew to move around the boat while it was underway and thus lessening the chance of accidents. A new seat design was also developed that reduced loadings on crew members' spines when the boat was travelling at full speed in rough weather.

The Tamar allocated for Longhope, *Helen Comrie* (ON.1284), arrived at the station after an extended period of crew training, with crew trials initially held in September 2006,

*The new 16m
Tamar lifeboat*
Helen Comrie
*passing Cantick
Head lighthouse
on her way to
Longhope, escorted
by relief 17m
Severn* Beth
Sell *from Thurso.
(Nicholas Leach)*

*The new 16m
Tamar lifeboat*
Helen Comrie
with The Queen
Mother *(right) and
relief 17m Severns*
The Will *(left)
from Stromness
and* Beth Sell
*from Thurso.
(Nicholas Leach)*

52ft Arun The Queen Mother *(left) leads the new 16m Tamar* Helen Comrie *to Longhope on 14 October
2006 escorted by lifeboats from Thurso and Stromness, as well as the Coastguard Emergency Towing Vessel* Anglian
Sovereign *and local harbour tugs. (Nicholas Leach)*

The new 16m Tamar Helen Comrie *makes her way towards Longhope pier on 14 October 2006 escorted by Thurso lifeboat* Beth Sell *and the Coastguard Emergency Towing Vessel* Anglian Sovereign *spraying her water cannons and providing a spectacular backdrop. (Nicholas Leach)*

Led by 52ft Arun The Queen Mother, *the new 16m Tamar* Helen Comrie *arrives at Longhope for the first time, 14 October 2006, with relief 17m Severn* Beth Sell *from Thurso in attendance. (Nicholas Leach)*

when the boat was taken on a short passage from the RNLI's Lifeboat College in Poole to St Helier, in the Channel Islands, including a visit to St Malo in France before returning to Poole. The four crew from Longhope on board for the short passage were Coxswain Kevin Kirkpatrick, Mechanic John Budge, and crew members Lorna Heddle and Matthew Budge. The boat was then used for further crew training out of Poole from 2 to 5 October and she departed Poole for her station on 6 October. During the long journey north, she called overnight at Salcombe (7 October), Padstow (8 October), Wicklow (9 October), Donaghadee

Longhope lifeboat crew, station officials and supporters gather on board 16m Tamar Helen Comrie *on the day the boat first arrived at the station, 14 October 2006. (Nicholas Leach)*

16m Tamar Helen
Comrie *on
exercise off Hoy,
October 2006.
With a top speed
of twenty-five
knots, she is the
fastest lifeboat to
serve at Longhope.
(Nicholas Leach)*

(10 October), Tobermory (11 October), and Oban, where there was a change of crew. She went on to Portree (12 October) and arrived at Scrabster on 13 October ready to make the crossing of the Pentland Firth to Longhope the following day. Coxswain Kevin Kirkpatrick and Mechanic John Budge were the only two crew away from station for the whole time, spending a week training and a week bringing the boat home.

Helen Comrie arrived at her new station on 14 October 2006 to an amazing reception at Longhope Pier. She was welcomed by no fewer than four lifeboats, including *Thomas McCunn*, which was specially launched for the occasion. *Helen Comrie* had stayed overnight at Scrabster on the last leg of her journey north, and reached Cantick Head lighthouse at 11.30 a.m. on 14 October accompanied by relief Severn lifeboats *Beth Sell* (ON.1262) and *The Will* (ON.1201) from Thurso and Stromness respectively. *The Queen Mother* (ON.1149) met the boats near the lighthouse, and the four all-weather lifeboats were led in formation to Longhope Pier by *Thomas McCunn* having passed the old boathouse at Brims on the way. Two local harbour tugs, as well as the Coastguard ETV *Anglian Sovereign*, were on hand for the event, spraying their water canons skyward, with the Coastguard helicopter 'Oscar Charlie' flying over the flotilla and completing a spectacular sight off Hoy. On reaching the berth at the pier, the Tamar was moored alongside the pontoon and friends, crew families and supporters went aboard to admire the new craft.

After a couple of weeks of intense crew training, the Tamar was officially placed on service on 26 October and became the latest in a long line of Longhope lifeboats. Within three weeks of going on station, she was called into action for real in very severe weather. On 11 November 2006, the oil tanker *FR8 Venture* was caught in violent storm conditions, with westerly winds of force eight to ten, south of the island of Swona in the Pentland Firth. Three men were seriously injured aboard the tanker, which was en route to Texas, after a large wave swamped its deck. The new Tamar lifeboat was requested to launch with medical assistance aboard and so Dr Christine Bradshaw joined the boat for what was the first sea search and rescue mission in which she had been involved.

On arrival at the scene, the lifeboat proceeded to the east of Swona to get some shelter to allow the doctor to be winched onto the rescue helicopter 'Oscar Charlie', which had flown from Shetland, and then to the casualty. The 42,000-ton tanker was pitching badly at times with the decks frequently under water, in winds at 70 to 80mph and waves up to fifteen

View over the small harbour at Longhope with the original pier centre right and the crew facility and workshop of 2001 on the left. 16m Tamar Helen Comrie *is moored at the berth, 52ft Arun* The Queen Mother *alongside the pier and the two relief Severns from Stromness and Thurso at the pier extension, October 2006. (Nicholas Leach)*

The impressive crew facility and workshop built at Longhope Pier in 2001 when the lifeboat had been placed on permanent moorings afloat. (Nicholas Leach)

metres high. Whilst the helicopter winched the doctor in the severe conditions, Longhope lifeboat circled to guard against any mishap in transfer. The doctor was dropped onto the tanker's wheelhouse and proceeded below to tend to the patients, two of whom had already died. Coxswain Kevin Kirkpatrick said, 'at the time the doctor was winched off the lifeboat, I reckon the wind was exceeding 70 to 80mph. Conditions couldn't have been worse and she did a really good job.' Dr Bradshaw and the injured crew were transferred back to the helicopter which flew both to the Aberdeen Royal Infirmary.

The *Venture* service is just the latest of many truly outstanding rescues performed by Longhope lifeboat crews who can be justifiably proud of the selfless service they have provided since 1874. To end the story of the Longhope lifeboats, the words of the Lifeboat Operations Manager Dr Tony Trickett are perhaps the most fitting:

Longhope is one of the finest lifeboat stations with generations of proud tradition of aiding those in distress. Whatever the weather, whatever the sea, the men of Brims never refused a call for help, often at great risk to themselves as we know only too well. We look back with great pride and remember the strength and determination and character of those who have gone before, while looking forward with enthusiasm to the challenges ahead.

CHAPTER SEVEN

A Lifeboat for Orkney's Capital

In addition to the stationing of a sturdy steel-hulled, self-righting lifeboat at Longhope during the 1970s, described in the previous chapter, the RNLI established a new station at Kirkwall, the capital and largest town of Orkney, to enhance rescue coverage of the seas around the island. Although the station was not formally established until 30 May 1972, the lifeboat, a new design of cruising vessel and the largest type ever built for the RNLI, had been operating in the area on an evaluation basis since the late 1960s. This lifeboat, one of two designed by John Tyrell of Arklow, was built for the RNLI by Yarrow & Co. Ltd, of Scotstoun, Glasgow. The boats were ordered in June 1964 after the Committee of Management had decided that a lifeboat larger than the existing 52ft Barnett, at the time the largest in the Institution's fleet, was required. The principal requirements for the new boat were an overall length of 70ft, a speed of eleven to twelve knots, the capacity to take approximately 120 survivors, a high endurance suitable for prolonged search and stand by operations, crew accommodation to permit evaluation as a cruising lifeboat with a full-time crew of five living aboard, and a twenty-knot inflatable inshore lifeboat carried on deck.

The specifications of the two boats were slightly different. The first was 70ft in length by 17ft in beam, while the second was slightly larger at 71ft by 18ft. Both were steel-hulled and powered by twin Gardner 8L3B diesel engines, each of 230hp, giving a top speed of just over eleven knots and a range of approximately 650 nautical miles. At a cruising speed of just over ten knots, a range of approximately 860 nautical miles was achievable. The boats carried 1,200 gallons of fuel and 70-002 had a displacement of 79 tons. The type was subsequently designated the Clyde class after the river on which the first two were built.

70ft Clyde cruising lifeboat Grace Paterson Ritchie *leaving Kirkwall harbour. (Orkney Photographic Archives)*

The first two Clyde class cruising lifeboats together, Charles H. Barrett (Civil Service No.35) *leading* Grace Paterson Ritchie. *The 70ft Clydes were the largest vessels ever built by the RNLI. (Supplied by Andy Anderson)*

The first of the Clyde class, 70-001 (ON.987), was named *Charles H. Barrett (Civil Service No.35)* as the cost of the boat, £63,907, had been met by the Civil Service Lifeboat Fund, long-time supporters of the RNLI. She was named on 4 May 1966 at St Katherine Dock, London, by Princess Marina, Duchess of Kent, president of the RNLI. From February 1966 until March 1968, this lifeboat undertook evaluation trials during which she carried out forty services and saved seven lives. In March 1968, she became permanently based at Clovelly as station lifeboat, for operations in the Bristol Channel. Meanwhile, the second boat, 70-002 (ON.988), began her extended trials out of Greenock, under the supervision of her builder, with a passage around the coast visiting many lifeboat stations. Starting from Troon, she went to Campbeltown, St Kilda, Thurso, Stornoway, Lerwick, Aberdeen, Buckie, Fraserburgh, Peterhead, Aberdeen, Dundee and from Leith to the Tyne. She then went via the Tees to Gorleston, and on to Tower Bridge in London for the capital's flag day on 22 March 1966.

After leaving London, she underwent further trials while on passage to the Channel Islands, where she called at Jersey, Guernsey and Alderney between 24 and 31 March 1966, before leaving for Cowes. She arrived there on 13 April 1966 and then continued her passage round the coast, calling at Plymouth, St Davids, Fishguard, Porthdinllaen, Holyhead, New Brighton and Fleetwood before crossing the Irish Sea. In the Irish Republic, she called at Arklow, Dun Laoghaire, and Belfast, staying for two days before going to Londonderry. On 2 May 1967, she made the passage back to Scotland calling at Campbeltown before returning to Yarrow Shipbuilders for survey at the end of May 1967. The extended trials were undertaken for operational reasons and to enable crew at many stations to familiarise themselves with and see the boat first hand. Although personnel crewing the boat could live aboard if necessary, conditions were considered somewhat spartan and overnight stays were rare.

On 6 September 1967, 70-002 was officially named *Grace Paterson Ritchie* at a ceremony held at Wemyss Bay Pier, Renfrewshire, Scotland. The new vessel was handed over to the RNLI by the trustee for the donor, Andrew Syme, and the Duke of Atholl proposed the Vote of Thanks before Mrs T. Lyle, a friend of the donor, formally christened the lifeboat.

Crew members on board Grace Paterson Ritchie *in Kirkwall harbour. (Orkney Photographic Archives)*

The donor wanted *Grace Paterson Ritchie* to be stationed in Scotland and so, after her extensive tour, she was sent to north-east Scotland and, based at Ullapool during the winter of 1966-67, carried out evaluation trials in the Minch under operational conditions. After the trials at Ullapool, she moved north to Orkney to provide cover for the Pentland Firth area. On 4 March 1968, it was decided that she should be based at Kirkwall with relief duties at Clovelly when necessary and, in July 1968, the Committee of Management decided her trials for the winter of 1968-69 should continue at Kirkwall. Before *Grace Paterson Ritchie* was officially installed as Kirkwall's lifeboat, however, as if to confirm that her station would be Orkney's capital, a portable TV set was presented to the boat's crew on 18 December 1967 while she was in the port.

Grace Paterson Ritchie moved around the coast and during her evaluation trials from 1966 until March 1968, she undertook a number of services from a variety of locations, including Lerwick, Loch Broom and Ullapool in Scotland, and Mumbles and Ilfracombe while in the Bristol Channel. One of the most testing of her early services took place on 26 October 1966, when she went to the aid of the motor vessel *Kathar* which had broken down in gale force winds off Cape Wrath. The lifeboat's services were not needed as, with the trawler *Marbella* on scene already, the vessel's crew effected repairs to the engine. However, *Grace Paterson Ritchie* and her crew had been out in severe weather for several hours.

The year 1969 proved to be a particularly testing one for the lifeboat service in Orkney as a result of the Longhope tragedy in March. The loss of that boat and her crew meant coverage in the treacherous Pentland Firth area had been significantly reduced and so *Grace Paterson Ritchie* and her Kirkwall crew were tasked to maintain coverage of the Firth while the station at Longhope was re-established with a new lifeboat and crew. During the night of 17-18 March, when the Longhope lifeboat had gone to the motor vessel *Irene* with such tragic consequences, *Grace Paterson Ritchie* had also been at sea in the appalling conditions. Under the command of Staff Coxswain Ian Cameron Ives, of Whitley Bay, she was tested to the limit, as Ives recalled afterwards: 'We encountered on that fateful night our worst seas off Mull Head. We hit one heavy sea, which was about 60ft high but the boat behaved beautifully and we have every confidence in her.' Over the whole period of the Longhope tragedy, *Grace Paterson Ritchie* was at sea for more than sixty hours.

Four days after the tragedy, she was taken to Longhope to attend the funeral of the Longhope lifeboat crew, but, just as her crew were preparing to go ashore, a message was received that the motor fishing vessel *Girl Mina*, with four persons on board, had broken down in the Pentland Firth. The lifeboat left at 2.23 p.m. and reached the casualty at 4.06 p.m. to find the fishing vessel eight miles off Rora Head and rolling heavily in the force six seas. *Grace Paterson Ritchie* took the vessel in tow and brought her to Stromness. With *Girl Mina* safely tied up, she proceeded to Longhope.

Four days later, *Grace Paterson Ritchie* was called into action again. On 26 March 1969, together with the Wick lifeboat *Sir Godfrey Baring* (ON.887), she went to the 666-ton trawler *James Barrie*, of Hull, with twenty-one men on board, which had gone aground on the Louther, one of the Pentland Skerries, about a mile south-east of Muckle Skerry. Standing by the stranded vessel was another Hull trawler *Loch Doon*. *Grace Paterson Ritchie* arrived at about 10.45 p.m. and Staff Coxswain G.G. Pegler immediately launched the inflatable lifeboat to investigate. The trawler had been driven hard onto the rocks just after 8 p.m. on the south-east side of the Louther and was on her port side. Although the crew were in no immediate danger and could get off at any time, both lifeboats, together with *Loch Doon*, stood by all night. As conditions began to worsen and the wind increased in strength, the trawler began to rock and the skipper decided to abandon ship. Despite a fouled propeller and manoeuvring with one engine, Wick lifeboat, under Coxswain Neil Stewart, picked up the twenty-one trawlermen who had taken to their two rafts and

Grace Paterson Ritchie *at moorings in Kirkwall harbour. She served as the Kirkwall lifeboat from 1968 to 1988 after operational trials in the area for several years and was one of only three Clyde class cruising lifeboats built by the RNLI. (Supplied by Tony Denton)*

A fine photograph of 70ft Clyde Grace Paterson Ritchie *at speed off Orkney. (Supplied by Andy Anderson)*

landed them at Wick. Before returning to Scapa, from where she had been called out, *Grace Paterson Ritchie* collected further life rafts from around the casualty. The abandoned trawler subsequently refloated and two local fishing vessels in the vicinity, *Kildinguie* and *Achilles*, made for the trawler while *Grace Paterson Ritchie* set out to help. Once alongside the abandoned vessel, the lifeboat started to pump the water out and then took her in tow stern first. Steered by *Kildinguie*, they started on a slow journey to Scapa but, when half a mile off Hoxa Head, the trawler sank, going down in less than a minute in twenty fathoms of water.

Grace Paterson Ritchie remained at Kirkwall until mid-May 1969, performing a number of routine services during that time. She then left for Bristol where she was overhauled and in her place came the relief lifeboat *The Princess Royal (Civil Service No. 7)* (ON.828), a 46ft Watson motor type, which performed one service before being replaced by another relief lifeboat. The second relief boat, 52ft Barnett *Hilton Briggs* (ON.889), was on station from August 1969 until April 1970 during which time she launched eight times on service before moving to Longhope. She performed a number of routine services during this period in Orkney, based at both Scapa and Kirkwall, including two medical evacuations from Hoy, taking patients to Scapa to be transferred to ambulances and then hospital. *Hilton Briggs* remained in the area for much of 1970 and 1971, operating from both Longhope and Kirkwall, before the station had been officially established.

Grace Paterson Ritchie returned to Orkney in 1970 and was based in Scapa for much of the summer, performing a number of services using the inflatable inshore rescue boat (IRB) carried aboard for rescues close to the shore. The craft was involved in an unusual rescue on 11 July 1970 when, at 12.19 p.m. that day, a flat-bottomed dinghy was reported missing from Weyland Bay. As *Grace Paterson Ritchie* was at Scapa, on the south side of Orkney mainland, it was quicker and easier to take the IRB two and a half miles overland by lorry to assist.

The IRB was launched at Kirkwall at 1.16 p.m. into a fresh west-south-westerly wind and moderate sea. At 1.59 p.m. the IRB found the dinghy ashore at Shapinsay, so the crew searched in the Helliar Holm area but again found nothing so returned to Kirkwall. The small boat arrived at 3.33 p.m. and was taken back to Scapa by road, by which time the missing seamen had been found by the police at Stromness.

In January 1971, *Grace Paterson Ritchie* returned to Kirkwall as the Longhope station was fully operational again and able to cover the Scapa area. But she left the area in the summer and between July and September 1971 operated from Clovelly, returning to Kirkwall on 16 September. She was then involved in cruising evaluation trials with a full-time crew starting in October 1971. The trials, which lasted until 31 March 1972, took her north of Kirkwall, to the Orkney North Isles where she was based mainly at Stronsay from Mondays to Fridays, and then she returned to Kirkwall Harbour at weekends. When the Kirkwall station was officially established on 30 May 1972, the station at Stronsay, in the north of Orkney, was closed.

During the trials, *Grace Paterson Ritchie* was involved in a particularly notable rescue on 8 November 1971 when, in deteriorating weather conditions, four Danish fishing vessels got into difficulty near the harbour. The pier was awash and the fishing vessels alongside were pitching dangerously. One of the fishing vessels, *Clupea*, had broken adrift and, as the lifeboat arrived, a second boat, *Kami*, also broke free. The former vessel then went aground to the east of Kirkwall Pier while Kirkwall Coastguard and others attempted to get lines aboard the stranded vessels to haul them back to the pier. Coastguards succeeded in getting headropes from the stranded vessels to the pier and prevented them from being driven further ashore, but could not rescue the crews. With the northerly wind force ten gusting to hurricane force twelve, the lifeboat crew assembled at 7.50 a.m.

70ft Clyde Grace Paterson Ritchie *served at Kirkwall lifeboat until 1988 and launched more than 150 times on service around Orkney, saving over seventy lives. (Supplied by Andy Anderson)*

Staff Coxswain Robin H. Dennison initially believed the Coastguard would be able to effect a rescue of the stranded crews unaided, but as the weather worsened he decided to take the lifeboat out of the harbour and into the rough seas and heavy swells. He intended to tow the remaining two vessels clear of the pier to safety and at 9.30 a.m. anchored to windward of one of them, *Rosslau*, and floated a rope down to her. Once the tow rope was secured, the fishing vessel cast off from the pier and was towed clear. This operation was repeated for *Anne Stranne*, which was towed clear at 10.50 a.m. By this time, virtually all the Coastguard equipment was in use holding the two stranded vessels, *Clupea* and *Kami*, from going ashore. Staff Coxswain Dennison decided that the safest way to save the crews was to tow the boats clear. With the lifeboat anchored, a cable was veered down until a tow rope could be secured to the end of the line holding *Clupea* to the quay. At 1.42 a.m. the Coastguard reported that the connection had been made and the lifeboat started to tow her clear, a task made more difficult by the failure of the casualty's power and steering. Once clear, the tow was taken over by *Rosslau*, which had earlier been pulled clear. Staff Coxswain Dennison then anchored the lifeboat again and repeated the procedure to secure a tow line to *Kami*. By 12.53 p.m., *Kami* was clear of danger and able to proceed under her own power. The four fishing boats were then advised to take shelter at Shapinsay, and *Grace Paterson Ritchie* returned to her berth at 1.40 p.m.

Between 8.35 a.m. and 1.40 p.m., *Grace Paterson Ritchie* and her crew had rescued twenty men and saved four boats, and the lifeboat had proved herself in the worst of weathers. For this excellent service, the Bronze medal was awarded to Staff Coxswain Dennison and medal certificates to the remainder of the crew D. Grieve, F. Johnston, A. Strutt, J. Craigie, I. Thomson, M. Drever and N. Sutherland. The official report of the service commented:

> The action taken by Staff Coxswain Dennison and his crew is to be commended. The highest praise for his seamanship and skill has been voiced by the skippers of the vessels concerned, the Danish authorities, HM Coastguard and all who witnessed the incidents. Not only did he ensure the safety of twenty lives without loss or injury, but almost certainly prevented the two stranded vessels from becoming total losses and the other two vessels sustaining

The 70ft Clyde cruising lifeboat Grace Paterson Ritchie *in service as the Kirkwall lifeboat. (Supplied by Andy Anderson)*

Douglas Currie (ON.1021) arriving at Kirkwall in June 1974 to take up duties as station lifeboat. A steel-hulled 48ft 6in Solent self-righter built at Cowes in 1973, and served the station for just over a year after which she was transferred to Macduff, and later to Fraserburgh, Portpatrick and Workington. (Orkney Photographic Archives)

considerable structural damage. The underwriters of the vessels . . . [stated] the lifeboat prevented in excess of £100,000 worth of damage and they made a voluntary payment to the funds of the Institution.

During 1972 and 1973, after the trials in the North Isles, *Grace Paterson Ritchie* was based at Kirkwall and undertook a number of rescues including searches for vessels reported in difficulty and escorting vessels. On 5 May 1973, she was called out just after midnight to the 1,024-ton passenger vessel *St Rognvald* which had run aground on Thieves Holm. As the vessel was hard aground, the passengers were transferred to the lifeboat to be landed at Kirkwall. After a change of crew, the lifeboat returned to stand by and assisted as the livestock was transferred to another vessel, the inter-island craft *Islander*, while the tug *Superman* arrived on 7 May to help *St Rognvald*. This tug tried several times to free the ship, but every effort was unsuccessful and so the vessel was left on the rocks until an ocean-going tug could help.

Between 5 December 1973 and 18 March 1974, the relief lifeboat *James and Margaret Boyd* (ON.913) was on duty while *Grace Paterson Ritchie* underwent a routine survey at Yarrow Shipbuilders on Clydeside. While on station, *James and Margaret Boyd* was involved in a difficult service carried out in severe weather. On 6 December 1973, the motor fishing vessel *Navena* went aground on Copinsay Island, in a north-north-west force twelve storm and very rough seas. The lifeboat was requested to launch and, although she safely got out of harbour at 7.12 a.m., manoeuvring in the severe weather proved very difficult. She proceeded to the casualty and arrived on scene at 9 a.m., standing by in extremely heavy weather. She stayed in attendance until just after 10 a.m. when the rescue helicopter arrived from Dyce (Aberdeen) airport and lifted the fishing vessel's crew off their boat. The operation was completed by 10.38 a.m. and the lifeboat then returned to station for 12.37 p.m. Following this service,

Kirkwall lifeboat crew on board Douglas Currie *in Kirkwall harbour, with* Grace Paterson Ritchie *in the background. They are,* left to right: Stewart Norse *(RNLI staff coxswain),* Dan Grieve, George Smith, Alex Strutt, Coxswain Billy Sinclair, S.P. Robertson *(Branch chairman),* Davie Peace, Bob Hall, Davie Johnston, Olaf Work *(deputy launching authority) and* Magnus Work *(honorary secretary). (Orkney Photographic Archives)*

framed letters of appreciation were sent to coxswain and crew as well as the honorary secretary for their part in this service.

James and Margaret Boyd performed a number of other services but none resulted in any lives being saved. She left Kirkwall in March having launched seven times in total. Meanwhile, *Grace Paterson Ritchie* completed her survey on 31 January 1974 after which she was used for further evaluation trials and returned to Kirkwall for the spring of 1974. When she was taken away from station again in summer 1974, the steel-hulled 48ft 6in Solent lifeboat *Douglas Currie* (ON.1021) was placed on temporary station duty having spent a week travelling north to Orkney. *Douglas Currie* served at Kirkwall from 1 July 1974 until 1 August 1975, during which time she launched eight times and saved twelve lives. Her first service was performed on 18 August 1974 when she went to the aid of the motor vessel *Shalder*, in difficulty a mile off Shapinsay, but on reaching the casualty the lifeboat crew found that the vessel's crew had effected repairs and so the lifeboat escorted her into Kirkwall.

On 27 December 1974 *Douglas Currie* launched just after midnight to the motor fishing vessel *Paramount*. The vessel was in difficulties in Kirkwall bay, dragging her anchor and slowly drifting ashore. The lifeboat attempted to tow the casualty clear of the rocks but in the gale force winds could not keep the casualty's head to wind and the vessel subsequently grounded. The lifeboat stood by throughout the night and a tug, *Baracuda*, was also engaged to assist in refloating the vessel in the morning. After the tug failed to pull the boat clear, the lifeboat returned to station in the evening. The following day, the lifeboat again put out and stood by while the tug attempted to refloat the vessel. After attempts had been abandoned at 10 p.m. due to insufficient water, the lifeboat landed the vessel's eight crew and returned to station.

In 1975 while away from station, *Grace Paterson Ritchie* spent several days in the Faroe Islands taking a delegation from the RNLI there to provide advice and information about the setting up of a lifeboat service. Leading the delegation was Lt-Cdr P.E.C. Pickles, RNVR, a deputy chairman of the RNLI, accompanied by Lt-Cdr Brian Miles, RNR, together with Les Vipond, T. Peebles, A. Strutt, J. Ross and S. Poulson. the Faroes Deputy Commercial Attaché in Aberdeen acted as interpreter for the trip, which was made at the request of the Faroese Lifeboat Service and paid for by the Faroese Government. *Grace Paterson Ritchie* left Buckie on 9 July in thick fog and made for Lerwick, berthing there with the Norwegian lifeboat *Ada Waage*, which had arrived in port the previous day. She left Lerwick the following day, rounded Sumburgh Head, and then set course for the Faroes, arriving at Tvoroyri, the main town on the south island Suduroy, at 9 a.m. on 11 July. From there, she visited Sandvik Pier and Sandoy, Sandur and many remote villages along the coast. On 13 July, *Grace Paterson Ritchie* went to Sandur and then to Midvag, where a cushion made out of Faroes wool was presented to the lifeboat's crew. The next calls took the boat to Streymoy, Vestmanna, Eysturoy, Fuglefjord, Runavic and Klaksvik, the main centres of the fishing industry with practical demonstrations given by the lifeboat crew. The visit ended with a luncheon, attended by all the local dignitaries, and a tour of Torshaven. The lifeboat then sailed for Kirkwall and arrived back at her station around 1 p.m. on 17 July.

Before her trip to the Faroes, *Grace Paterson Ritchie* had been on relief duty at Clovelly from September 1974 to July 1975, but eventually returned to Kirkwall on 8 August 1975. She remained at Kirkwall, with the exception of short periods away for survey and overhaul, until the late 1980s as the station's lifeboat. During the late 1970s, she was called out most often to assist fishing vessels in difficulty and in most cases these were routine calls involving a vessel aground or broken down. On 5 March 1976 she assisted in freeing the Danish motor fishing vessel *Mariane Booker*, which had gone ashore at Coubister Skerry. On 5 February 1977, she went to the fishing vessel *Monica Croan*, ashore on the west side of Vasa Skerry, and stood by until the vessel refloated on the tide.

Relief 70ft Clyde Charles H. Barrett (Civil Service No.35) *(ON.987) tows in the fishing vessel* Evangeline *(LK.182) on 30 August 1976, which was on temporary duty at Kirkwall at the time.* Evangeline *had broken down to the east of Orkney and was taking in water, so the lifeboat launched at 12.14 p.m. While she was en route, the supply vessel* Scandia Service *took the* Evangeline *in tow. When the lifeboat reached the two vessels, she took over the tow, returning to Kirkwall at 2.58 p.m. (Orkney Photographic Archives)*

As well as helping fishing vessels, the lifeboats of Orkney have been frequently involved in medical evacuations from the outer isles when other means of transport have not been available, and on 21 May 1978 *Grace Paterson Ritchie* undertook such a service. At 2 a.m., the Coastguard contacted the honorary secretary stating that two persons had been seriously hurt in an accident on Stronsay. With thick fog blanketing the area, the air ambulance could not fly and so the lifeboat was tasked to help. She reached Stronsay Island at 4.23 a.m., took on board the injured men and conveyed them to the mainland, arriving at Kirkwall at 6.35 a.m. to transfer the casualties to a waiting ambulance. For this service, a Letter of Appreciation from the Director was sent to Coxswain William Sinclair

On 28 August 1980, *Grace Paterson Ritchie* was involved in another notable medical service after, at 7.06 p.m., the Coastguard had informed the station that a sick person on Westray needed hospital treatment in Kirkwall. *Grace Paterson Ritchie* left Kirkwall at 7.18 p.m. and arrived at Rapness Pier on Westray at 9.15 p.m. after a crossing in calm seas but with fog hampering visibility. Just before leaving Rapness a message was received that another patient, this time on Sanday, also needed to be collected. The lifeboat arrived there to find insufficient water to go alongside and so the boat's ILB was launched to pick up the patient for transfer to the lifeboat. Once this had been successfully done, the lifeboat left Sanday at 11.12 p.m. and, at 12.48 a.m. on 29 August, arrived back in Kirkwall where the two patients were transferred to a waiting ambulance. In recognition of this fine service, a Letter of Appreciation was sent to the station from the Chief of Operations.

During the winter months in Orkney, the weather can become extremely harsh, and on 31 January 1983, the motor boat *Summer Isles* was caught out in typically severe conditions. At 11.05 p.m. a message was sent to the honorary secretary that she was in difficulties beside the Haston Slip and was being pounded by heavy seas whipped up by the gale. *Grace Paterson Ritchie* launched at 11.30 p.m. and proceeded at half speed through the easterly force twelve storm,

Kirkwall lifeboat crew receiving their awards for the rescue on 22 January 1984 of the crew of three of fishing boat Benachie. *Coxswain Billy Sinclair was awarded the Bronze medal and the remainder of the crew were presented with medal service certificates. The awards were presented by Vice Admiral Sir Peter Compton (deputy chairman of RNLI), right. The crew are, left to right:* Mike Drever, Bobby Hall, Alec Strutt, unknown, Dan Grieve, Billy Sinclair, Geoff Gardens. *(Orkney Photographic Archives)*

avoiding mooring buoys in the area that could have fouled her propellers. After making VHF contact with the casualty, the lifeboat crew dropped anchor and veered down wind towards it. After two attempts to get close to the motor boat, the lifeboat was eventually close enough to fire a rocket line. When this had reached the casualty, those on board secured a heavy towline from the lifeboat. The casualty was then pulled clear of the jetty at 12.30 a.m. and, as the motor boat had no power, was brought well clear before the tow rope was shortened. The casualty was eventually brought into Kirkwall harbour at about 3 a.m. on 1 February.

The ILB carried aboard *Grace Paterson Ritchie* was used to good effect again in another well executed rescue on 18 September 1983. On this occasion, the ILB D-218 was launched to a single-handed sailing dinghy which had capsized about a mile north-north-east of Kirkwall Pier. Manned by Mechanic Alec Strutt, Dupre Strutt and W. Swanney, the ILB set out at 11.10 a.m. and was alongside the dinghy within five minutes. The dinghy was then righted and, as its occupant was too tired to continue sailing, the ILB towed it back into Kirkwall reaching the harbour at 11.30 a.m. Although *Grace Paterson Ritchie*, did not leave her moorings, the quick thinking and swift actions of the three lifeboat men undoubtedly saved the dinghy sailor's life. For his part in this service, a Letter of Appreciation signed by the Chief of Operations was sent to Mechanic Strutt.

On 22 January 1984, *Grace Paterson Ritchie* and her crew were involved in a very fine service, probably the most outstanding rescue undertaken during her time at Kirkwall. At 9.15 a.m., Pentland Coastguard alerted the station that the sixteen-ton fishing vessel *Benachie*, of Ronsay, had parted her moorings and gone ashore on the south of the Island of Rousay, nine miles north of Kirkwall. Her owner and two of his crew had managed to board and were trying to salvage the vessel. At 10 a.m., *Grace Paterson Ritchie* left her station under Coxswain William Sinclair and headed north at full speed into a force ten gale. Very heavy seas were encountered as the lifeboat cleared Shapinsay and the seas became even heavier between the islands of Wyre and Egilsay, with the wind running against a flood tide.

At 11.15 a.m., the stranded fishing vessel was sighted by the lifeboat men. She had been blown along a sandy beach and was between rocks in a position from which her crew could not leave her. The vessel was rolling heavily and the heavy seas were breaking over her. By this time, the storm was gusting to violent storm force eleven and snow showers had turned into a blizzard. Coxswain Sinclair anchored 200 metres offshore, up tide of the casualty, and veered down until the lifeboat was about forty metres away. The line that was fired landed two metres down wind of Benachie but the line drifted close enough for the casualty's crew to grab it. A towline was then passed to the vessel which was pulled clear of the rocks. The lifeboat escorted the casualty to Wyre Pier for inspection and when it was ascertained *Benachie* was okay, *Grace Paterson Ritchie* set off on her return journey. The passage back to Kirkwall was made at reduced speed because of the very rough conditions which continued until the lee of Shapinsay was gained. By 1.25 p.m. the lifeboat was back on station and ready for service after a very difficult rescue in which three men and their fishing vessel had been rescued. For this service, the Bronze medal was awarded to Coxswain Capt. W.S. Sinclair and medal service certificates were presented to Second Coxswain Andrew Grieve, Mechanic Dupre Strutt, Second Mechanic Robert Mainland, Emergency Mechanics Michael Drever and Michael Foulis, and crew members Robert Hall and Geoffrey Gardens.

During the 1980s, the RNLI was developing faster all-weather lifeboats to meet changing demands. The faster the lifeboat, the less time it took to reach an incident, thereby reducing the chances of a situation deteriorating and making a rescue more difficult. The first fast lifeboat type, the 44ft Waveney, was introduced in the early 1960s and by the end of the decade

Grace Paterson Ritchie *at Buckie in March 1989 during the handing over ceremony to the Lifesaving Association of Iceland, for whom she was renamed* Henry H. Halfdanssen. *(Andy Anderson)*

a 52ft type had been designed, the Arun class. Many Aruns were built during the 1970s and 1980s, including that sent to Stromness. In the mid-1980s, as part of the policy to operate fast lifeboats at all stations, the RNLI formulated plans to replace the Clyde class cruising lifeboats and in 1988 allocated a new 52ft Arun to Kirkwall. During the first half of 1988, *Grace Paterson Ritchie* continued her work and performed three services, assisting in a search for a man overboard from the fishing vessel *Bon Ami* on 24 April and going to the aid of the motor vessel *Tommeline* which had gone aground on 20 May. The last service by *Grace Paterson Ritchie* as the Kirkwall lifeboat took place on 6 June 1988. After reports that a diver was missing from the motor fishing vessel *Our Lorraine*, she put out at 2.14 p.m. and proceeded to the fishing vessel, which was a mile north of Damsay in the Bay of Firth. While en route, a message was received that the diver had been recovered and was safe, so the lifeboat returned to station.

Grace Paterson Ritchie left Kirkwall on 25 July 1988 and was taken to Herd & Mackenzie's boatyard at Buckie where she was stored before being sold out of service. During her career with the RNLI, she launched on service 197 times and is credited with saving eighty-six lives, as follows: 1966 to March 1968 on passage, Scotland and Bristol Channel, twenty-two launches, no lives saved; March 1968 to June 1974 at Kirkwall, eighty-two launches, forty-six lives saved; September 1974 to July 1975 relieving at Clovelly, twenty launches, eleven lives saved; August 1975 to July 1988 at Kirkwall, seventy-three launches, twenty-nine lives saved.

Grace Paterson Ritchie remained at Buckie until being sold out of service on 10 February 1989 for £60,000 to the Lifesaving Association of Iceland. She left Buckie in March 1989 and sailed for Iceland, where she was used as a lifeboat based at Reykjavik. She was renamed *Henry A. Halfdansson* after the Icelandic Association's then chairman. The Kirkwall crew had kept the boat's bell as a memento of her service in Orkney when she departed from the station but they decided, when they knew she was continuing to save lives at sea, to return it to the Iceland crew, who were pleased to receive it. As *Henry A. Halfdansson*, the lifeboat served at Reykjavik as a lifeboat for more than a decade, until in 2002 she was replaced by a faster lifeboat and then sold by the Icelandic Association. She has since returned to UK waters and, named *Grace Ritchie*, is maintained in private hands, based at Largs Yacht Haven.

Fast Lifeboats at Kirkwall

The 70ft Clyde lifeboat *Grace Paterson Ritchie* performed sterling service throughout her time at Kirkwall but, by the late 1980s, as the RNLI was looking to provide fast lifeboats at all lifeboat stations, a decision was made to replace the Clyde with a new 52ft Arun lifeboat. The Arun class building programme lasted from 1971 until 1990, during which time a total of forty-six boats were built. The boat allocated to Kirkwall *Mickie Salveson* (ON.1135) was the thirty-ninth, and was built by Halmatic Ltd, at Havant, at a cost of £587,133. Funded from the bequest of the late Mrs Mary 'Mickie' Salvesen, the new lifeboat was named after her donor, who also provided the lifeboat *Norman Salvesen* (ON.1121) which was placed on service at Wick and later moved to Sennen Cove.

Above: *52ft Arun* Mickie Salvesen *(ON.1135) during trials after completion by Halmatic Ltd and before going on station. She served at Kirkwall for ten years during which time she saved thirty-five lives. (RNLI)*

Right: *Arrival on station of* 52ft Arun Mickie Salvesen *in July 1988, escorted by* Grace Paterson Ritchie. *(Donald Budge)*

The new lifeboat was formally named *Mickie Salvesen* at a ceremony on 20 August 1988 at Kirkwall's old harbour. With 500 guests in attendance, including members of the Christian Salvesen company and the donor's family, the ceremony was held on a damp day with Brigadier Robertson, chairman of Kirkwall branch, overseeing proceedings. Sir Charles McGrigor, Convener of the Scottish Lifeboat Council, acknowledged the donor's generosity and formally handed the lifeboat to Honorary Secretary Capt. Bill Spence. Historic links with Norway were maintained by the presence of the Norwegian lifeboat *Dagfinn Paust* at the ceremony and Admiral Steimler, president of the Norwegian Lifeboat Society. After the service of dedication led by the Revd Cant, minister of St Magnus Cathedral, Mrs Doris Sutcliffe named the boat to the memory of her late sister, who was known as 'Mickie' Salvesen.

The extra speed of the Arun over the Clyde was put to good effect on her first service, on 2 July 1988, before she had officially been placed on station. A message was received that a premature baby had been born on Sanday, and a doctor and midwife with incubator were urgently required there. Thick fog prevented the air ambulance from flying and so, with doctor and midwife aboard, *Mickie Salvesen* left Kirkwall at 8.56 a.m. and reached Sanday just over an hour later. The baby was placed in the incubator and the lifeboat returned to Orkney mainland where an ambulance was waiting at the harbour. The baby and his parents were transferred to an RAF helicopter, which had managed to fly almost blind from Lossiemouth. The helicopter then took the baby to hospital in Aberdeen, where he made a full recovery.

After a couple more routine services during 1988, *Mickie Salvesen* was involved in a fine medal-winning service towards the end of the summer. On 13 September the bulk cement carrier *BC Mercurius*, with six persons on board, suffered engine failure two and a half miles north of Noup Head in Westray in northerly gale force eight conditions. She was slowly being driven ashore in the appalling conditions, and so *Mickie Salvesen* slipped her moorings at 7.20 a.m. under Coxswain Capt. William Sinclair. The lifeboat negotiated the narrow channels out of Kirkwall, then experienced a heavy swell in the more open waters of Westray Firth. Meanwhile, the Coastguard rescue helicopter from Sumburgh had also arrived on scene and managed to winch four crew members of *BC Mercurius* to safety. The master and chief engineer stayed on board their vessel, hoping to save her and help the lifeboat crew with a towing operation. The lifeboat maintained full speed in spite of 20ft seas and arrived on

52ft Arun Mickie Salvesen *arriving at Kirkwall for the first time, after coming north from the RNLI Depot at Poole, where the crew underwent training on the new lifeboat. (Donald Budge)*

Mickie Salvesen *moored in Kirkwall harbour in 1994 with, on inside, relief 52ft Arun lifeboat* Newsbuoy
(ON. 1103). (Donald Budge)

Mickie Salvesen *at her moorings in Kirkwall's old harbour alongside the shore building constructed on the West Pier
in 1990. The building consists of a crew room, workshop, changing room and toilet/shower facilities. (Nicholas Leach)*

scene just after 9 a.m. The 160ft coaster was lying across the sea, rolling heavily and shipping
seas across her foredeck. A team of Coastguard auxiliaries had assembled at Noup Head
lighthouse as the coaster, about 800 yards offshore, drifted slowly towards them.

The ship's master made it clear that he wanted the coaster towed clear, and so despite *BC
Mercurius* rolling and pitching violently, the lifeboat was manoeuvred close to the casualty in
the very rough seas and heavy rain squalls ready to take the two men off if necessary. The
coaster appeared to be out of imminent danger and the Coastguard radioed to say that a tug
had been arranged. However, less than half an hour later the situation had changed and the
coaster was just 400 yards off the land and drifting closer. With the Coastguard helicopter

52ft Arun Mickie Salvesen *at her moorings. Built in 1988, she served at Kirkwall for ten years, and then after a short stint in the Relief Fleet went to Aberdeen in 1998. She spent two years here, then was a relief lifeboat for a further three years and in August 2003 was placed on station at Barry Dock in South Wales. (Nicholas Leach)*

refuelling at Kirkwall airport, the lifeboat moved in to take up the tow. Coxswain Sinclair made a few trial runs to see if it was possible to get close enough to the coaster to pass a line without damaging the lifeboat. He was also checking to see if it was safe enough for the two remaining crew on *BC Mercurius* to get to the bow as the vessel was now in a perilous position close to the rocks. The helicopter was requested to stand by in case the tow attempt failed, as there would be little time to lift the crew off before the casualty hit the rocks.

On the first attempt, a heaving line and tow rope were successfully passed to the vessel and made fast. The lifeboat then managed to turn the vessel to the north, clear of the rocks, which were just 300 yards astern of the casualty. During this procedure, both lifeboat and casualty were rolling and pitching violently with the tow rope parting on three occasions. On each occasion, the lifeboat rapidly retrieved it and manoeuvred alongside to secure it again. By preventing the casualty from drifting downwind towards the shore, the lifeboat enabled her to be carried east with the tide. By 11.15 a.m., the casualty was 800 yards north west of Our Ness and in 80ft of water in the Bay of Noup, so Coxswain Sinclair requested that *BC Mercurius's* master anchor. The vessel dropped her two anchors in the hope that these would prevent her being driven ashore.

With the anchors holding, *Mickie Salvesen* let go the towline and stood by the vessel, which was still pitching and rolling violently and shipping seas. At 2 p.m., the tug *Kintore* arrived and, after considerable difficulty, managed to pass and make fast a tow line. At 3 p.m., the tug departed with the coaster in tow and the lifeboat proceeded to Pierowall, Westray, to pick up the coaster's four crew who had been landed there by the helicopter. The lifeboat then escorted the tug and coaster to Kirkwall, arriving at 8.55 p.m. For his outstanding seamanship during this arduous service in gale force winds, Capt. Sinclair was awarded the Bronze medal.

The other members of the crew, Second Coxswain James Mitchell, Mechanic Dupre Strutt, Assistant Mechanic Robert Mainland and crew members Geoffrey Gardens, Robert Hall and Smith Foubister were all awarded medal service certificates. This was Capt. Sinclair's last service as Coxswain before his retirement.

During the early 1990s, the majority of calls involved assisting fishing vessels that had broken down, but the lifeboat was also called upon to help yachts, dinghies and search for missing persons. Many of these services were in comparatively calm weather, but on 17 January 1993,

17m Severn Margaret Foster *passing a snowy Heliar Holm lighthouse as she heads for Kirkwall to take up duties alongside, in the snow, March 1998. (By courtesy of Kirkwall Lifeboat Station)*

Newly arrived 17m Severn Margaret Foster *at the West Pier with 52ft Arun* Mickie Salvesen, *the boat she was about to replace, moored alongside in the snow, March 1998. (Donald Budge)*

17m Severn Margaret Foster *at Buckie Boatyard, Buckie, August 1998, being cleaned and readied for her naming ceremony the following month. This photograph of the boat out of the water gives a good impression of the hull design, with the bow thruster and the bilge keels which provide protection to the propellers. (Nicholas Leach)*

Mickie Salvesen put out in storm force ten winds after the motor vessel *Euro Clipper* had radioed Pentland Coastguard to say one of her crew was injured. The man had severed two fingers in an accident and the ship was east of Copinsay on passage to Kirkwall. The skipper of the vessel initially wanted to berth at Kirkwall Pier, but was advised that conditions would make this impossible. So, at 10.51 a.m., *Mickie Salvesen* put out to assist, requesting that *Euro Clipper* head to the west side of Kirkwall Bay and make a slow turn to port to enable the lifeboat crew to transfer the injured man in the lee. This was successfully completed at 11.15 a.m. and the lifeboat returned to Kirkwall ten minutes later, where the injured crewman was transferred to hospital by ambulance.

Another unusual service took place on 20 August 1997, when *Mickie Salvesen* was launched at 4.10 p.m. to a party of sea kayaks that had become separated off the Galt Buoy in deteriorating conditions. The lifeboat crew found one group of kayakers who had made it ashore on Shapinsay, and sighted another group on Grassholm. A search was started for further missing kayakers, and eventually all were found and taken on board the lifeboat, with the Arun's inflatable 'Y' boat being launched to assist in the rescue. All were landed at Balfour pier on Shapinsay and the lifeboat returned to Kirkwall at 7 p.m. This was the last service performed by Mechanic Alec Strutt after thirty-three years in the service. When he got ashore afterwards, he handed his pager to the honorary secretary while his son, Dupre, took over as mechanic.

What proved to be the last service performed by *Mickie Salvesen* took place on 27 December 1997 after a small boat was reported overdue after a visit to Damsay. After launching at 4.50 p.m., the crew of *Mickie Salvesen* searched the area and found three persons near a beached boat. The inflatable Y boat was launched and transferred the three persons to the lifeboat, while the lifeboat crew managed to refloat the small boat. This was taken in tow and all arrived back at Kirkwall at 6.20 p.m. This low-key rescue ended the Arun's operational service at Kirkwall, and in April 1998

Above: *The scene at the West Pier in the harbour during the naming ceremony of* Margaret Foster *on 26 September 1998. (Andy Anderson)*

Right: Margaret Foster *puts to sea for a short trip with invited guests at the end of her naming ceremony on 26 September 1998. (Andy Anderson)*

she left the station having saved thirty-five lives in eighty-nine launches during her ten years in Orkney. She was transferred to the Relief Fleet for five months before going to Aberdeen as temporary station lifeboat for two years. She left Aberdeen in July 2000 to again become a Relief lifeboat. A further three years in the Relief Fleet ended in August 2003 when she was placed on station at Barry Dock in Wales where she remained until 2006.

In April 1997, it was announced that a new 17m Severn lifeboat had been allocated to Kirkwall, named *Margaret Foster* and funded from the legacy of Miss Margaret Ellen Foster, of Emsworth. The new boat, which cost £1,580,000 and was similar to that stationed at Stromness, was fitted out by at the FBM yard, Cowes, after the hull had been moulded of fibre-reinforced composite by Green Marine at Lymington. Fitted with twin 1,050hp engines, she had a maximum speed of twenty-five knots making her not only larger but also much faster than the 52ft Arun. Given the enormous area covered by the Kirkwall station, this extra speed meant she could provide a more effective service. Commodore George Cooper, RNLI Chief of Operations, when recommending the allocation of the Severn to the station, explained:

17m Severn Margaret Foster *with relief 52ft Arun* Davina and Charles Matthews Hunter *(ON.1078) at the West Pier, 2001. The Arun was stationed at Mallaig from 1982 to 2001 and then used as a relief lifeboat for two years, standing in for the Severn while she went for refit and overhaul. (Donald Budge)*

Kirkwall is a key station providing all-weather lifeboat cover for the waters of the northern group of Orkney Islands. It is a fairly quiet station having carried out an average of 10.8 services since 1991, mainly to fishing vessels...A Severn class lifeboat is best suited to provide lifeboat cover from this exposed lifeboat station in terms of weather and open sea conditions and where all-weather lifeboat flank cover was not immediately available.

After completing her fitting out and contractor's trials in November 1997, she was taken on a series of proving trials. During these, she stopped overnight on 10 November 1997 at Alderney in the Channel Islands and spent a couple of days at St Helier on Jersey before an overnight stop at Weymouth on 13 November. She then spent almost two months at Souter Marine Ltd, Cowes, before coming to the RNLI Depot at Poole on 20 January 1998 ready for crew training. During her passage from Cowes to Poole, she stopped at Emsworth Marina so that local people could see the boat bearing the donor's name. The donor had been a keen supporter of the lifeboat service and was well known to local RNLI Branch at Emsworth. The Kirkwall crew were trained on the new boat at the end of February 1998 and on 27 February set off for Orkney. After an overnight stop at Dover on 27 February, *Margaret Foster* headed across the Channel to IJmuiden in Holland where she stayed for another night. She stayed overnight at Lowestoft on 1 March, she diverted to Grimsby with mechanical problems on her starboard engine on 2 March before continuing north. She called at Tynemouth on 3 March after the problems with the starboard engine had been resolved and new parts fitted to the injector connections. She stayed overnight at Aberdeen on 4 March and on 5 March set off on the final leg of her journey to station, arriving at Kirkwall on 5 March to be greeted by the boat she was to replace, 52ft Arun *Mickie Salvesen*.

17m Severn Margaret Foster *leaving Kirkwall harbour on exercise, August 2001. (Nicholas Leach)*

17m Severn Margaret Foster *in the berth alongside the West Pier and adjacent to the crew facility in Kirkwall's old harbour, August 2001, before the pontoon had been installed to improve boarding arrangements. (Nicholas Leach)*

Margaret Foster with relief 17m Severn Fraser Flyer (Civil Service No.43) *(ON.1237) alongside the West Pier, 2003. (Donald Budge)*

Further crew training took place at Kirkwall on 5 and 6 March before *Margaret Foster* was taken on an extended crew training passage to Stornoway on 6 March, and then via Portree for an overnight stop at Lochinver. The training passage was completed on 8 March and she returned to Kirkwall for a further two weeks of crew training. After a propeller change at Wick on 24 March, she was officially placed on station two days later. Before being placed on service, however, *Margaret Foster* had performed her first service. On 16 March 1998, the local trawler *Aalskere*, with steering failure, had gone aground on Egilsay. With the tide falling, reaching the casualty quickly was essential and so the new Severn put out at 4.20 a.m., reaching the casualty half an hour later. A towline was rigged and, as the tide turned, the lifeboat managed to pull her clear. The lifeboat then escorted the casualty to Kirkwall.

The naming ceremony of *Margaret Foster* took placed on 26 September 1998 at the West Pier in the harbour. The ceremony was opened by Bill Spence, chairman of Kirkwall Lifeboat Station, and the lifeboat was handed to the RNLI by Victor Cornish, Executor of Miss Foster's estate. She was accepted by David Acland, RNLI chairman, and passed into the care of Kirkwall Lifeboat Station, being formally accepted by Honorary Secretary Capt. Stephen Manson. The service of dedication was conducted by the Revd Ron Ferguson, of St Magnus Cathedral. Brigadier Sidney Robertson MBE, president of Kirkwall Station Branch and a life vice-president of the RNLI, then named the new lifeboat, pressing the button to release the bottle of Highland Park whisky which smashed across her bow.

Since her inauguration, *Margaret Foster* has given good service undertaking some challenging services in difficult conditions. On 24 July 1999, she went to the aid of the barque *Regina Caellis* in force seven winds with moderate seas and swells. The barque, with six persons on board, had gone aground on the Green Holms. The lifeboat reached the casualty at 12.26 p.m. and attempted to tow the vessel off, but the tow rope parted and Coxswain Geoffrey Gardens decided to wait until the tide turned before making a further attempt. When the tide turned, the casualty started to swing and list, so the towline was reconnected but parted twice more. At the third attempt, the barque was pulled clear and at 6.50 p.m. the lifeboat began the tow back to Kirkwall. The barque was taking on water and her rudder was stuck hard to port making berthing difficult when the boats finally reached port at 9.20 p.m. Strong winds combined with the stuck rudder made the vessel sheer about wildly, but the lifeboat crew managed to berth the vessel alongside the east side of the pier with Coxswain Gardens showing good skill in handling the lifeboat and casualty in the confined waters and poor weather.

Less than two months later, on 10 September 1999, *Margaret Foster* and her crew were involved in another well-executed service. At 9 p.m., Honorary Secretary Capt. Stephen Mason was informed by Pentland Coastguard that a crew member on the rig support vessel *Stream Truck* had suffered a suspected heart attack. The vessel was thirteen miles east of Stronsay and seventeen miles north-east of Kirkwall with conditions on scene reported as south-easterly gale force nine winds, and a ten to twelve metre swell with very rough seas. At 11.21 p.m., *Margaret Foster* slipped her moorings under the command of Coxswain Geoffrey Gardens with Second Coxswain Smith Foubister, Mechanic Dupre Strutt, James Budge, Michael Foulis and Robert Hall forming the crew. Also on board was Dr Peter Faye of the Skerryvore Practice, Kirkwall, who volunteered to assist.

Once clear of Kirkwall harbour, the lifeboat was exposed to the full force of the prevailing conditions but managed to make moderate speed into very rough seas. The conditions were so severe that the impact from one large wave caused the laser plotter navigation system to fail, although it was soon restarted. At 10.46 p.m., the lifeboat rendezvoused with *Stream Truck* but the conditions made it impossible to transfer Dr Faye and crew member Robert Hall.

Margaret Foster *bringing the fishing vessel* Steadfast IV *to safety at Westray, August 2000. (Donald Budge)*

Margaret Foster and Shetland-based Coastguard helicopter G-BDOC 'Oscar Charlie' in Shapinsay Sound, June 2004. Two lifeboat crew are being winched aboard the helicopter as part of a routine exercise. (Nicholas Leach)

Coxswain Gardens therefore decided to escort the vessel to Deer Sound where the transfer was undertaken without too much difficulty, keeping the lifeboat's port shoulder alongside the vessel and maintaining a headway speed of eight knots. Dr Faye was suffering from seasickness but, despite this, immediately set up a defibrillator which had a cardiograph facility and monitored the patient's condition. Despite his seasickness, Dr Faye raised a vein in the patient's arm and administered medication intravenously. With conditions still very poor, Dr Faye and crew member Hall stabilised the patient, but the prevailing weather precluded moving the patient to the lifeboat. More medical supplies were transferred to *Stream Truck* at the doctor's request, including a basket stretcher and the lifeboat's oxygen set. At 11.35 p.m. the lifeboat and *Stream Truck* made best speed towards Kirkwall Bay and, once in the shelter of the Bay, the patient was transferred to the lifeboat for passage back to harbour. The lifeboat returned to her berth ten minutes after midnight and transferred the patient to a waiting ambulance.

For his work in saving the life of the heart attack victim, Dr Faye was awarded the RNLI's special Doctor's Vellum, the first to be awarded by the Institution since 1981. Although he had rarely been on a lifeboat, Dr Faye volunteered to go out despite the severe weather conditions. In his report, Deputy Divisional Inspector of Lifeboats for Scotland, Dave Holden, said, 'his courage and determination are without question'. Crew member Robert Hall received a Letter of Appreciation signed by the RNLI's Director for his part in the service.

During a period of severe weather in January 2000, *Margaret Foster* was called out on three occasions, starting on 21 January when she went to the aid of a diver who had lost contact with his boat south-east of Egilsay. After a search involving several other vessels, including the local ferry and the Sumburgh rescue helicopter 'Oscar Charlie', *Margaret Foster* located the diver on the face of a very large wave. He had drifted ten miles in two hours in very strong tidal conditions, but the lifeboat crew soon recovered him and treated him for hypothermia. The diver was only found because of Coxswain Gardens' local knowledge which led him to search west of Killiholm after suspecting that the tidal rips would have carried the casualty out into the Rost. The lifeboat delivered the diver into the care of an ambulance on the quayside at Kirkwall at 4.50 p.m. A Letter of Appreciation signed from the Chief of Operations was sent to the crew after this service.

The following day, *Margaret Foster* was out again after the fishing vessel *Be Ready*, with five persons on board, was reported on fire twenty miles north of Westray. The lifeboat put out in force nine winds and six to eight metre seas and, at the west end of Westray, a large sea passed right over the lifeboat causing some damage to her fittings. In the severe sea conditions, with at least another three hours until she would reach the casualty, *Margaret Foster* hove to as Coastguard helicopter 'Oscar Charlie' had reached the scene and managed to winch the survivors to safety. Once all the survivors had been picked up by the helicopter, *Margaret Foster* was released from duty and returned to station. She reached Kirkwall after a difficult passage during which further seas broke right over the deck and wheelhouse. She handled the conditions extremely well and reached her berth safely after several hours in difficult sea conditions.

The last of the three services took place on 29 January when the Honduran coaster *Brio*, with four persons on board, started dragging her anchor and was in danger of being driven ashore in Kirkwall Bay in exceptionally bad weather with wind speeds in excess of seventy knots, gusting at times to over one hundred knots. *Margaret Foster* reached the casualty at 11.10 a.m. and the crew, after numerous attempts to pass a line across had failed, established a tow. The task was made particularly difficult by the position of the coaster's anchor chain, the very

Margaret Foster *at full speed in Shapinsay Sound, June 2004. (Nicholas Leach)*

An aerial view of the old harbour at Kirkwall showing the lifeboat at her moorings alongside the crew facility, with the inter-island ferry terminal to the right. (Supplied by Kirkwall Lifeboat Station)

rough seas and the language difficulties with the men on the coaster. The vessel was brought head to wind and the lifeboat eventually managed to tow her into deep water across the bay. At one point during this operation, one of the lifeboat crew lost his footing in the violent rolling, fell and hurt his back. He was put in a stretcher and given first aid.

When the towline parted as the coaster sheered to starboard, the Coastguard's emergency towing vessel (ETV) *Anglian Monarch* was on scene and able to establish a tow, leaving *Margaret Foster* free to land the injured crewman at Kirkwall before returning to the casualty. The tow by *Anglian Monarch* parted when the coaster's towing bitts were ripped off the deck leaving both vessels drifting onto the shore near Thieves Holm. As the crew of *Brio* were unable to see properly, *Margaret Foster* took up station to lead the vessel to safety, with the coaster making very slow headway against the weather and anchor. Coxswain Gardens decided to lead *Brio* towards Finstown, where the anchor was recovered in safety. The lifeboat then guided the coaster to Isbister Bay, where she was anchored at 4.10 p.m., enabling the lifeboat to return to station. Honorary secretary Stephen Manson commented afterwards that he could not remember such bad conditions in what should have been sheltered water and commended coxswain and crew for their efforts in such dangerous circumstances. Extremely skilful boat-handling was coupled with good local knowledge to enable the successful execution of this service as, had the lifeboat not pulled the bow of the coaster into the wind, the casualty would have been aground in seconds. The RNLI recognised the crew's efforts and a Letter of Appreciation was sent by the Chief of Operations.

On 24 May 2002, Shetland Coastguard requested the assistance of the lifeboat after a helicopter crashed into the sea near the Broch of Birsay. *Margaret Foster* departed station at 11.38 a.m. arriving at the search area an hour later having been diverted to Rousay to collect two local divers and a dive attendant from Leask Marine of Kirkwall. The Coastguard helicopter

The impressive sight of Kirkwall lifeboat Margaret Foster *heading out to sea at full speed. (Nicholas Leach)*

Kirkwall Lifeboat Station 2006: 17m Severn Margaret Foster *at moorings alongside the pontoon installed in 2003 adjacent to the crew facility on the West Pier. (Nicholas Leach)*

'Oscar Charlie' was despatched from Sumburgh to assist with the search, together with an RAF helicopter and Nimrod aircraft. Once at the scene of the crash, *Margaret Foster* searched with the Stromness lifeboat until being requested to take on board more divers from helicopter Rescue 137. *Margaret Foster* then proceeded to the position where oil was seen to be surfacing and the local divers dived on the wreckage to investigate. They found the body of the pilot in the cockpit still strapped in his seat and were able to bring the body to the surface where it was taken aboard the lifeboat's small inflatable 'Y' boat and transferred to *Margaret Foster*. The RAF divers were then transferred to Stromness lifeboat and *Margaret Foster* departed the scene at 2.40 p.m., returning to station via Tingwall Pier to pick up a doctor, and Rousay, where the local divers were landed.

In the early hours of 5 March 2004, Shetland Coastguard received a call for help from the fishing vessel *Elegance* which was on fire off Start Point. *Margaret Foster* left her berth at 2.25 a.m. and found the casualty just over a mile east of Start Point at 3.45 a.m. A tow rope was passed by the crew of *Elegance* with a chain bridle that was too short, so the lifeboat's own tow rope was used to lengthen it and within half an hour the tow was under way at just over two knots. An hour later, the Coastguard helicopter 'Oscar Charlie' arrived to lower a salvage pump aboard the casualty, a difficult operation due to the heading needed for a safe transfer. Despite the pump coming aboard, at 6.03 a.m. the skipper of *Elegance* decided to abandon ship and so the lifeboat slipped the tow to manoeuvre alongside. By 6.11 a.m., the three crew were safely aboard *Margaret Foster* enabling 'Oscar Charlie' to return to Sumburgh. The Coastguard ETV *Anglian Sovereign* was also on her way by this time, arriving at 8 a.m. by when the Fisheries Patrol Vessel *Norna* was helping with pumps and dinghies. With the ETV on scene, Shetland Coastguard asked *Margaret Foster* to take the survivors to Kirkwall, where she arrived at 9.43 a.m. The survivors walked ashore with no injuries and the vessel was later taken in tow by the ETV. She was brought to Kirkwall pier but, as she was entering the String, she healed over and was about to sink so was towed away from the local coastlines for fear of pollution. She eventually sank east of Shapinsay.

Appendices

Appendix One: Lifeboat Summary

Stromness Lifeboats

On station	ON	Name Donor	Type Year built	Launches/ saved
8.1867–91	286	*Saltaire* Gift of Sir Titus Salt, Bt, Leeds.	33' x 8'6" Self-righter 1867	3/5
6.1891– 4.1909	299	*Good Shepherd* Loyal Order of Ancient Shepherds.	42' x 11' Self-righter 1891	11/18
4.1909–28	561	*John A. Hay* Legacy of John A. Hay, Cheltenham.	42' x 11'6" SR (M) 1908	32/90
3.1928–5.55	702	*J. J. K. S. W.* Legacy of Miss J. Moody, Mr J.P. Traill, Mr W.M. Aitken, Mrs E.J. Hanson, and Mr W.M. Notting.	51' x 13'6" Barnett (M) 1928	92/139
5.1955–6.84	924	*Archibald and Alexander M. Paterson* Gift of Miss Margaret M Paterson, St Petersburg, Florida, USA.	52' x 13'6" Barnett (M) 1955	123/52
10.1984–98	1099	*Joseph Rothwell Sykes and Hilda M.* Bequests of J. Sykes, Nora Sykes, Doris Rothwell and Hilda Vyvyan.	52' x 17' Arun (M) 1984	89/8
10.1998–	1236	*Violet, Dorothy and Kathleen* Bequest of Miss Violet Jane Matton, Seaford, East Sussex, and her sisters, Dorothy and Kathleen.	17.28m x 5.5m Severn (M) 1998	

(M) indicates motor lifeboat
ON stands for RNLI Official Number

Stromness lifeboat Violet, Dorothy and Kathleen *is one of forty-five Severn class lifeboats in the RNLI's fleet; at 17m in length, the Severn is the largest all-weather lifeboat in service. (Nicholas Leach)*

Longhope

On station	ON	Name Donor	Type Year built	Launches/ lives saved
1874–91	—	*Dickinson Edleston* Gift Mr D. Edleston, Sowerby Bridge.	37' x 9'2" Self-righter 1874	4/0
2.1891–1904	307	*Samyntas Stannah* Legacy of Mrs E.M. Stannah, Surrey.	39' x 9' Self-righter 1891	4/52
4.1906–26	550	*Anne Miles* Gift of Miss A. Miles, London.	43' x 12'6" Watson 1905	7/8
9.1926–33	698	*K. T. J. S.* Legacies of William G. King, J. Turnball, M. Jesset and Mrs S.H. Sandford.	45'6" x 12'6" Watson (M) 1926	24/25
1.1933–62	759	*Thomas McCunn* Legacy of Mr William McCunn, Largs.	45'6" x 12'6" Watson (M) 1933	101/308
4.1962–3.69	962	*T. G. B.* Anonymous gift.	47' x 13' Watson (M) 1962	34/24
1970	889	*Hilton Briggs* Legacy of Mrs A. Briggs, Southport.	52' x 13'6" Barnett (M) 1952	6/0
12.1970–3.88	1010	*David and Elizabeth King & E. B.* Legacy of Miss Charlotte E. King, of Edinburgh, and an anonymous gift.	48'6" x 14' Solent (M) 1970	77/32
3.1988–99	1138	*Lord Saltoun* Bequest of Mrs Mary Salvesen.	47' x 15' Tyne (M) 1987	41/9
8.1999–2004	1098	*Sir Max Aitken II* The Beaverbrook Foundation.	52' x 17' Arun (M) 1984	20/0
6.2004–10.06	1149	*The Queen Mother* Legacy of Miss Sarah Sinclair Gray, Dunoon, and RNLI funds.	52' x 17' Arun (M) 1989	14/4
10.2006–	1284	*Helen Comrie* Legacy of Thomas L. M. Comrie.	16m x 5m Tamar (M) 2006	

Longhope lifeboats The Queen Mother *(left) and* Sir Max Aitken II *together at Longhope Pier in June 2004
during the changeover from the latter to the former. (Nicholas Leach)*

Kirkwall lifeboat Margaret Foster *in Shapinsay Sound, to the north of the Orkney captial. (Nicholas Leach)*

Stronsay

On station	ON	Name Donor	Type Year built	Launches/ lives saved
4.1909–15	565	*John Ryburn* Legacy of Mr William McCunn, Largs.	43' x 12'6" Watson (M) 1908	11/4
10.1952–55	707	*Edward Z. Dresden* Legacy of Edmund Dresden, London.	45'6" x 12'6" Watson (M) 1928	11/0
1955–72	923	*John Gellatly Hyndman* Legacy of Elise A. Hyndman, Greenock.	52' Barnett (M) 1955	116/47

Kirkwall

On station	ON	Name Donor	Type Year built	Launches/ lives saved
3.1968–74 & 8.1975–88	988	*Grace Paterson Ritchie* Legacy of Miss Grace P. Ritchie.	70' x 17' Clyde (M) 1966	82/46
6.1974–8.75	1021	*Douglas Currie* Gift from Douglas Currie Trust, legacy of Mr J. J. Davidson, Glasgow Ladies Lifeboat Guild and other gifts.	48'6" x 14' Solent (M) 1973	8/12
7.1988–3.98	1135	*Mickie Salvesen* Bequest of Mrs Mary 'Mickie' Salvesen.	52' x 17' Arun (M) 1988	89/35
3.1998–	1231	*Margaret Foster* Legacy of Miss Margaret Ellen Foster, Emsworth, Hampshire.	17.28m x 5.5m Severn (M) 1997	

Appendix Two: Lifeboat Sites in Orkney

Visiting the Lifeboat Stations

It is possible to visit the lifeboat stations of Orkney and, as all the lifeboats are kept at moorings, the boats themselves can easily be seen. At Stromness, the boat is moored alongside the South Pier, south of the Scrabster Ferry terminal. At Kirkwall, the lifeboat has a purpose-built boarding pontoon alongside the West Pier of the Old Harbour, with the crew facility adjacent. Longhope Pier accommodates the Longhope lifeboat, which is moored behind a protective breakwater at a purpose-built berth close to the modern crew facility.

Old Lifeboat Houses

Four old lifeboat houses can be seen in Orkney, two at Stromness and two on Hoy. At Stromness, the first lifeboat house, built in 1867 to the south of the town at the Ness, remains in use as a store for the local golf club, and can be seen from the ferry as it enters and leaves harbour. The lifeboat house built on Stromness Waterfront was used as a crew room until being sold by the RNLI in December 2001 to become the headquarters for Scapa Scuba, a dive school and drysuit shop. On Hoy, the lifeboat houses built at Brims in 1874 and 1906 are both still standing. The earlier house, built on a neck of land connecting North and South Walls, known as The Ayre, is used as a local store and remains largely unaltered externally. The later boathouse with its slipway is now home to the Longhope Lifeboat Museum (see p.184).

Stromness Museum

Stromness Museum is located at 52 Alfred Street. Inside is a small display on lifeboats alongside exhibits relating to local shipwrecks and the lighthouses around Orkney. Orkney's proud

The lifeboat house and slipway on the waterfront at Stromness remain in more or less original condition externally but inside the house has been converted into a shop called Scapa Scuba with the service boards on display. (Nicholas Leach)

Headstones in Kirkhope burial ground at Osmondwall on Hoy of two of the lifeboatmen lost in the Longhope disaster of March 1969 including, on the right, that of Coxswain Dan Kirkpatrick, 'Anchored safe, where storms are o'er'. (Nicholas Leach)

seafaring tradition and maritime heritage is covered with exhibits relating to the whaling industry of the eighteenth and nineteenth centuries, when many Orcadians left Stromness to join the ships of the Hudson's Bay Company for a new life in Canada. A large display is devoted to the scuttling of the German Fleet in Scapa Flow. The museum is open every day between October and April but for opening times and details of admission charges, contact the museum on 01856 850025.

Longhope Lifeboat Museum

The old lifeboat house at Brims, built in 1906, is now home to the former Longhope lifeboat *Thomas McCunn* which forms the centrepiece of the local lifeboat museum (see Appendix 3). The lifeboat house can be seen from the main road between Houton, the ferry terminal, and Longhope village.

Longhope Lifeboat Memorial

The Kirkhope burial ground at Osmondwall is dominated by the lone bronze figure of a lifeboatman, erected in honour of the eight crewmen of the lifeboat *T.G.B.* which capsized on service on 17 March 1969.

Lifeboat Reminders on Stronsay

The lifeboat station at Stronsay was operational from 1909 to 1915 and 1952 to 1972. The supporting structure is all that remains of the lifeboat house built in 1911. The cottage built the following year for the mechanic, named Ryburn, still stands and is maintained in good condition. The station's service boards are on display in the local community centre.

Appendix Three: Longhope Lifeboat Museum

The lifeboat museum at Longhope was established in 2000 after the station's former lifeboat, *Thomas McCunn*, became available for display and the old lifeboat house at Brims was no longer required for operational purposes. *Thomas McCunn*, sold out of service in August 1972, had been acquired by J. Spiers, of Walton-on-the-Naze. She was re-engined with two 80bhp Mermaid 397 four-cylinder diesels in 1973, altered only internally, and maintained much as she was when in service as a lifeboat. Renamed *Pentland Speir*, she was initiaslly kept at Walton-on-the-Naze in Essex, until being moved to Hampshire during the 1980s, and by the 1990s, was at Hayling Island, moored at the local Yacht Club.

In 2000, her owner Peter Roberts, of Midhurst, Sussex, was looking to sell her and, with the 1906-built lifeboat house at Brims becoming empty, the opportunity to take the vessel back to Orkney presented itself as purpose-built accommodation was available to house the lifeboat. So, on 29 July 2000 she was sold by Mr Roberts to the Longhope Lifeboat Museum Trust for the sum of £1 Scots. With the sale complete, *Thomas McCunn* was sailed back to her original home from Hayling Island by a crew made up of past and present lifeboat men. During the passage up the east coast, she visited eight lifeboat stations and arrived in Longhope on 7 August 2000, back at her original home. She was recovered up the old slipway and was once again housed inside the building that had been her home for almost thirty years.

The Princess Royal became Patron of the Longhope Lifeboat Museum Trust on 1 March 2002 when she assumed the role from the original patron, HRH Queen Elizabeth the Queen

Thomas McCunn *calls at Wick on her way north to Longhope from Hayling Island. (By coutesy of Andy Anderson)*

Thomas McCunn *inside the lifeboat house at the head of the slipway, surrounded by photographs and mementoes from the station's history that make up the exhibits in the Longhope Lifeboat Museum. (Nicholas Leach)*

Mother, who accepted the honour just months before her death. On 28 May 2002 the Princess Royal came to Hoy to officially open the museum at a special ceremony, which took place in blustery weather. During the ceremony, she met past and present Longhope crew members as well as the many local people who had given their time to the project. Many of the local population were on hand to greet their royal visitor and, after a short speech of welcome by Dr Tony Trickett, she formally opened the museum. She was then taken on a tour of the exhibits inside the museum and looked over *Thomas McCunn* on her cradle at the top of the slipway. After this, she accepted the chance to be launched down the slipway for a trip back to Longhope Pier on board the old lifeboat accomplished in a force five to six south-easterly wind. Accompanied by the operational lifeboat *Sir Max Aitken, Thomas McCunn* reached the pier and the Princess disembarked to return to the mainland at the end of a memorable day.

The museum now forms an essential part of Hoy and is on the tourist trail for visitors coming to this unique island. Inside, the story of *Thomas McCunn* is told, together with accounts of the Longhope lifeboat disaster of 17 March 1969 when eight brave lifeboatmen from the station were lost in the lifeboat *T.G.B.* on service to the freighter *Irene.* The museum project has been funded entirely by public donations with all restoration works, collections and displays being carried out voluntarily.

Appendix Four: What Became of the Lifeboats?

John Ryburn (Stronsay 1909-15)

After serving at Stronsay, John Rynburn served as the Peterhead No.2 lifeboat for five years before being transferred to Broughty Ferry where she stayed for a further fourteen years. She was sold out of service in February 1935 to T.J. Hughes, of Rhyl. She was based in North Wales, registered in Carnarvon in 1952 and owned by a succession of different individuals who used her as a private motor boat. In 1959 she was fitted with a 40bhp Ailsa Craig four-cylinder engine. Since at least the early 1990s she has been kept at Caernarvon River Quay, opposite the Castle, with her wheelhouse covered by sheeting and gradually deteriorating, as pictured. (Nicholas Leach)

K.T.J.S. (Longhope 1926-33)

K.T.J.S. was sold out of service in May 1952 after serving at Aith, Arranmore and in the Reserve FLeet. She was converted for stern trawling and used as a fishing boat out of Lowestoft during the mid-1950s, renamed Alton (LO.511). By 1980 she had become B.M.160, and was fishing from Brixham in Devon. She was then put up for sale during the winter of 1980-81, but was wrecked before any sale went through. (Supplied by Tony Denton)

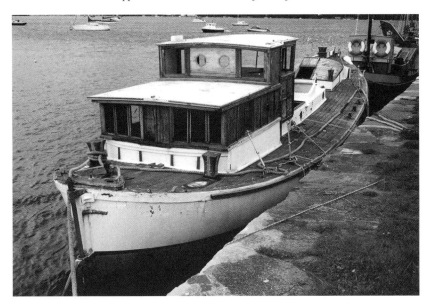

J.J.K.S.W. (Stromness 1928-55)

After leaving Stromness in May 1955, J.J.K.S.W. was placed in the Reserve Fleet and served at stations throughout the country until being sold out of service in 1965. She was based at Port Penryn and Bangor in North Wales, having been renamed Jon Dee, and during the late 1970s was used to take angling parties out. During the 1980s she was taken out of the water at Dickie's Boat Yard, Bangor, with the then owner looking to dispose of her to anyone willing to restore her. Throughout the 1990s she was kept at Dickie's, usually out of water, undergoing gradual restoration, with her hull painted orange and white and a wheelhouse added. In 2000 she was back in the water and kept at Port Penrhyn, but in poor condition, but her more recent whereabouts are unknown. (Nicholas Leach)

T. G. B. (Longhope 1962-69)

T.G.B. *served at Arranmore from 1970 to 1978 and then in the Relief Fleet until being sold out of service in 1986, since when she has been on display at the Scottish Maritime Museum, Irvine. (Nicholas Leach)*

John Gellatly Hyndman (Stronsay 1955-72)

John Gellatly Hyndman *was sold out of service in 1985 after a twelve-year career in the Relief Fleet during which time she saved forty-five lives. After sale during the late 1980s, she was renamed* Stronsay *based in the north east and kept at Hartlepool and Yarm on the River Tees. By the 1990s, she had been moved to the Boathaven at Littleport, near Ely, where she remained until being bought in 2002 by Peter Lucas, who moved her by low-loader to Plymouth. She was then sold to Andy Ashley who took her to Mashford's Boatyard, Cremyll. Here she was restored and then sailed to her permanent home in Portishead where she was based at the marina. (Nicholas Leach)*

Grace Paterson Ritchie (Kirkwall 1968-88)

After being replaced at Kirkwall, Grace Paterson Ritchie *was sold to the Lifesaving Association of Iceland on 10 February 1989 for £60,000. She sailed for Iceland in June 1989 to take up duty at Reykjavik and continue as a life-saver, a role for which she was renamed* Henry A. Halfdansson *after the Association's chairman at the time. The Kirkwall crew had kept the boat's bell as a keepsake when she left Kirkwall for what they thought would be the last time. However, they decided once they knew she was to continue in her role as a life-saver, that her bell should be returned to her. The bell was therefore presented to the Iceland crew, who were delighted and very surprised to receive it, when the boat made a courtesy visit to Kirkwall before taking up her life-saving duties at Reykjavik. She served in Iceland for more than a decade until, in 2002, the RNLI sold the former Lerwick Arun* Soldian *to the Icelandic Association as a replacement for* Henry A. Halfdansson. *Replaced in Iceland, she was then sold to a new owner in Scotland who used her as a diving boat out of at Largs Yacht Haven as* Grace Ritchie, *as pictured. (Nicholas Leach)*

Archibald and Alexander M. Paterson (Stromness 1955-84)

After a long career at Stromness, Archibald and Alexander M. Paterson *was sold out of service in 1989 from the boatyard of Herd & MacKenzie, at Buckie. She was bought by Mark Wakelin, harbour master at Padstow, who took her to north Cornwall and kept her unaltered in Padstow Harbour. In 1993, Richard F. Palmer, of Gerrards Cross, bought the boat, which by now had been renamed* St Issey. *He used her mainly for cruising and fishing and took her to Maldon. She spent about three years in Poole until in June 1993 she went to Cork Harbour where she was moored between the Ferryport and the Naval Base. The only alterations made were internal ones with the forward air boxes removed, a door made in the forward bulkhead and the lateral air cases removed to make space for bunks on each side. She was used for day cruising and sea angling. After her time in Cork, she was moved to Fishguard Harbour, where by October 2002 she was being offered for sale. In 2003, her end almost came when she broke from her moorings in the harbour and sustained severe damage when she was driven ashore. She was transferred to Pembroke Dock for repairs but, in 2004, Andy Ianetta of Gloucester acquired the boat and took her to Portishead for repairs. She was returned to the water fully refitted and used for cruising around the South West, including attending the historic lifeboat rally at Fowey in Cornwall, where she is pictured. (Nicholas Leach, left)*

David and Elizabeth King & E. B. (Longhope 1970-88)

David and Elizabeth King & E. B. *was sold out of service on 15 March 1990 to Erik A. White. She was taken from Buckie to Castletown on the Isle of Man where she was refitted and renamed* Island Lass. *She remained at Castletown for several years and then moved to a number of different places, mostly in south-west Scotland. In 2002, she was offered for sale from Kirkcudbright Marina, still with her twin Gardner 6LX diesel enginess, de-rated to 80hp, and described as needing 'minimal conversion with excellent potential'. In 2003, she had been moved to the canal basin at Bowling, Dumbarton, where she is pictured, and was renamed* Storm. *(Nicholas Leach)*

Joseph Rothwell Sykes and Hilda M (Stromness 1984-98)

After service at Stromness, Joseph Rothwell Sykes and Hilda M *was allocated to Broughty Ferry in January 1999 where she served until April 2001, launching fifty-two times on service. After a further year as a Relief lifeboat, she was sold out of service in 2002 to the Finnish lifeboat service. She is now based in the west coast town of Uusikaupunki on the Gulf of Bothnia, renamed* PR Janne Malén. *At the same time as the Finnish service bought* Joseph Rothwell Sykes and Hilda M, *they also bought* Marie Winstone, *another 52ft Arun.* PR Janne Malén *is supported by* PK Vekara, *an Atlantic 21 rigid-inflatable also acquired from the RNLI. The Finnish lifeboat service has five former RNLI Arun lifeboats and twelve Atlantic 21s in its fleet, which totals 140 vessels.*

Lord Saltoun (Longhope 1988-99)

After service at Longhope, Lord Saltoun was placed in the Relief Fleet and she has served at stations throughout Britain and Ireland in place of other Tyne class lifeboats. She is pictured on exercise at Baltimore, in south-west Ireland, in April 2004. (Nicholas Leach)

Mickie Salvesen (Kirkwall 1988-99)

After a decade at Kirkwall, Mickie Salvesen was placed in the Relief Fleet for a few months until going to Aberdeen in August 1998 to temporarily replace another, older Arun. After two years at Aberdeen she returned to the Relief Fleet and spent three years relieving at stations while their lifeboats went for refit. In August 2003 she was placed on station at Barry Dock, South Wales, where she is pictured in October 2004. She served here until January 2006, after which she was sold by the RNLI to ICE-SAR in Iceland for further service as a lifeboat. (Nicholas Leach)

Together again: now under private ownership, 52ft Barnett sister vessels, Alexander and Archibald M. Paterson *and* John Gellatly Hyndman *(on right), from Stromness and Stronsay respectively, pictured at Fowey in July 2006 during the Cornish port's annual historic lifeboat rally. (Nicholas Leach)*

Bibliography

Allen, Anne (1997): *Orkney's Maritime Heritage* (National Maritime Museum).

Anon (1977): *For Those In Peril: Orkney Lifeboat History* (Stromness Museum).

Burgher, Leslie (1991): *Orkney – An Illustrated Architectural Guide* (Royal Incorporation of Architects in Scotland).

Cameron, Ian (2002): *Riders of the Storm* (Weidenfeld & Nicholson).

Davies, Joan (1984): Stromness: 'First Lifeboat Station in Orkney', *The Lifeboat*, Vol. XLIX, No. 487, Spring, pp. 16-19.

Ferguson, David M. (1988): *Shipwrecks of Orkney, Shetland and Pentland Firth* (David & Charles, Newton Abbot, Devon).

Leach, Nicholas (2002): 'Orkney Odyssey: The Road to the North', *Ships Monthly*, Vol. 37, No. 5, May, pp. 34-8.

Leach, Nicholas (2002): 'Extreme Search and Rescue', *The Lifeboat*, No. 566, Winter 2003/4, pp. 33-35.

Manson, Stephen M. (2001): *Grace, Mickie & Margaret: Kirkwall Lifeboat Reports 1966-2001* (The Orcadian Ltd, Kirkwall, Orkney).

Marwick, Ernest W. (1967): *The Story of the Stromness Life-boats 1867-1967.*

Morris, Jeff (1990): *The History of the Longhope Lifeboats.*

Morris, Jeff (1999): *The History of the Stromness Lifeboats* (2nd Edition).

Warner, Oliver (1974): *The Lifeboat Service* (Cassell, London).

Wilson, Bryce (1965): *The Lighthouses of Orkney* (Stromness Museum).